SOCRATES

in Love

Philosophy
for a Die-Hard Romantic

CHRISTOPHER PHILLIPS

W. W. NORTON & COMPANY

NEW YORK • LONDON

Disclaimer: To guard participants' privacy, names have been changed; occupations and other biographical information, and the specific locales at which dialogues occurred, have at times been changed. Sometimes, participants portrayed in this book are composites of those who took part in actual dialogues, and some dialogues are composites.

For information about permission to reproduce selections from this book,
write to Permissions, W. W. Norton & Company, Inc.,
500 Fifth Avenue, New York, NY 10110

Manufacturing by Quebecor Fairfield
Book design by Chris Welch
Production manager: Julia Druskin

The Library of Congress has catalogued the hardcover edition as follows:
Library of Congress Cataloging-in-Publication Data

Phillips, Christopher, 1959 July 15–
Socrates in love : philosophy for a passionate heart /
Christopher Phillips. –1st ed.
Includes bibliographical references.
ISBN-13: 978-0-393-06017-1 (hardcover)
ISBN-10: 0-393-06017-9 (hardcover)
1. Love. 2. Philosophy. 3. Socrates. I. Title.
BD436.P44 2007
128'.46–dc22

2006026681

ISBN 978-0-393-33067-0 pbk.

W. W. Norton & Company, Inc.
500 Fifth Avenue, New York, N.Y. 10110
www.wwnorton.com

W. W. Norton & Company Ltd.
Castle House, 75/76 Wells Street, London W1T 3QT

1 2 3 4 5 6 7 8 9 0

Praise for Christopher Phillips and
SOCRATES *in Love*

"When I read the words 'Where Is the Love?' in the introduction to this book, I immediately heard the singing voices of Roberta Flack and Donny Hathaway. That kept me going, despite my fear of being confused once more by Socrates. I discovered an important mosaic of ancient tales and current opinions, and that *Socrates in Love* breathed compassion, curiosity, and intrigue into the dusty world of empirical philosophy. And I can still hear the song."
—Bob Kerrey, president, The New School

"It's clear that Phillips is on to something. . . . [*Socrates in Love*] is a response to our greatest societal need: the need to connect with one another in meaningful discourse and to find, in that process, our common humanity. For this, Phillips should be applauded."
—*Portfolio Weekly*

"[We] are left hoping that Phillips, by returning to the methods of the first Western philosopher, has created a template for philosophical exploration that many others will emulate."
—*Christian Science Monitor*

"*Socrates Café* beautifully . . . tells you how and why the questioning style of Socrates works with children and adults." —*Washington Post*

"Christopher Phillips has the genius to raise the dead philosophers' society to life. [*Socrates in Love*] is a pleasure to read and touches on the crucial issues of love that inspired Plato. Whoever hasn't read Plato is probably dead to his soul, and whoever hasn't read Phillips probably doesn't know how alive Plato is." —Thomas Moore, author of *Care of the Soul* and *Dark Nights of the Soul*

"[*Socrates Café* is] a bracing, rollicking read about the spark that ignites when people start asking meaningful questions."

—*O, The Oprah Magazine*

"Here is ancient wisdom in all its complexity brought vividly to life— rendered accessible to readers today. Here is a traveling, inquiring teacher become a wonderfully engaging writer, whose reflecting mind becomes a companion for us needy readers."

—Robert Coles, Harvard University

"These timely seminars provide many welcome insights into the controversial problems of our daily lives and induce further reflection about who we are and where we are going."

—*San Antonio Express News*

"Like a Johnny Appleseed with a master's degree, Phillips has gallivanted back and forth across America, to cafes and coffee shops, senior centers, assisted-living complexes, prisons, libraries, day-care centers, elementary and high schools, and churches, forming lasting communities of inquiry."

—*Utne Reader*

"I am excited about Christopher Phillips's effort to bring philosophy out of the ivory tower and back into the lives of ordinary people, where it belongs."

—Rabbi Harold S. Kushner, author of *When Bad Things Happen to Good People*

"Phillips' presentation is skillful in his ability to weave threads of references to Socrates' society and his own opinions into the fabric of each question. He is artful in his choices of which cultures best illustrate an original perspective on the question at hand."

—*Charlotte Observer*

"A modern-day Socrates . . . who's chosen the world, not just the agora, for his stage . . . [with] a model discourse that elevates working lives and reduces intellectualism's pretensions."
—*Richmond Times-Dispatch* (Virginia)

"[Phillips] winningly showcases a tantalizing method for getting philosophy to thrive more widely."   —*Publishers Weekly*

"*Socrates Café* is a testament to Phillips's conviction that Americans are hungry to start probing questions the way Socrates did more than two millennia ago in Athens."   —*Arizona Republic*

"Highly accessible. . . . Alive with the passions of ordinary people from a dozen cultures, these colloquies dramatize the universality of Socrates' deeply humanizing concerns. . . . Readers will applaud Phillips for once again making philosophy a living enterprise beyond the lecture hall and the faculty lounge."   —*Booklist*

CONTENTS

For

CECILIA

La mia principessa

and for

CALIOPE ALEXIS

La mia piccola principessa

And for

MARGARET ANN PHILLIPS

ALEXANDER PHILLIPS

MICHAEL PHILLIPS

BELOVED MOM, DAD, AND BROTHER

INTRODUCTION

Where Is the Love?

"I'm embarrassed to report that not only do I know both of them, but they're two of my favorite dance partners," Alexandros, eighty-one, says to me. The people in question are two older women engaged in a heated exchange. One is taking part in an abortion rights rally organized after President George W. Bush made his first appointment to the United States Supreme Court; the other is front and center in a counterprotest. Finally, the pro-abortion protester tells her foil in no uncertain terms that she is full of you-know-what. In reply, her anti-abortion counterpart directs a gesture her way that is understood the world over as the furthest thing from complimentary.

Alexandros shakes his head and sighs. "There's such an invisible wall between people today. This scene brings to mind the Simon and Garfunkel song: 'People hearing without listening.'" He then says, "The not-so-funny thing is that on my date with one of those ladies the other night, she bemoaned that young people no longer practice the values we old folks hold dear. Thank heavens they don't!"

Alexandros gazes at the bronze sculpture of Socrates, a rare full-length representation of the fifth century B.C. Greek philosopher, and says to the statue, or no one in particular, "Where is the love?"

He and I are seated on a bench in Athens Square Park in the New York City neighborhood of Astoria, in the northwest part of the borough of Queens. Even on this sultry midsummer afternoon, no one is deterred from gathering at the park, whether it's to partake in their democratic freedom of assembly and expression, to be alone, or to enjoy the ample space for family outings and other benign social gatherings. When I first came to Astoria as a child to visit relatives, Greek was the predominant language spoken, even more so than English, and the borough is still home to more Greeks than any other community in the United States. But now I'm also treated to nearly 150 other languages in this vibrant fifty-eight-neighborhood borough, the most culturally diverse area in the United States.

Alexandros fixes his attention on a woman passing out meals to the homeless, many of whom greet her with tight hugs. "Ah, the language of love," he says.

It's a language he's fluent in himself, though he's had his share of heartbreak and tragedy. An only child, Alexandros came to the United States from Greece as a young teen in the 1940s. He was sent here by his parents at the height of the Greek civil war, a bloody conflict that pitted communists against Greek nationals. Children and adolescents, particularly in the northern mountainous areas of Greece, were routinely abducted and sent by communist insurgents to camps inside the iron curtain or were forcibly conscripted into their army. Alexandros's parents spent every penny to their name to have him spirited out of Greece so he could make a new life for himself in a country with boundless promise.

After becoming a U.S. citizen, Alexandros lied about his age and promptly enlisted as a volunteer in the army. He went on to fight in the Korean conflict; he has never talked—much less boasted—about his acts of courage under fire, nor has he complained about his debilitating war wounds. In the late 1950s, he settled in Washington, D. C. He worked his way from busboy to cook to owner of a restaurant-deli. His business, uninsured, was burned down during the riots that followed the killing of Martin Luther King, Jr., in 1968. "If setbacks don't kill you, they make you stronger," he is fond of saying.

Alexandros came to the Tidewater Virginia area and started life anew, eventually becoming owner of a diner, which I frequented during my days as an undergraduate student at the College of William and Mary, in nearby Williamsburg. If Alexandros ever slept, I didn't know about it. Many a night after closing, he would come to my dormitory, rouse me from slumber, and take me to his favorite nightclub so I could "learn to dance like a Greek." He never married. He had left behind the love of his life when he came to America. "I don't believe in that nonsense that you have many possible soul mates," Alexandros said to me the night of his fifty-fifth birthday, after uncharacteristically having a few too many. "If you're graced by God, you find your true love once—but only once. I found mine, and for that I am blessed."

Although Alexandros did not spend his adult life with his true love, he has lived every moment with unbridled passion, limitless energy, unquenchable curiosity, and caring concern, whether carrying out his labor of love at the restaurant—a home away from home for a motley group of all ages from all walks of life—or learning new languages, one of his favorite pastimes, or serving as a permanent fixture at local city council meetings to give his two cents' worth, or acting as a philanthropist, though he would have rejected that term. Although he is a soft touch for any cause that helps lift up needy people or perpetuate democracy, he believes that the "tithe" he gives—nearly half of his earnings—is the least anyone should give who is "blessed to live in a great democracy."

Alexandros left his restaurant open into the wee hours whenever I had to cram for an exam—and whenever my classmates and I, at times with a professor or two, would venture over to continue the rich dialogues begun in class. To my delight, other restaurant habitués often would sidle over and join in, offering their perspectives on questions such as, "What is a good citizen?" "Are all humans endowed with inalienable rights?" and even "What is love?"

After I graduated in 1981, we stayed in close touch at first, but less so over time as I became immersed in the hurly-burly of everyday living. Fifteen years later, in 1996, we had a joyous reunion. Alexandros was then living in semiretirement (though in truth more active and involved than ever) with relatives in Astoria, where he helped out running their restaurant. I had recently moved to northern New Jersey, and he took me up on my invitation to attend one of the first Socrates Café philosophical dialogues I ever held. This normally loquacious man didn't say a word during the dialogue. "I was too busy thinking," he said afterward, adding, "And to think it all started at my humble restaurant."

Alexandros and I have since had frequent reunions, particularly in summer, when Cecilia and I take advantage of relatively cheap Manhattan rents to carry out a number of philosophical outreach projects with marginalized groups in the tristate region. Today at our latest get-together, Alexandros is frowning, though it goes so much against the grain of his buoyant nature that his face hardly seems to know how to frown. He launches into an impassioned lament.

"Ronald Reagan, one of my favorite actors, called the United States 'a shining city on a hill' whose 'beacon light guides freedom-loving people everywhere,'" Alexandros says. "Each citizen is supposed to be a ray of that beacon light. That requires more than a passionate show of your own right to freely express yourself. You have to show with equal passion that you embrace and cherish others' right to do the same. To do that, you have to tear down the walls between yourself and others, and build bridges, of love."

His words are almost drowned out by the two antagonists who have resumed their screaming match nearby. Alexandros looks their way and says, "Even our own First Lady has got in on the intolerance act. At her campaign event in New Jersey before the last presidential election, Mrs. Bush's security detail had a woman handcuffed and forcibly evicted after the woman screamed out that she'd lost her son in the Iraq War. This grieving woman, instead of being hugged and commiserated with over her loss, was scolded and humiliated. Mrs. Bush told her audience that people like this woman didn't understand the pain of those who died on 9/11, didn't realize the sacrifice needed to keep our country free. The fact is, *no one* realized the sacrifice more than that woman, yet Mrs. Bush couldn't open her heart to her."

Alexandros points to the bronze sculpture of Socrates. "His society didn't collapse because of an outside aggressor. It collapsed from within, from the complete breakdown of communication between citizens, and the breakdown of loving sentiment for one another. They came to have disdain for anyone who didn't see eye to eye with them. They ganged up and got rid of Socrates because he was an uncomfortable reminder of the glory days of ancient Athens, when *demokratia*—'people power'—reigned and citizens worked toward a greater good. He epitomized the fact that you're meant to stay open to all views, to all human experiences, because that's how you deepen your love for people and of wisdom. That amazing man sacrificed his life in the name of classic Athenian values of excellence and honor and compassion, so one day they might live on. And they did, here in America, for more than two centuries. I'm worried my beloved America is becoming as loveless as ancient Athens in its days of decline."

Alexandros looks at Socrates again, then at me, and says, "Constantine Cavafy, the 'poet of the Greek diaspora,' was a peer of your grandparents. Cavafy, like them, left Greece for the boundless promise of the United States. Cavafy lamented: 'Without consideration . . . they built great high walls around me. . . . Now I sit here and despair.'

"I'm *not* despairing, not just yet," Alexandros is quick to assure me. "But each of us has to do everything he can to bring back the love." With that, he hoists himself up. "Time to do my part."

He walks over and puts himself between the two screaming women. At first, I think they are going to come together in common cause and punch his lights out for daring to intervene. I can't hear what he says, but before long he has them laughing, then hugging each other. He looks my way and winks. I look up at Socrates.

Socrates in Love

Socrates was "the first theorist of love," as Eva Cantarella, the prominent scholar of ancient Greece and Rome and professor at the University of Milan, puts it. As Socrates makes clear in Xenophon's *Symposium*, he "does not remember a moment of his life during which he was not in love." Socrates was not satisfied with only further sculpting and refining existing forms of love. He aspired to create new pathways, possibilities, and incarnations—at a time, no less, when his fellow Athenians, after their decisive defeat in the second Peloponnesian War, had come to shun all but the most narcissistic forms of love.

Socrates tested the limits of love as conventionally conceived, seeking to discover more about its nature, workings, objectives, and objects. The fount of Socrates' love is typically explained away as coming from a single source—*eros*, or erotic-romantic love. Yet Socrates, along with most of his fellow Athenians—until the polis entered a period of irreversible decline in his adult years—was informed and inspired by five types of love: *eros*; *storge* (familial-type love); *xenia* ("stranger love"); *philia* (communal and friendship-based love); and *agape* (self-sacrificial and even unconditional love). Socrates showed that there were no tidy divides between these forms of love; he acted in the world from the premise that one could not remake oneself, one's society, one's universe if one did not harness all these types of love in concert.

Heart-Shaped World

Where is the love?

What is the state of love in our world today? Is it in the same dire straits as in Socrates' time, heralding another downward spiral in human civilization? Can the Greeks of the halcyon days of ancient Athens, and in particular can Socrates—the Western world's greatest lover—show us the way to make ours a more loving world today?

A promising way to gain enlightenment about Socrates' philosophy of love, and his approach to learning about its mysterious ways and applying what he learned, is not had just by delving into the past in general, or even his past in particular, though both are vital aspects of the undertaking. Nor is it just a scholarly exercise, though this too is a critical component of such an investigation. If one is to gain fruitful insights into love the Socratic way, one must do what Socrates did: inquire about love, experiment with love in theory and practice, and look for love in lots of places, from the predictable to the unfamiliar.*

With the five traditional types of Greek love as the springboard for my investigations, I embarked on something of a global quest for love, locking hearts and minds with people in places such as a gambling den in Las Vegas on the hundredth anniversary of its founding; at a peace park in Hiroshima; in a home in Havana, Cuba, where a special family reunion was taking place; in the Czech Republic just as it was set to enter the European Union; in Soweto and Pretoria, South Africa, during the heady days of the presidential inauguration and celebration of the nation's tenth anniversary of freedom from apartheid; at a restaurant in Belfast, Northern Ireland, on Easter Sunday; at a diversity celebration in the Bay Area of California; at the Wounded Knee memorial on the Pine Ridge Sioux Reservation in South Dakota; at a park in

---

*One must also do what Plato did—craft, and reflect on, Socratic discourses on love. Like Plato, I do at times use some license in fashioning the dialogues adapted here from the actual dialogues in which I participated—to mirror more faithfully the tone and tenor and substance of what took place. Consequently, the actual dialogues can be best seen as a template from which to cull and structure and compose. What is more, framing philosophical questions within timely contexts does not make them dated, and so does not diminish them, but rather helps us to see how certain universal patterns and lessons emerge—enabling us better to apply them as we wrap our hearts and minds around, and grapple with, the most pressing and vexing conundrums of today and tomorrow.

Greenwich Village during the biggest blackout in U.S. history; at a special fellowship gathering of evangelical Christians, Jews, and Sikhs at renowned evangelical leader Billy Graham's last revival.

I learned still more about love by inquiring with homeless children and adults in the United States; with Muslim students, including Sufi Muslims, as well as with Buddhists in Toronto; with American soldiers and with Cuban war veterans; with a family on the Mexico–United States border that assists immigrants. My explorations included dialogues with inmates in a maximum security prison, with Katrina refugees, with Mardi Gras celebrants in New Orleans, with youth in a gang-ridden area in East Los Angeles, with moms and a dad in a Texas exurb, with people around the globe during a real-time Internet dialogue, and with elementary age children on the steps of Capitol Hill.

I communed about love with many so-called ordinary people who are living lives of great heart. Their insights on love—which spring from their passionate and compassionate works and deeds, from their continued cultivation of feeling minds and thinking hearts—made my quest one of continual revelation. Because of them, I discovered cultural, spiritual, and philosophical traditions and practices of love that serve as compelling and hopeful antidotes to the concerted efforts of those hell-bent on making ours a world of fear and hate. Standout theorists and practitioners of love in their own right, they would have made Socrates proud.

PART I

EROS

A Brief History of Eros

The Eros myth advanced by Socrates in Plato's *Symposium* was the latest in a long line fashioned by the mythmaking Greeks. Hesiod, the Greek poet and historian of mythology who lived around 700 B.C., recounts in his *Theogony*, or "Origin of the Gods," that in initial incarnations, Eros shares equal billing with the other gods present at the world's birth. Right on the heels of the gods Chaos (air) and Gaia (earth), Eros emerged from the primordial darkness and joined them as the first "deathless ones who hold the peaks of snowy Olympus." Eros was the force behind the birth of all things in the universe. Eventually Eros came to be opposed to Eris, the god of strife. While Eros strove to give birth to all the entities that would fill out the canvas of the universe, Eris was intent on undoing all his creations. In Eros myths that followed, Eros' nature and objectives became murkier: Eros himself could be the source of such strife, undoing at times his own creations, so Eris was dispensed with.

Eros was soon transformed from an amorphous primordial deity to one with distinctive features. He became "the fairest of the deathless gods," and the most beguiling—the one "who unnerves the limbs and overcomes the mind and wise counsels of all gods and all men within them." Eros now was the god who could engender uncontrollable lust, passion, desire, sensual longing. Even the most sage were not immune to his powers.

In these accounts, Eros was no longer one of the original gods but one of the Erotes, or "love gods," each of whom possessed the power to provoke desire in humans—and in some cases other gods—at whim. Among the Erotes, Eros is first among equals, the fairest and most powerful. Various accounts depict Eros sometimes as a child, sometimes an adolescent, sometimes a man; sometimes he has brothers, and at others he is an only child. Always, he is at the center of "desire matches," some for the good—some even leading to celestial sex romps among gods—but many destructive in bent, bringing about someone's undoing.

Finally, Eros comes to be the son of Aphrodite, the Greek goddess of beauty, love, and desire. Depending on the account, Eros was the scion of a range of fathers, but Aphrodite was always his mother, and the only one who had some sway over him; many of his acts that stoked the passions of people and gods were at his mother's bidding.

In all latter accounts, Eros is charming and beautiful, crafty and manipulative, capricious and mischievous, at times cunning and cruel. Always he can prod the most sensible into doing the insensible—with no motivation, typically, other than because he can, and because he derives great pleasure from doing so. In one account, Eros isn't immune to his own powers: At the behest of Aphrodite, who was jealous of a beautiful mortal named Psyche, Eros shot an arrow into her heart, prompting her to fall in love with the ugliest mortal alive. But Eros was struck partially by his own arrow, and he himself became enrapt by Psyche's beauty and consumed by desire for her. In the one and only time that he defies his mother, against her express command he whisked Psyche off to a hideaway before any harm could befall her. After a harrowing romance, Zeus, the ruler of gods and men, allowed them to marry, and Psyche herself became a goddess.

Eros and True Arête

Eros' origins as limned by Plato's Socrates are a marked variation on the traditional versions of Eros myths, though Plato does give the god an aura of familiarity—the better to couch some radically different notions of the god's objectives and capacities. Socrates suggested that Eros did not directly intervene in the affairs of man, but was an intermediary. Although Eros did indeed plant within all humans the seeds of sensual desire, or *eros* with a small "e," by Socrates' account that's where his intervention ended. After that, it was up to humans to determine how to nurture or satisfy this *eros* bequeathed to us.

As Socrates says, Eros "is the source of our desire to love each other." But humans then determine how to act on that source. Socrates dispelled the idea that Eros controlled human will, able to subvert or pervert it to his whim. Rather, each can choose to spend his life sating *eros* in base ways, or foster it in ways that lead to higher forms of self and social goods.

SOCRATES RELATES THAT on Aphrodite's birthday, the beggarly god Poverty took advantage of Plenty in his inebriated state, as he lay in Zeus' garden, to make a baby with him. The baby conceived was Eros, whom Socrates characterizes as "naturally a lover of the beautiful" and "no seeker after wisdom, for he is wise already." Yet humans, endowed with *eros*, are not innately wise or lovers of the beautiful. Unlike Eros, we *do* have to be seekers. For, as Socrates says, to be "as Eros" should be the quest of each human, because "wisdom is a most beautiful thing, and love is of the beautiful."

Put another way: The most beautiful thing one can love, according to Socrates, is wisdom. We demonstrate this most beautiful love in our striving to become wise—which is tantamount to the quest to discover and realize more about the nature and potential of *arête*, or all-around human excellence. It is "love of beauty" in action. In this dedicated endeavor, we rub shoulders with the immortals.

True Arête

In the *Symposium*, Socrates says his exchange with Diotima ends with this insight:

> What if man had eyes to see true beauty. . . . [I]n that commu-
> nion only, beholding beauty with the eye of the mind, will he be
> able to bring forth, not images of beauty, but realities, and so
> nourish true *arête*, in order to . . . be immortal.

As you cultivate the ability to see true beauty with your mind's eye, you come to desire more than anything to bring forth this beauty through your works and deeds. You might do this by making a baby with the one you love most in the world, creating a work of art such as a novel or a painting or a play, campaigning for social change, engaging in philosophical inquiry on human excellence, seeking to discover elegant physical laws of the universe, or forming pioneering political institutions—always with the end of nourishing true *arête*.

Arête, as the classical Greek scholar H. D. F. Kitto puts it, is the quest to be an excellent all-rounder, to become someone with "a respect for the wholeness or oneness of life," with an understanding that achieving harmony "exists not in one department of life but life itself." To the Greeks, this wholeness was a specific type of order and harmony between self and society—a type in which every deed undertaken by a member of Athenian citizenry was with a keen mindfulness of its impact on everyone else, and a recognition that one could not attain greater personal excellence without also paving the way for everyone else in society to attain it as well.

"Would that be an ignoble life?" Diotima rhetorically asked Socrates of this quest. To the contrary, it is man's shot at immortality.

Desire and Beauty

In the *Symposium*, Socrates impresses upon us what a driving force desire is in our lives, how it has the potential to lead us terribly astray in ways in which we waste our lives pursuing the wrong kinds of desire—or how it can set us on a course that brings us into direct contact with the divine.

As eminent humanities scholar Stringfellow Barr eloquently writes in his history of the Greeks, Socrates posits in the *Symposium* that *eros*, if properly tapped into,

> could lead a man up a kind of ladder from perceiving and loving a beautiful form to loving all beautiful forms, to the beauty of institutions and laws, to the beauty of the various sciences, to a science of beauty everywhere, until at last such a man could behold beauty itself, beauty bare, unspecified, simple, everlasting.

But the process itself of perceiving and loving has to be one of beauty; it must entail a method and ethos of discovery that teaches one how better to perceive and love what is beautiful in both the particular and the abstract. Bereft of this, progressing in our ability to see—much less create—beautiful forms remains out of our reach.

Moreover, Socrates in fact indicates that, with each step we advance up the ladder, perceiving a particular form and perceiving beauty in its essence go hand in glove; as one ascends the ladder, one is better able to see both universal and particular beauty and how they are woven together at every turn. Ascension up the "*eros* ladder" is equivalent to developing the capacity to see abstract beauty in particular objects, and concomitantly to see in each particular object a manifestation of *eros* at its most ethereal and abstract.

What are the components of this ladder? All the foundational forms of Greek love. They must be nurtured together to create the conditions necessary for *eros* to work its magic. *Eros* can never be all it can be if it is divorced from the complementary nourishing of *xenia*, *storge*, *philia*, and *agape*.

Thus, *eros* in its highest manifestation is not equivalent to arriving at a sort of mountaintop where one eventually beholds "beauty itself," disembodied from the beholder and what one is beholding. True *eros* is not a static concept equivalent to a fixed end point where we behold an immutable essence of beauty. Instead, it is the continual cultivation of our capacity to perceive, create, realize ever newer and more divine forms of beauty. Consequently, Socrates would never agree that the beauty born of *eros* is a simple essence unto itself. Rather, to him, it is the most integral part of the elegant yet complex process of human perception, invention, creation.

The Ways of Eros

Eros is not just that which enables one to visualize or write a poem or compose a symphony or produce some other original aesthetic work. Rather, it is the ability to produce something that opens our lenses to new possibilities or dimensions of human being. The same goes when one is making a contribution to a scholarly discipline, setting forth a new juridical law, founding a new type of science, or catalyzing the formation of a new social institution or political system. Not all such endeavors are equivalent to *eros* in action. To Socrates, only those that expand our ways of looking at and being in the world—that advance true *arête*—are equivalent to functional beautiful forms. In order to make such forms, one must develop imaginative abilities along with rational acumen, and one must simultaneously foster both social conscience and autonomy.

In saying that *eros* is an acquisitive and possessive sort of love, Socrates was not diminishing it, only clarifying its nature, so it can be recognized, tapped into, and harnessed properly. To do this, one has to learn what is worth acquiring and possessing. This requires continual inquiry and experimentation and testing with diverse others, with the shared end of realizing forms of beauty—aesthetic, professional, humanistic, spiritual—that advance us further along the path toward true *arête*.

Drinking Party

Symposium is Greek for "drinking party." Socrates' inquiry into the nature of *eros* takes place during a symposium with friends and acquaintances. They have been drinking steadily, engaged in ribald revelry throughout the night. Yet no one, least of all Socrates, deems it incongruous that serious philosophical inquiry would take place in such environs. In fact, they couldn't imagine such inquiry occurring anywhere *but* in an atmosphere suffused with the playful, the passionate and erotic. If you're going to discuss matters of the heart in ways that will bear fruit, you should not seek out sterile surroundings and merely intellectualize.

To discover Socrates' outlook on *eros*, one must take into account not just the formal dialogue presented to Plato, but the drinking party itself, the repartee and asides among participants, the sexual tension and attraction among them—and toward Socrates. Often in the process of their sexual banter, the participants reveal more about their notions of *eros* than they do in the formal philosophical exploration. Then one can appreciate how, in the course of the dialogue, the participants grow in their insight into *eros* and in their capacity to develop it in the name of *arête*.

Eros *Outlet*

Someone in the throes of *eros* is driven by a spirit and force—what the Greeks of antiquity called a daimon—to fill a void within. The earliest Greek societies believed that one needed the opportunity from time to time to "vent" this daimon. Long before the birth of Socrates, they held festivals in honor of the Greek god Dionysus, whom classicist E. R. Dodds says is the mythic representation of the "mysterious and uncontrollable tides" of human compulsions and passions that "ebb and flow" within us.

According to early Greek mythology, it was Dionysus who on occasion spurred Greeks to give in to their irrational impulses with abandon. The trick was to find just the right balance: if you don't vent your lower impulses intermittently, in orgiastic and other frenzied displays, you become repressed and stifled in a way that can lead to abrupt and violent outbursts, the Greeks maintained. But if you overdo it, you become captive to these impulses. The earliest Greek societies held that the ideal balance—in which one learns to vent and channel sexual desires properly, in the right measure and for the right ends—can compel one to become more adept at discovering, contemplating, and fashioning beauty in its higher forms. It can lead to the cultivation of rational, constructive, creative impulses, enabling one to develop talents in ways that make an optimal contribution to society.

If It Makes You Happy

"*Eros* is 'free love,'" April tells us. "It is a love, not a sex, free-for-all."

I, along with several others, am in a tavern off Bourbon Street, in New Orleans, amid the raucous festivities of Mardi Gras. I've been attending Mardi Gras, a tradition in the "Big Easy" starting in the 1870s, for more than a dozen years. Of course, none of us has any idea that the coming fall, a category 4 hurricane will devastate the region and render much of it uninhabitable. I'd met April, an organic gardener and jewelry designer, and many of the rest of those sandwiched around me during the several years I lived in Hattiesburg, Mississippi, plying my trade as a magazine writer. As we watch those outside engaged in a gleeful struggle to catch trinkets thrown from the passing gaudy floats, including one from the Krewe of Eros, we explore the question, "What is *eros*?"

"'Free love' was the philosophy of us 'flower children' of the 1960s," April goes on. "The counterculture was about exploring and experimenting with sex, drugs, the pill, and rock and roll—in the name of a more liberating love—*eros*. It wasn't just, or even mostly, about individual freedom, but about human emancipation. Part of this was celebrating, rather than being ashamed of, diverse dispositions toward sex—and protesting the severe limitations on *eros* that the puritanical and hypocritical establishment had placed on it."

Comments Tommie, a reflexologist, "I never went as far as Alfred Kinsey [the human sexuality research scientist], who said 'the only unnatural sexual act is one you can't perform.' And I believed that sexual experimentation should always be in the name of discovering a more universal love. If that wasn't the goal, then there was no *eros* in the picture."

"Tommie and I lived in a commune for a while," April explains. "All of us shared the same values—sharing everything we had, including our bodies. We were intimate, with our love for one another—

rather than promiscuity—our justification for coming together this way."

Says Clarence, a dentist and sometimes nudist, "Uninhibited *eros* is far from the same thing as uninhibited sex, which trivializes *eros* because it can be sans love. Uninhibited *eros* means that sex is just one among an arsenal of emancipating tools. The sexual revolution has to be tied to the political and spiritual and economic revolution—making a world of love, not war, making a world where everything we do, everything we produce, is a form of expression geared toward greater emancipation. We believed back then that 'free love' was not value free but the highest value. Everything you make, say, do should be a creative expression of free love—it should be a gift you give of yourself to others freely, with no coercion. That is *eros*."

We watch a group strip on a balcony across the street as they're egged on by bystanders below. "Today in America, it's a free sex sideshow," says Tommie. "It's about gratuitous sex, sex completely demystified, devalued, diminished. When I hear young people talk about sex, it makes me blush, and I'm from the sixties. They talk about sexual encounters and positions like they're comparing toothpaste brands. *Eros* is nowhere to be seen or heard or experienced. It can never mean you 'value' one another only as sex objects, people to help you get off."

Clarence's friend Charles, who plays in a blues band, says, "Endless orgies and all-around lewdness are false *eros*. This one-night-stand stuff, getting so drunk you can't stand up, showing your privates from the balcony, is the opposite of *eros*."

He soon goes on: "*Eros* sometimes is best expressed in other ways besides outright loving sex. Sometimes you give it fullest expression when you're no longer sexually intimate with the one you love. Like, the best blues songs are often those about a romantic love lost, about a former lover now getting it on with another. They're an 'aesthetic venting' that oozes an *eros* that otherwise would have stayed bottled up and died inside."

"I do enjoy Mardi Gras," Clarence then says. "But contrary to popular belief, it is not about *eros*. It is about excess, plain and simple, a venting of your wild side. That's nothing to be ashamed of, but you shouldn't make it more than it is, or you make it less than what it is."

"Well, to me, Mardi Gras is *eros*," says Hank, a bartender, his bald pate painted the colors of the rainbow, his biceps decked out with tattoos of naked women in various compromising positions. "*Eros* is sating your deepest desire, no matter what that desire might be."

"No matter how base?" I ask.

Hank thinks long and hard about this. "'Base' is in the eye of the beholder. Those who've spoken so far believe that the desires of their parents were base, and their parents thought the same about the desires of these 'free love radicals.' I don't think anyone on this planet would ever consider their own deepest desires base.

"*Eros* is what you covet so much you're a slave to it," Hank then says. "It's what you can never get enough of, no matter how often you get a fix of it. It leaves you in a euphoric, ecstatic state—but, alas, a temporary one—so you're always wanting more. It can be chocolate; politics; sex, drugs, and rock and roll; or playing shuffleboard and gorging at buffets on a cruise ship—whatever floats your boat. For me, it's New Orleans vice—the unabashed celebration of the hedonistic, the orgiastic, the pornographic."

"So to you, it doesn't have to involve love?" I ask.

"Not romantic love," Hank replies, "at least not as others here have posited the term. It does involve a romance—one involving the satisfaction of what gives you the biggest personal thrill, the greatest high. It doesn't have to involve erotic intimacy with another or with others, but with whatever object or activity gets you to that highest point of ecstasy."

"Translated from the French, Mardi Gras means 'Fat Tuesday,' a day of gorging, of going absolutely hog wild," says Hank's friend Paul. "That is *eros* in action."

Paul goes on to tell us, "Mardi Gras has pagan origins. Even by the extremely permissive standards of the Greeks back in the pre-Hellenic days, its celebration was considered wild. Eventually it became incorporated into the Christian church, but it never lost its lascivious nature. Institutionalized religion recognized the need to satisfy primitive desires from time to time—not base desires, but primitive ones that we all have and that we all, deep down, need to satisfy. *Eros* is the satisfaction of these desires, which brings you a type of atavistic pleasure."

Charles says after a good while, "Some desires can't be reconciled. Since I married over ten years ago, my highest desire has been to be a loving husband in a monogamous relationship. But sometimes I have a desire—call it primitive, call it base—to be with others, to 'get wild' with them. I try to convince myself that, hey, I've got 50 percent of my dad's genes, and he was quite the sexual carouser, so it's natural that I have these desires. But 50 percent of my genes aren't from him. And even if all my genes came from him, I'm not him, I'm me.

"The point I'm getting at is that my desire to be with others conflicts with my image of who I desire to be as a husband and father. If I gave in to this desire to 'just do it' with others—with whom I may not have any emotional attachment—it would lead me away from becoming the person I 'desire to aspire' to be.

"My wife would never stray. It wouldn't even occur to her to. It bothers me that it does occur to me. I also know she loves me so much that even if I gave in to this desire, and she found out, she'd forgive me. But she'd never look at me quite the same way again. And I'd never look at me the same way again."

Then Charles says, "*Eros* is knowing what you should desire, and acting in such a way that you fight to overcome all those other desires of yours that conflict with it, so you can come closer to realizing your 'higher desire.'" He sighs. "So I go on fighting these lower desires of mine. I hope twenty years from now, I'm still just fantasizing, and am still as loyal to my wife as ever. All this fantasizing hasn't made me a worse lover with my wife, I'll tell you that."

"How do you know what you should desire?" I ask the group.

Tommie replies, "Let me answer it this way: If you fulfill a desire, yet afterward it leaves you feeling empty or ashamed, then you haven't fulfilled *eros*. A 'higher desire' can only be one that makes you happy and that makes happier all those with whom you are doing the fulfilling.

"All of us in the commune desired a kind of utopia back then," she goes on after a pause, "a world where there was no cheating, no adultery, no hypocrisy. But after a while I and others came to realize that what we really wanted was to have one soul mate for life. I had to take a journey to realize that I'd been rebelling against the 'older generation,' which had cheapened the whole notion of being with just one person, what with all their philandering. I came to see that what I wanted was a genuine equal, an intimate partner with whom I could have a truly freeing love in a monogamous relationship—something that most in my parents' generation couldn't have because men and women weren't equals. Our free love movement set the stage for men and women to have monogamous partnerships with true equality—making true *eros* possible."

"I left the commune after a year, and Tommie left not long after I did, and eventually it disbanded," April now says. "Even with all the drugs to free us from our inhibitions, I found the sex with others at best so-so. I don't think we came close to achieving the intimacy we'd hoped for. Yet I consider it a success in its way, because it was a noble experiment, undertaken out of loving intent, to emancipate love from its patriarchal shackles."

April goes on: "I've been happily married for over two decades to a man who is so loving and understanding that, out of true *eros*, he is devoted to helping me satisfy my desires. True *eros* can only exist with that kind of intimacy between equals who desire to fill one another with ecstatic pleasure in *all* their life pursuits, not just sexual ones."

I ask, "Can your notion of what specifically constitutes 'eros in action' and how it should be satisfied change a great deal over time?"

"It can, and does," replies April. "I honestly wouldn't want our children to know all the details of how I practiced and explored *eros* in my youth—not out of shame but because that's no longer the path that I believe a person should take to fulfill her highest desires. But the elements that make up true *eros* don't change—play, creativity, desire, commitment, inventiveness, sexual fulfillment."

Then Hank chimes in: "I still insist that *eros* is whatever most or best gives you an ecstatic rush—whether it's good, bad, base, sublime, what have you."

He pauses, sighs, and seems to reconsider. "I wonder, though, if those things I do that give me a cheap, momentary thrill or high, but make me feel after a while like I've cheapened myself or someone else, can really be considered *eros*. Because the high that comes from *eros* should never make you feel miserable, should it?"

Making Sex Taboos Taboo

Bertrand Russell (1872–1970), who made seminal contributions to formal logic, mathematics, and analytical philosophy, was demonized in his time for asserting that societal taboos about sex were almost always "totally irrational and very harmful" (for example, the old wives' tale that masturbation causes insanity). Though Russell was denounced as a sexual libertine, Russell scholar Al Seckel notes that in truth he was a romantic in matters of sex and love: Russell saw no conflict between rationalism and romantic love; he believed, as did Socrates, that rational inquiry aided and abetted the discovery and elevation of romantic intimacy and creativity. In Russell's view, it is only when one can consider and cultivate a sexual ethic "freely and fearlessly" that one can set forth rational sexual mores:

> The doctrine that I wish to preach ... involves nearly as much self
> control as is involved in conventional doctrine. . . . The doctrine
> that there is something [inherently] sinful about sex has done
> untold harm to individual character. . . . By keeping sex love in a
> prison, conventional morality has done much to imprison all

forms of friendly feeling. . . . Whatever sexual ethic may come to
be ultimately accepted must be free from superstition and must
have recognizable and demonstrable grounds in its favor.

Russell also faced social opprobrium for asserting that the institution of marriage was greatly diminished by existing puritanical stric-
tures. For advocating premarital sex, and even trial marriages in some
instances, and for maintaining that infidelity wasn't necessarily auto-
matic grounds for divorce, Russell became a pariah on both sides of the
Atlantic. A successful effort was led by social puritans in cosmopolitan
Manhattan to prevent him from accepting a teaching position there.
      This is the "radical" view he propounded:

> Love is what gives intrinsic value to a marriage . . . it is one of the
> supreme things which make human life worth preserving. But
> though there is no good marriage without love, the best marriages
> have a purpose which goes beyond love . . . infinite with the infin-
> ity of human endeavor . . . [with] that deep intimacy, physical,
> mental and spiritual, which makes a serious love between man
> and woman the most fructifying of human experiences.

Al Seckel notes that "Russell's revolt did not overturn all the
oppressive ideas, and recently, with the tremendous resurgence of
religious fundamentalism, there has been something of a . . .
re-establishment of some of the old conventions."

Sex Appeal

French feminist and existentialist philosopher Simone de Beauvoir
(1908–1986), following Socrates and Diotima, called *eros* the portal to
the divine, that which makes "significances and goals appear in the

world" and leads one to discover "reasons for existing." De Beauvoir believes that those segments of society that repress or oppress one gender or class in effect repress themselves as well, because true *eros* can be experienced only between equals.

French-born American author Anaïs Nin, a contemporary of de Beauvoir and known for her explicitly erotic writing, didn't think women were men's equal but their betters. Nin asserted that in women *eros* still exists in its pure state—one in which love and sensuality are enmeshed—whereas for men these two fundamental elements of *eros* long ago went their separate ways. Thus, for men, all that remains is the striving to satisfy their base urges.

The other lamentable result, Nin said, is that women engaged in relationships with men cannot fully evolve their *eros*. But rather than give up on men altogether, she believed that women must "stop listing their griefs against men" and focus instead on reeducating them about the true ways of *eros*, so they can resume a mutual striving that pushes outward the boundaries of erotic discovery. In all cases, regardless of with whom women have relationships, Nin asserted that it must be their dedicated task to take the lead in "linking eroticism to love, to emotion, to a selection of a certain person," because women are the only gender still fully in touch with true *eros*.

> The true liberation of eroticism lies in accepting the fact that there are millions of facets to it . . . a million objects of it, situations, atmospheres and variations. We have . . . to dispense with guilt concerning its expansion, then remain open to its surprises, varied expressions. . . .

But its "highest potency," she believed, can be fused only "with individual love and passion for a particular human being."

To de Beauvoir and Nin as to Socrates and Diotima, principled pleasure-seeking entails that you never see others—whether that "other" is another person, your society, your universe—only as a means to your own satisfaction, but that you also see them as ends in themselves. Socrates believed that only by fulfilling the love mandate of Diotima could you grow in ways that would enable you "to see true beauty . . . and so nourish true *arête*, in order to become the friend of God, and be immortal."

Forbidden Fruit

Martha Nussbaum, the distinguished feminist philosopher and social activist with appointments in the University of Chicago's schools of philosophy, law, divinity, and classics, points out the critical role that societal mores play in determining those objects we desire in sating our sexual *eros*.

> We see this quickly in the tremendous variety of what is found erotically appealing in different societies—and, of course, by different individuals in different societies: different attributes of bodily shapes, of demeanor and gesture, of clothing, of sexual behavior itself.

What this really underscores is the pivotal role of society in dictating what we *should* desire. But this may conflict with what, or whom, we actually desire. When this is so, what we desire becomes forbidden fruit, so to speak, and we may feel deep dissatisfaction if this desire is unfulfilled, and deep shame if it is consummated.

Scholar K. J. Dover writes that the culture of ancient Athens for a while was "free to select, adapt, develop—and above all—innovate." It's not just that there were blurred boundaries between various orientations but that there were no boundaries to be blurred in the first place, because of their holistic outlook on such matters. What mattered to them was that the "orientation" of erotic satisfaction was principled—that no matter how one went about realizing one's erotic desires, one did so in a way in which those involved first and foremost saw one another as ends in themselves. So one was more oriented toward those "significances and goals" of Simone de Beauvoir, and Anais Nin's prescription for "true liberation of eroticism," which steer one further toward *arête*.

When Athens went into deep decline in Socrates' latter years, so did the pervasive practice of this norm and form of erotic realization.

Crazy Love

Socrates says in the dialogue *Phaedrus* that *eros* unchecked will drive a person mad. Far from proposing that *eros* should be suppressed, he meant it should be properly understood so it can be exploited to maximum effect. When this is what takes place, he says, "*eros* can be one of life's blessings." In *Phaedrus*, Socrates and Phaedrus—who hint they have a mutual erotic attraction—engage in a discourse on how to solve "the problem of *eros*." Socrates tells Phaedrus that "within each one of us there are two sorts of ruling or guiding principles. . . . One is the innate desire for pleasure, the other an acquired judgment that aims us at what is best. . . ." *Eros*, to Socrates, is the merging of acquired judgment with our instinctual desire for pleasure. *Eros* is neither reason nor instinct, but both, entwined in the service of *arête*, to ensure that the pleasures we pursue are principled.

Great Escape

"This place feeds passions of mine that no other place could ever satisfy," says Denny, a high roller who's feeling no pain as he makes a wobbly but nonetheless sweeping gesture meant to take in all our surroundings. "Here, I can get in touch with and nurture my inner 'wild child.'"

With his booming voice, he has no trouble making himself heard above what some might call revelry and others might call racket. We are surrounded by many of the most popular gambling attractions known to man (slot machines), along with two adjoining nightclubs that seem in competition over which can bombard us louder with aesthetically challenged 1970s music.

We are holding a dialogue on the question "What feeds your passions?" The motley gathering consists of fellow passengers I'd met on the plane flight to "Sin City," hotel housekeeping staff who had just ended their shift, local residents who "happen" to find themselves here in the casino at least once a week, and other assorted gamblers and passersby willing to engage in philosophical discourse, as long as they are also within arm's reach of the slot machine levers.

Today is the hundredth anniversary of Las Vegas' founding. We are at ground zero of Glitter Gulch—named for its endless miles of near-blinding neon—the downtown site where on May 15, 1905, a land auction of 110 acres took place. It converted Vegas from a no-horse town into a formal municipality to serve as a base to house and entertain all those working on the western expansion of the massive cross-country railroad. The casino where we're holding philosophical court was one of the first built here after gambling was legalized in the state in 1931. The casino paved the way for Las Vegas eventually to become known as the Entertainment and Gambling Capital of the World, where gaming, prostitution, and quickie marriages and divorces were par for the course. Once upon a time the likes of the Rat Pack—Frank Sinatra, Dean Martin, Sammy Davis Jr., Joey Bishop, and Peter Lawford—made the city even more notorious with their frequent visits for bacchanalian binges with some of their acquaintances in the mob, which in the 1950s had controlling interests in many of the casinos.

"As I was telling you on the plane," Denny, a life insurance salesman with a penchant for inordinately loud Hawaiian shirts, says to me now, "many think of this place as a den of iniquity. Which it is.

Some think this makes it a microcosm of everything that's wrong with this country. But it's America at its best, a place to feed those passions we all have but have few outlets for anywhere else, because we have to be prim and proper."

He explains himself further: "I work hard at my job. You might even say I have a certain passion for it. Salesmen are the backbone of our great economy. If I exceed my sales target by 10 percent, my boss rewards me with a weekend trip here. It's something out of the ordinary. If you were from Omaha, it'd be out of the ordinary for you too. Here, I feed my 'baser passions' for intense forty-eight-hour stretches. I drink more than I should, fool around more than I should, gamble more than I should—and then go home able to work better at my job, be a better husband and father, with the memory of my visit here still vivid. That motivates me to do all I can to be rewarded with another trip here."

Says Rosie, who is here on her monthly sojourn with a group of girlfriends from Salt Lake City, "Vegas' longtime motto is, 'What happens here stays here.' It's meant to be a great, brief escape from family responsibility and all normality. If I didn't have Vegas to escape to, I'd truly be a desperate housewife. By coming here periodically with 'the girls,' letting it 'all hang out' for a short spell, I go back home and can actually be passionate about suburbia and the life of a soccer mom."

Jake, an instructor at a nearby college, says, "I agree that sometimes you need to separate your baser from higher passions, to cultivate one not at the expense of the other but to the advantage of the other. Even the Greeks and Romans, the fathers of the 'civilized' Western world, permitted bacchanalian revelry on occasion. Instead of putting blinders to their more primal passions, they faced them squarely, reveled in them from time to time in ways that made them more pure and productive citizens. By allowing people to have orgies and other passionate feeding frenzies, they produced some of the most timeless works of art ever. There's a connection between the two."

Says Kep-Tian, who has ventured here from Taiwan, "It's part of the eastern tradition too. Even the legendary sixth century B.C. Taoist moral philosopher Lao-tzu invented a gambling game in China. He recognized the healthiness and necessity of such diversions and the role they played in channeling our more reckless passions, so we were responsible the rest of the time."

"Why not feed your baser passions all the time?" I ask.

"It'd be like having Christmas everyday," Denny says. "It lessens the value of your base passions if you give in to them all the time. Same goes with feeding your higher passions, or middling passions. If you feed any of them too much, they overload and become counterproductive."

Interjects Lupe, a housekeeper at a resort casino, "I think you should feed only your higher passions. Vegas feeds mine. A passion, as I understand it, is what you're most devoted to, what you have the greatest conviction and commitment to. Vegas feeds my passion for putting food in the mouths of my children."

Lupe continues. "I know, for many, Vegas is a great escape from somewhere else, but for me, this was a place permanently to escape *to*. It was an escape *from* hell. I came here from Juarez, Mexico, with my two young children five years ago. We crossed the Sonora Desert. Some might say I was foolhardy for risking our lives, but it was worth the risk, to get here to the promised land.

"After my husband abandoned us [in Mexico], I worked seven days a week, twelve hours a day, at a *maquiladora*, making blue jeans for fifteen dollars a week—slave wages. Here I have a good-paying job, good benefits, my boys go to a good school. We have a good, safe roof over our heads. I can spend quality time with my kids rather than coming home so bone-tired that I collapse in bed. Someday, my sons will be mayor and governor here. Here in Vegas, 'anything goes'—and by that I mean the sky is the limit for anyone who works with enough drive and discipline."

Says Evan, a taxi driver, "Vegas also has fed my higher passion—for becoming the person I'd long dreamed of being. My life sucked in small-town New England. People have you pegged a certain way, and that's that. Here people let you be who you are or become who you want to be, and they'll do whatever they can to help you along."

According to an article in *U.S. News & World Report*, "tens of thousands of Americans" see Vegas as the new mecca where they "reinvent their lives." With its "robust economy that services more than 30 million visits a year," Vegas today "lures upwards of 6,000 a month," and it "increasingly draws seekers of a normal, middle class life"—a far cry from its earlier days, when it was primarily a magnet for "misfits, gangsters and gamblers seeking refuge from America's mainstream."

"Look, I'm really glad for people like Evan and Lupe that Vegas is their pot of gold at the end of the higher passion rainbow," Denny says. "Like the McDonald's commercial goes, they're 'lovin' it' here, and I'm lovin' it here. We just have different reasons for escaping here and lovin' it."

"This place is purely impure," says Shelley, a dancer at a strip club. "You can be whoever you are—transvestite, transsexual, straight, diehard Christian or atheist, a bit of all the above, whatever. It's genderblind, class-blind, colorblind. No one could care less where you're from, what your politics are, your ethnicity, your academic pedigree or lack thereof. Our philosophy is 'live and let live.' Imagine what a lovely and lovable world it would be if all of it was like Sin City."

Harold, a lay minister, comments, "Just about an hour down the road is the Nevada Test Site, where the United States has conducted its nuclear weapons tests. It's the 'temple' of destructive base passions. I've spent a lot of my life protesting at its entrance with other peace activists. People say, 'Oh, we'd never use nuclear weapons.' Yet we have them, we have used them, and I fear we'll use them again. I've met many who love the idea of what a nuclear weapon is capable of doing. And look at how so many these days, of so many religious persuasions, find the ultimate passion in killing the innocent—the more the better. Vegas is harmless in comparison, even beneficial in some ways as an outlet for venting one's darker impulses from time to time—but in moderation."

Harold continues. "A few blocks from this glitz and glitter, there are so many who are down and out, who destroyed their livelihoods, their relationships, because they couldn't keep their baser passions in sufficient check. I counsel those addicted to gambling—who came thinking they were going to cart money away from here in truckloads, only to lose it all."

"Look, I know that while I and millions of others feed our baser passions in Vegas, there's a big bad world out there," remarks Denny as he impatiently tries to flag down a cocktail waitress for another drink. "I know there's down-and-out people a few blocks away. I know that thousands of miles away, our soldiers are risking it all so that others can live with the type of hope and opportunity that so many risk it all to come to America to enjoy. I know that, and I appreciate it deeply.

"I still have to go on living to the hilt sometimes, don't I? I've still got to have a reason to bounce out of bed in the morning. Hell, our president told us the most patriotic act we could do after 9–11 was go out and keep spending money. That makes me a patriot, doing my part here for the cause."

Denny continues before anyone else can get a word in edgewise. "Whether you escape to Vegas for a better job or to escape from your job and the overall humdrum, whether you come here to spend a few nights or the rest of your life, as the case may be, whether you come here with great expectations and you fail miserably or you succeed beyond your wildest dreams, you gotta love a place that lets you feed the passions—whatever they are—that most need feeding." Denny pulls the slot, and a few second later, out tumbles $250 in quarters. He lets out a shout of atavistic joy. "It doesn't get better than this, baby."

Eros *Run Amok*

What happens when most members of society become captive to their more reckless passions? *Eros* unchecked was considered a principal catalyst behind Athens' demise. As it is typically explained away, Athenians had lost their collective heart for cultivating their higher passions after their devastating loss in the Second Peloponnesian War. But what is rarely stressed is that it was the Athenian leadership's decision to launch this war—and the reasons for doing so—not its outcome in defeat, that led to Athens' decline and fall. This war was the first ever precipitated by the Athenians for reasons other than to spread democracy. In this instance, their motivation was a naked landgrab. As their premier historian Thucydides put it, Athenians had become "ungovernable in passion"; lust for power and wealth and self-gratification were the new virtues, supplanting those they'd long held dear and prompting militaristic fanaticism. By war's end, scholar Donald Kagan writes, there was a "collapse in the habits, institutions, beliefs and restraints" that had made Athens the greatest civilization. But in truth, this collapse came about at the war's outset, not its end.

Loving and Loathing in Las Vegas

In his most famous work, *Fear and Loathing in Las Vegas: Savage Journey to the Heart of the American Dream*, gonzo journalist and quintessential American gadfly Hunter S. Thompson embarked on a six-month journey to discover what he called the real American dream. In a book that was otherwise impossible to take seriously, it becomes clear that Thompson wrote more than two hundred pages of farce just to make even more poignant his brief exploration of a very serious and heartfelt question: what does one do after the greatest love-in in U.S. history is no more? It turns out he wasn't going to Vegas to discover the American dream as it had become. That most everyone, in his view, had sold out was all too obvious; it certainly didn't need any reportorial exposé. Rather, his trip into the world of Vegas, the poster child of American lasciviousness, was an opportunity to reflect on the dream that America had almost realized, the bright, shining moment that had just recently been, and died. His journey to Vegas was a "sort of atavistic endeavor, a dream-trip into the past—however recent—into the sixties." Already the great call to civic and social change that spoke to people of all walks of life—the young in particular—seemed but a distant memory, almost as if it had never been.

Thompson called his 1971 Vegas sojourn a chance to remember the recent "sixties trip" that captivated his generation and stirred it to revive America's original dream—namely, to create a world in which all citizens had not just the right but a bona fide opportunity to pursue a liberating life. He considered his work a peonage, a "reluctant salute to that decade that started so high and then went so brutally sour."

Just six years earlier, Thompson said he had been blessed to be part of "a very special time and place," in which it "*meant* something" to be alive and participating in a higher cause, one so passionate and joyful that "no explanation, no mix of words or music or memories can touch that sense of knowing that you were there and alive in that corner of time and the world."

Thompson said Vegas was the epitome of the American dream as it had come to be—a place that did not tolerate losers; for them, it was "the meanest town on Earth." He saw himself as a quintessential loser, and felt it proper punishment that he should banish himself to Vegas for six months. There, he mused that the only option remaining to a socially conscious person in a sea of social unconsciousness was to "lash down the screws and get on with what one has to do"—to keep fighting the good fight to resurrect the 1960s activist ethos more heartily than ever, especially now that the American ship was clearly sinking.

Thompson was at turns praised and vilified by liberals and conservatives alike. He was a gadfly's gadfly, an exemplary bad conscience of his time—once famously called "a Socrates who cursed and drank Wild Turkey." For Thompson, there were no sacred cows, and this poster child for excessive living and scintillating journalism was just as hard, in fact harder, on himself and his own failings than anyone else. His goal was to prompt and prod Americans to shun the type of numbing security that had won the day. Hopeless as his task might have seemed, he was unrelenting in his pursuit of reporting the "[a]bsolute truth," which was "a very rare and dangerous commodity in the context of journalism." According to his biographer,

Paul Perry, Thompson was heartened once his adopted hometown of Aspen became, for a while at least, a place of gatherings that brought together "'the unwashed American businessman' . . . with the likes of Robert Kennedy . . . to discuss topics like the relevance of Good and Evil to modern man and mankind's possible spiritual links to Socrates."

Thompson best articulated his philosophy of living in an essay he wrote in the 1950s. It couldn't have been said better by Socrates himself:

> Security . . . what does this word mean in relation to life as we know it today? . . . by this term, I mean a man who has settled for financial and personal security for his goal in life. . . . His ideas and ideals are those of society in general and he is accepted as . . . respectable. . . . A man is to be pitied who lacked the courage to accept the challenge of freedom and depart from the cushion of security. . . .
>
> Turn back the pages of history and see the men who have shaped the destiny of the world. Security was never theirs, but they lived rather than existed. Where would the world be if all men had sought security and not taken risks or gambled with their lives on the chance that, if they won, life would be different and richer? . . . [W]ho is the happier man, he who has braved the storm of life and lived or he who has stayed securely on shore and merely existed?

In the eyes of Hunter Thompson, Americans no longer gambled in the true American tradition of those who "shaped the destiny of the world." A place such as Vegas made a mockery of what real gambling, for the greater good of citizenry and humanity, was supposed to be all about. Even if we win big in Vegas, we lose big, because we don't advance one iota the original American dream. On February 20, 2005, Thompson died at his home in the Aspen, Colorado, area at age sixty-seven, of a self-inflicted gunshot wound to the head.

———

SOCRATES, ALARMED THAT his peers increasingly pursued a life that promised only "the semblance of success," was determined to inspire them to pursue a life that no amount of money or material goods could buy. So it is, he said, that "I spend my time going about trying to persuade all of you, young and old, that your first and chief concern should not be for your bodies or possessions, but for the highest welfare of your soul." Yet some forms of excess can elevate the human experience, can make it possible for us to be more loving and caring. Socrates believed there were certain types of wealth of which one could never have too much—a wealth of empathy, of goodness. Xenophon, the Greek historian and contemporary of Socrates, notes that Socrates praised those who choose "rather to hoard up a treasure of learning and knowledge than of money." Socrates called these the "true riches" because they "enrich with virtue the minds of those that possess them."

Oedipus

Oedipus the King and *Oedipus at Colonus*, part of the Theban trilogy written by Greek tragedian Sophocles (496–406 B.C.), a contemporary of Socrates, were the inspiration behind the Oedipal complex of Sigmund Freud (1856–1939), founder of psychoanalysis. Freud believed that the play served as a dramatic case in point that a central feature in the lives of the young is that they harbor such an erotic attraction for one parent and hatred of the other that they fantasize about having sex with one and killing the other. To Freud, such "wish fulfillment" must be dealt with openly and treated as a normal part of a child's development, lest it exacerbate severe neuroses in later years. However, the fact is that though the Oedipus plays have their erotic components, they in no way treat an Oedipal complex as Freud construes it.

Oedipus and Socrates have this in common: both sought knowledge that would enable them to best serve their beloved societies. In Oedipus' case, he sought to know who murdered the former king, specifically because this knowledge would arrest the plague that beset his people. Unbeknownst to Oedipus, he himself had murdered the king—his father—during a fight. He had then become king and married Jocasta, whom he did not know was his mother, with whom he had four children. He had no way of knowing that the stranger who provoked him into a lethal fight was his father, any more than he knew that the woman he ended up marrying was his mother. This was a contrivance of Sophocles, to make the play's outcome as tragic as possible.

Yet it is not at all clear that Oedipus himself had an Oedipal complex. According to Freud's own criteria, Oedipus would have had to know his father's and mother's identities, then wished to murder one and marry the other.

Oedipus, himself now King of Thebes, was told by the Delphic oracle that discovering the former king's killer was the only way to prevent further suffering among his people from a devastating plague. Oedipus persisted in his search out of love for his people, even after being warned off by many who knew the truth. Likewise, out of love for Oedipus, those in the know about who the killer was tried to derail his pursuit, even if it brought them further harm.

Both Socrates and Oedipus believed that self-discovery was always related to the goal of advancing their respective societies. Digging into their past with no greater purpose or objective than past-dwelling introspection would have made no more sense to Sophocles' Oedipus than it would have to Socrates.

Complex Oedipus

Where does this leave the Oedipus complex of Freud? Its conceptualization was driven by Freud's own call to "know thyself." Freud's reasons for doing so were similar to those of Socrates and Oedipus: to discover knowledge that would keep human civilization, or their respective corner of it, from dissipating. Freud, who in 1938 at age eighty-two fled Vienna with his family for England to elude Nazi persecution, wanted to understand how we could confront and come to grips with our destructive and irrational tendencies.

Freud's notion of an Oedipal complex originated with his own admitted sexual feelings toward his mother and his concomitant animosity for his father. Freud discovered in analyzing other patients that many confessed to harboring similar sentiments toward their own parents; he extrapolated from this that it must be "a universal childhood event." But although some children surely do have some combination of erotic and aggressive feelings toward their parents, there is no evidence to support Freud's theory that it is universal. Socrates, for one, apparently never had such a complex. Where Socrates would have agreed with Freud is that honest acknowledgment of and confrontation with such feelings can lead to healthy growth. For Freud, the only unforgivable thing is a society that does not allow its members to better understand such feelings.

If someone as nonjudgmental and perceptive as Freud had been there for Oedipus in his time of crisis, perhaps his rash act could have been prevented. Freud dedicated himself to keeping many from harming themselves out of misplaced guilt or shame because of a lack of understanding of their erotic feelings. He knew that the most sensitive didn't need the harsh judgment of society to torture themselves; they were their own harshest and most unforgiving critics. In this vein, no one was a harsher critic of Oedipus than Oedipus himself. He was a complex being deeply in love with and committed to his wife and children, and deeply committed to and loving toward his subjects.

Freud and Socrates

Like Socrates, Freud believed that knowing the truth about *eros* could set us free. Unlike Socrates, he believed that *eros* was solely a matter to be plumbed psychologically. Socrates and Freud, though, shared the view that virtually every relationship has its erotic element, no matter how sublimated. To Socrates, *eros* was no fixed entity housed in a physical-psychic loci, such as a libido, but a dynamic, functional, and evolving one that could be better understood and discovered only by exploring our inner and outer cosmos in tandem.

Freud believed that sex was the instinctual fount of human nature, and therefore of all our constructive and destructive tendencies. Writing about *eros* at a time of growing anti-Semitism and fascism, Freud was pessimistic over whether humans had not learned anything of worth in the interim since World War I—three of his sons fought in the war, in which more than 15 million died, and one daughter died in the famine and influenza epidemic that ensued— about the darker aspects of their nature that would prevent another violent conflict of its magnitude. Interestingly, he constructed his own mythology of humans' basic instincts, not for philosophical purposes but to make more compelling his psychological notions. In his myth, Freud opposed "two 'heavenly powers'"—eternal Eros and eternal Thanatos—the life-affirming Greek god versus the Greek god of death and destruction.

Our sex drives, Freud maintained, were the wellspring for both. According to him, if we act merely to sate ourselves sexually, we are not acting in the best interests of society, and so in fact may bring down the societal curtain, because acts that give pleasure to an individual may well be in direct conflict with that which best perpetuates society. If man makes "genital eroticism the central point of his life," Freud claimed in his *Civilization and Its Discontents*, he will have no energy or inclination to devote himself to culture- and civilization-building endeavors, and society will suffer. Consequently, Freud avers, "the wise men of every age have warned us most emphatically against this way of life." To Freud, we each must willingly agree to a "restriction of sexual life" if we are to foster "a humanitarian ideal."

Because, according to Freud, we do not have unlimited quantities of psychosexual energy at our disposal, we can undertake culture-building only by repressing our sexual drive; in his view, only this "aim-inhibiting" behavior is conducive to the perpetuation of civilization. To Freud, individual happiness per se, as achieved through personal sexual gratification, is of no cultural worth, because it can unravel society. Gratifying oneself in such a way, Freud believed, often conflicts with acts that can best serve to evolve society.

Freud versus the Greeks

The Greeks of antiquity believed that their shared aim should be to tap into their primitive energies in ways that enabled them continually to expand and enhance their energy supply. They did not consider human sexual and aggressive instincts as necessarily pitted against each other, as Freud did. To them, such impulses need not be suppressed, but properly channeled. Indeed, they believed that the proper harnessing of one's sex drives was *itself* a paramount humanitarian ideal. They would have agreed with Freud that the sex instinct should not be vented willy-nilly; but to them, the answer was not to repress it. The Greeks operated from the premise that if one's sexual energy were tapped into properly, the individual self and the societal self, wholly interdependent in their view, would evolve optimally.

FREUD SURELY ERRED in asserting that we must always inhibit our sexual appetites if we are to flourish artistically, culturally, and politically. Rather, we must learn how to utilize our sexual appetites in ways that can contribute to such advances. Although in some instances it may well be the case that the failure to satisfy (or the conscious effort to suppress) our sexual urges leads some to create great works of art and literature, or make lasting contributions in other fields, it can just as well be the case in many instances that such failure inhibits greater artistic, scientific, and humanistic achievement. It depends on the culture, the society, the individual, and the ends.

Eros *and Civilization*

German-American philosopher Herbert Marcuse (1898–1979), a favorite of the New Left in the 1960s and 1970s—his work spawned such slogans as "Make Love, Not War" and "Free Love"—wrote *Eros and Civilization* as a rebuttal to Sigmund Freud's views about sexual suppression. Marcuse asserted that the suppression of *eros* does not lead to the safeguarding of civilization, but its converse. Until and unless we consciously work to create societies in which the nurturing of our sex lives, work lives, political lives, and spiritual lives are complementary, and so are equally valued as principal, interrelated ends by members of society, Marcuse maintained we will end up less, rather than more, evolved.

Whereas Freud believed that "civilization is based on the permanent subjugation of the human instinct" for the greater good of society, Marcuse asserted that only a "nonrepressive society" can perpetuate and advance itself. Unlike Freud, Marcuse did not adhere to the notion that there is an inherent biological clash between sex and civilization. In modern industrial societies, he said the evidence shows that sexual repression has served only to contribute to the marginalization of the poor and of women. Rather than exploiting our "social wealth for shaping man's world in accordance with his Life Instincts," Marcuse argued that we have become "an acquisitive and antagonistic society in the process of constant expansion." Thus instead of furthering human liberation, he asserted that sexual repression has led to "the destruction of life (human and animal)," generating a state of affairs in which "cruelty and hatred and the scientific extermination of men have increased." In his view, repressing our sexual instincts has played a decisive role in contributing to the very problems that Freud believed it would remedy.

The solution, Marcuse maintained, is not to redouble our efforts to create a leisure society. Over the long haul, he averred, it would make a bad problem worse, because we would remain as alienated from our work as ever, and as alienated from a creative and liberating sex life—no matter how much free time we had to engage in sex—of a sort in which it was an integral and redemptive part of all dimensions of human existence. According to Marcuse, the only answer is to create a type of society in which all our waking moments, especially our working ones, are creative expressions of and outlets for our passions, particularly our sexual ones. He asserted we should *not* strive toward ever more leisure, but live a multidimensional creative life that blurs the bounds between work and nonwork hours, between overt sexual expression and other forms of creative expression.

Marcuse, however, did not believe that reviving the type of society cultivated by ancient Athens was the answer; rather, he asserted that only a Marxist society could lead to the human fulfillment he envisioned. To date, though, no society that has billed itself as Marxist has come close to achieving the ends he has described and that the Athenians accomplished for a while.

Reason and Instinct

Herbert Marcuse asserted that *eros* was purely instinctual, something that needed to be wedded to reason, or Logos, in order for us to best harness and channel it creatively. Socrates, on the other hand, believed that *eros* itself had reason embedded within it, and we must try to discover the combination of erotic reason and instinct that best serves the ends of true *arête*. It was this philosophy of *eros* that, for a while, spurred Athens' Golden Age.

The Last Temptation of Eros

In Eva Cantarella's view, Socrates would be the last person to succumb "to the temptations of sex," because maintaining control over his sexual impulses "was an ideal which fitted in with [his] general aspiration towards self-control," and this control was but one demonstration of the sort of "rigour which he believed indispensable, in every area of experience, if one was to reach the fullness of being." But it was a fullness that a love such as *eros* would never be sufficient in itself to bring into being.

Cantarella, though, insists that for Socrates and his fellow inquisitors, "the theme of Eros [is] at the centre of their moral and political reflections." Whereas love informed and drove their inquiries, *eros* was but one of the types at the center. By equating *eros* in particular with love in all its dimensions, she diminishes the full nature and scope, breadth and depth, of their inquiries and insights, of all that "fullness of being" can be.

On the other hand, the preeminent classical scholar Benjamin Jowett says that one can never leave *eros* completely behind. As he writes in the introduction to his translation of Plato's *Symposium*, Plato is "conscious that the highest and noblest things in the world are not easily severed from the sensual desires." But why would you want to sever the sensual from the high and noble? One's sensual desires themselves can be high and noble, prompting creativity, experimentation, and discovery. Conversely, spiritual desires can be more primitive at times than the sensual. Many of the most barbaric acts in human history were carried out by those moved by what they deemed unalloyed, sublime spirituality. Perhaps if their spiritual and sensual sides had been cultivated in tandem, as Socrates modeled and exhorted, they might have acted with more humanity.

One of the most important insights on this subject comes in Plato's *Republic*, in a brief encounter between Socrates and Cephalus, who engage in a short dialogue that precedes a much more involved one on the nature of justice. Socrates asks Cephalus if, with the advantage of age, he has learned anything of particular merit regarding whether his sexual appetites of his more youthful years are something to be missed or, now that he is no longer under their control, he feels more liberated. Cephalus reports that he is glad to have gained a considerable measure of control over the sexual and material appetites of his youthful days, that it has freed him up to devote himself more fruitfully to the pursuit of becoming wiser. Like Socrates, Cephalus is able not so much to deny but to control and channel his passions in ways that lead to the loving pursuit of those things that matter the most—how to become a more excellent human being, how to make ours a more loving world. One does not have to be an ascetic to deny one's sexual urges, to sublimate them in every instance. Yet, as Socrates and Cephalus seem to conclude, one does need to have some degree of mastery over them if one is not to be mastered by and captive to them, thereby failing to discover and hone other kinds of love that can have an impact on one's society, and perhaps on humanity as a whole.

From its lowest to highest manifestations, from its most destructive to constructive outcomes, what distinguishes *eros* in all instances is that it drives a person to fill something lacking within. Because Socrates' works and deeds were largely undertaken out of expansive love rather than any perceived emptiness within or without, and moreover were not directed just at enhancing immediate interpersonal relations but at deepening redemptive bonds between self and a larger world, *eros* cannot be the sum total of Socratic love.

Eros *Middle Way*

In Plato's *Symposium*, Alcibiades is feeling no pain when he equates Socrates with both the goat-hoofed creatures from Greek mythology that were devoted to wine and excess, and to the semidivine acolytes of the sexually charged gods Pan, who resembles a satyr, and Dionysus. But although the mythical figures whom Alcibiades mentions represented the rapture and ecstasy that could drive a person to madness, he overlooks that Socrates himself was the picture of control. Socrates was expert at harnessing the Dionysian aspects of his nature and wedding them to the Apollonian—the refined and aesthetic and spiritual. Going to either extreme, the Dionysian or Apollonian, to Socrates would steer one away from, rather than toward, true *arête*.

The drinking party, with Socrates at the helm, is never allowed to devolve into drunkenness and debauchery any more than it is steered toward the decidedly stoic and intellectual. He deftly navigates a middle course between the two, because this is what will lead them to new insights into and possibilities for *eros*. There is controlled chaos as he channels the participants' passions between physical and spiritual extremes, resulting in the gradual maturation of their outlooks on love, their enhanced ability to visualize beauty in new ways, and their desire to bring to light what they see.

In Book Nine of Plato's *Republic*, Socrates provides a road map—one of the middle way—for how one should properly channel and nurture *eros*. He says that one should have "first indulged his appetites neither too much nor too little, just enough to lay them to sleep, and prevent them and their enjoyments and pains from interfering with the higher principle . . . to contemplate and aspire to the knowledge of the unknown." If one does not follow such a prescription, Socrates asserts that these drives will become more unwieldy and uncontrollable, until "the wild beast within us, gorged with meat or drink . . . goes forth to satisfy his desires; and there is no conceivable folly or crime" that one will not engage in to sate them. But by learning to confront and harness these impulses, one can become a person whose "pulse is healthy and temperate," and so better able to focus "on noble thoughts and inquiries."

SOCRATES' PHILOSOPHY OF cultivating *eros* resembles the Buddha's notion of the Golden Mean. *Eros* at its best, to Socrates, is the midpoint between poverty and plenty. There is another "*eros* middle ground" as well: Poros was a god, an immortal, and Plenty was mortal—so the proper fostering of *eros* is tantamount to traversing the middle ground between the ethereal and eternal world.

Socrates also indicates in Xenophon's version of the *Symposium* that *eros* can be a prison if we don't exploit it properly. If we go to extremes in spiritual love any more than in physical love, *eros* is constraining rather than liberating; spiritual lust is as deformative as physical lust. For us to be wardens rather than prisoners of our *eros*, we must learn how to tap into it in ways that transform us and our world.

What is more, to Socrates, *eros* should never be considered in a vacuum but always in the context of developing together the five fundamental forms of love—*eros*, *storge*, *xenia*, *philia*, and *agape*. Thus, to him, one must strive to discover the Golden Mean among them, the ideal mix of the five forms that will best advance true *arête*.

Constant Craving

In Plato's *Symposium*, Socrates says Diotima instructs him that *eros* is the spirit that first stirs the embers of passion between two people. Diotima says that if you stay mired in mere "sexual *eros*," you'll be obsessed with sating your bodily appetites at the expense and neglect of all else; consequently, you must learn to gain mastery over it and steer it toward "heavenly *eros*." She tells Socrates that the window of opportunity for weaning yourself from more base desires and appetites and the concomitant notions of beauty derived from them, and coming to understand and revel in its more sublime forms, is when your physical love with another is at its peak, because this is when you are most inclined to search within your beloved for such manifestations of beauty. This in turn ensures that over time your love will deepen, your bond will strengthen, until you come to the epiphany that "the beauty of people's souls is more valuable than the beauty of their bodies." Diotima warns that if this isn't what comes to pass, then when physical looks and the attraction based on them fizzle, you will have missed out on an unrivaled and perhaps not-to-be-repeated opportunity for growth in affairs of love, and your commitment to another will go by the wayside. You'll never learn what it is to forge deeper commitments of lasting worth, and will be fated to remain in a state of all-consuming craving, "committed" only to sating your basest lusts.

IN PLATO'S *PHAEDRUS,* an allegorical follow-on to the *Symposium,* Socrates distinguishes between types of lovers. On one end of the spectrum is the "evil lover," who is "out to serve himself." For him, the beloved is only a means to sate his own passions and appetites, someone for whom he has no true tenderness or solicitousness, though he pretends he does at the outset, making himself "most agreeable" in order "to enslave and deceive another" for his own manipulative and controlling ends. Preeminent classical scholar Benjamin Jowett notes that only when the evil lover's affection is no more does it become apparent to his putative beloved that he is "the enemy" and loves only "as wolves love lambs." Then there's the so-called "non-lover," who evokes no emotional response from others with whom he interacts, because he evokes no sentiments—neither jealousy nor possessiveness nor any other romantic feeling. As a consequence of his excessive "prudence," he does not stir one to have any emotional attachment to him. Then there is the "noble lover," who does not seek that which is best for himself but is concerned only for his beloved. A noble lover would never intentionally or knowingly do harm to the beloved; rather, his every action is geared to do that which is in his beloved's best interests and holds the greatest promise of furthering his objectives.

Jowett points out that Socrates makes these distinctions between lovers in this dialogue in order to further bring home the acute differences between lower and higher love: "the one answers to the natural wants of the animal, the other rising above them and contemplating with awe the forms of justice, temperance, holiness." In both instances, love is depicted as "one of the great powers of nature," but only in the case of noble love is there a commitment that turns a couple's thoughts "toward beauty of divine origin."

Commitment

"All commitments are a type of marriage. They entail responsibility, devotion. But the best ones have a romance to them; they're creative and loving. They make you feel more free than you were before you entered into them," says Rachel, a physician's assistant gathered with me and about twenty others at a Diversity Celebration in the Bay Area of California. We're holding a dialogue on the question "What are the best commitments?"

"A commitment of this kind with the one you love most in the world," Rachel goes on, "expands your world. There's a thread of creativity, exploration, discovery in just about all your interactions with one another."

Ray, forty-five, is a charter member of the first Socrates Café group I started in the Bay Area in the late 1990s while I was living there. He says, "The best commitments—at least of the loving, romantic kind, which seem to be the type we're talking about—are your ticket to the best sex in the world. You can be so open and honest about your needs and desires, and you're both devoted to satisfying them. Fulfilling someone erotically is never 'just about sex,' but the sex is without compare, the best, because those involved love one another. Sex without love can be great, but sex with love is the ultimate."

Then he says, "There's that exchange in Philip Roth's *The Human Stain* where classics professor Coleman Silk, after having sex with thirty-four-year-old Faunia, a janitor with whom he wants to have a serious relationship, insists to her, 'This is more than sex.' Faunia adamantly says, 'No it's not. . . . This is sex. All by itself. Don't fuck it up by pretending it's something else.' She's mad at him for breaking 'the rules of engagement,' for having higher aspirations for their relationship other than sex. Faunia thinks sex is at its best when unalloyed with romance, when a couple has no mutual feelings other than those generated by pure sexual arousal. But even so-so sex with love is far better than the best 'just sex' with no love. To hit the sublime, there has to be an intimacy between those involved, so that every time you think you've hit the peak, think again—there's an even higher one just around the bend."

Rachel, nodding, says, "My partner and I practice Tantra, the ancient art of cultivating sexual awareness. Tantra means 'loving sex,' engaging in sex in such a way that you become one with your partner. *Pinde So Brahamande*, in Sanskrit, means that your body is a divine temple, a microcosm of the universe itself, and with Tantra yoga and meditation, you tap into and expend sexual energy in ways that lead to greater sexual and spiritual awareness at the same time."

"My 'sex Bible,' the *Kama Sutra*, is also my life Bible, my 'commitment Bible,' " says Ana, a friend of Ray's who came from Atlanta to take part in the celebration, organized after President Bush declared he would spearhead a movement to enact a constitutional amendment banning same-sex marriages. "I don't see it, as many do, as first and foremost a primer on sex," she says of the writings composed by the enigmatic Vatsyayana, about whom virtually nothing is known, between the first and sixth centuries A.D. "Its chapters cover everything from specific sexual positions, how to bring about the highest forms of erotic arousal, the links between the erotic and the epistemological, to insights on love in general.

"*Kama* is Sanskrit, and means both 'sex' and 'love'; the two are bonded together. In terms of 'best commitment,' it doesn't mean, if you love somebody set them free, but rather make love to somebody in a way that makes them feel freer, more liberated. The *Kama Sutra*, or 'aphorisms on love,' is meant to show how to wed *Kama* with *Artha*, your overall well-being, and with *Dharma*, your virtuous code of conduct. Your sex life is the pathway to becoming more in touch with all dimensions of yourself and more committed to the world. It means sex is holy, as long as it is never frivolous or promiscuous, but engaged in with someone with whom you're committed in a loving relationship. The objective of making the best love is for you to be moved to throw yourself more completely into the world, to nurture the erotic in ways that deepen your bonds with the world, your commitment and sense of responsibility to it."

After a pause, Rachel says, "Another aspect to the best romantic commitments is that you and your partner love each other for who you are, not hoping or expecting you'll 'change.' My partner and I have total acceptance for each other. She's the nonjudgmental mirror into my soul. Knowing she loves me warts and all, I'm continually driven to take a hard look at my weaknesses and examine how I can become a better person. Because I don't have to; I want to."

"Are acceptance and nonjudgment equally indispensable for 'best commitments'?" I ask. "Cecilia, the love of my life, loves me warts and all too. She's *judged* that she loves my warts every bit as much as the rest of me. To her, glaring faults of mine that drive others—and me—crazy, she somehow finds marvelous, even endearing, as perfect as my perfections."

"Well, I'd always thought love was blind to judgment," Rachel replies after a while. "But yes, it's even better if there is a type of judgment involved. Each of you, with eyes wide open, judges the other and decides that you love the entire package. Otherwise, it's more like you're overlooking the other's faults rather than lovingly accepting them."

"The first and best commitment you must make is to yourself—to find out who you are at your core," says Muriel, a house mate of Ray's. "If you're ever going to make a best commitment with another, then you have to be comfortable in your own skin. You know that song, 'love the one you're with'? Well, the only one you're with 24-7 is yourself."

"Is it necessary to be completely comfortable in your own skin before you can commit meaningfully to another?" I ask. "Or can the deep commitment you and another make to each other—accepting one another for who you are, discomfort zone and all—be what helps you become more comfortable with yourself?"

"You certainly don't have to be perfectly comfortable with yourself to enter into a committed relationship, but you have to have a pretty darned decent idea who you are," Muriel replies. "Sometimes you can be in a loving, committed relationship and come to realize, not that you were living a lie, but that you didn't know the whole truth about yourself—for instance, that you're gay—and once that truth becomes apparent, it ends that relationship."

She then says: "The best commitments are ones of unconditional acceptance, but they're not unquestioning. Only fanatics never question their commitments. Rather, you should question your commitments all the time, in light of further discoveries about who you are as a person."

"Sometimes," Ray interjects, "you have to be willing to give offense, to yourself and to your nearest and dearest, in coming to grips with the unique truths about yourself—and that means you have to be committed first and best to knowing yourself as fully and honestly as you can. You can't be your best self, and so never make a 'best commitment' to anyone or anything else, without that knowledge."

"Exactly," says Muriel. "You may have to weather a deep crisis of faith, of identity, face a great deal of persecution—even from those who are supposed to love you more than any other. But it's worth it, because then you can really make a deep commitment to your world."

Ana becomes even more animated and says, "I realize finally the word I've been searching for since this dialogue began: sacred. The best commitments are sacred ones. They begin with two or more people accepting a deep responsibility for each other's well-being. But they don't end there. You become more passionate about nurturing everyone in your orbit."

"That's certainly the ideal, but I'm afraid I fall short of it," says Ana's friend John, with whom she and her boyfriend are staying while in the Bay Area, and who had been content until now just to listen. He continues, "I was riding down the elevator in my building the other day with my partner, and an elderly man in the car with us said, 'I hate faggots.'

"My first impulse was to slug him. But then I said, to his and my surprise, 'Why?'

"He didn't reply. As soon as the elevator door opened, he stormed off and again muttered 'faggots.' Because I was holding hands with my partner, all he saw was a gay man—not even that, he saw a 'faggot.' He didn't see a professional violinist. He didn't see a father of two lovely adopted boys from China. He didn't see the first person in his entire extended family ever to set foot in a college, much less to graduate summa cum laude. He didn't see a man with a world of sacred commitments, because of his blind prejudice."

"What did you see in him?" I ask.

"A scared, hate-filled old homophobe. But later on, I began to think: wouldn't it be something if I could've coaxed him into sitting down with me, so we could talk. I hate to think he'll go out of the world that way, never knowing why he hates or fears people who are 'different'. But I also hate to think I'll go out of the world with my own fears and prejudices. I bet if we'd taken the time to get to know each other, we'd have found something we have in common, like maybe a shared love for stamp collecting. That would have been a 'best commitment,' for two people who patently dislike each other to get to know each other, see if maybe they're wrong about each other. Even if it doesn't go the way of this best-case scenario, at least you've tried, and surely you'll have learned a lot about yourself."

John looks at us and says, "More than anything, the best commitments are those in which you become more closely 'wedded' to yourself. You have a sacred selfishness to know yourself as fully as you can, so you can become a better you, which to me is the best lifetime commitment you can make. To do that, we need others—friends, strangers, antagonists—to be mirrors into our soul. The more the better."

Sex and the Society

Martha Nussbaum testified before the U.S. Supreme Court during its 1996 deliberations on a Colorado statute that prohibited the enactment of any laws that would extend basic civil rights to homosexuals. Nussbaum said that in all classical "traditions and civilizations, same-sex romantic relationships, attachments, and sexual conduct were highly regarded." Before the advent of Christianity, she says there is no evidence in any of the Western cultures, much less their legal statutes—on which our own country's are largely based—that they "regarded same-sex erotic attachments as immoral, 'unnatural,' or improper." Indeed, she testified that there is clear evidence that during the halcyon days of ancient Athens, "homosexual acts between consenting males, and in rarer cases between consenting females, are attested as received with great approval." Ultimately, the Supreme Court struck down Colorado's notorious Amendment Two.

IN HER BOOK *Sex and Social Justice*, Nussbaum says that all laws should be geared to reflect and promote the core value that all human beings have dignity "just in virtue of being human, and this respect should not be abridged on account of a characteristic that is distributed by the whims of fortune." Today's gay rights movement, in her view, is one such attempt to realize further the humanism inspired by democratic Athens of old. Nussbaum notes how "reading the Greeks has value in our moral and legal deliberations" today on matters of gender rights and same-sex relationships "for the way in which they invite us to share the passionate longing of these same-sex lovers, to be moved by their hopes and anxieties and their eventual joy." In doing so, we are likely to discover that their longings are not "alien" to those who engage primarily or exclusively in heterosexual relations.

Mirror Mirror

James McGreevey, in announcing his resignation as governor of New Jersey for having had what he described as a consensual affair with another man, said that all his life he had "grappled with my own identity, who I am." The married father of two, raised a Catholic, went on to say, "At a point in every person's life, one has to look deeply into the mirror of one's soul and decide one's unique truth in the world, not as we may want to see it or hope to see it, but as it is."

Can a mirror ever accurately reflect who you are? Can you ever "see" yourself completely, accurately, honestly? Or is it the "trying to see" that matters? Does it depend on your purpose or goal? If the "unique truth" you come to know serves only to depress or traumatize, is it worth discovering?

IN PLATO'S ALCIBIADES, Socrates muses what it would be like if his command from the Delphic oracle had been "see thyself" rather than "know thyself." He notes that there is "something of the nature of the mirror in our own eyes," that when you look into them there's "a sort of image of the person looking." Socrates goes on to say that being able to see your physical reflection does not amount to seeing yourself. To do this, he says you must look into the mirror of your innermost self—your thoughts and feelings, intentions and objectives. You must also look at your outermost self—not your physical features but your works and deeds. Ideally, you look at both congruently.

How does one do this fruitfully? In Plato's *Phaedrus*, Socrates says that "the lover is [the beloved's] mirror in whom he is beholding himself" in such a way that the beloved comes to understand how elements of his way of living love might distance him from self-knowledge, put him at a further remove from others and his world. At the same time, the beloved recognizes how he can make headway in doing away with blinders that prevent greater self-illumination, breaking down partitions between self and other, between inside and outside.

TO HAZRAT INAYAT KHAN (1882–1927), the first Sufi master of the West, who made it his life's work to bridge eastern and western spiritual approaches, the human mirror is composed of equal parts mind and heart. "Mind is the surface of the mirror and the heart its depth," and, with both combining to serve as a prism into the soul, "all is reflected." Like a particle and a wave, both are manifestations of one and the same thing, but each is a critical component in providing a more complete picture of what one is seeing. Khan distinguishes between types of moral mirrors: that of "the insincere person," whose reflections reveal only surface—of himself and those who would seek to know more of themselves through him—versus the mirror of "the sincere person," whose reflections permeate surface and depth at once. When two sincere people are "focused on one another . . . with love," each helps the other gain greater literal and figurative vision of who they are and still might be.

TO ISLAMIC PHILOSOPHER and mystic Rumi (1207–1273), one of the greatest expositors of love of all time, your beloved's nonjudgmental mirror is the catalyst by which your own heart opens further, until it is so clear and pure that it is like a mirror without images.

But the best mirrors are of a lovingly *judgmental* sort. They contain potentially infinite images rather than none, all geared to help us show that we are works in progress capable of sculpting selves that can give new meaning to all we've been and done so far. This is what a Socratic mirror would do.

Can someone who doesn't love us, someone insincere or even hateful, hold up a mirror to us that is worth peering into, contribute to our store of knowledge about ourselves that we can draw on in constructive ways, helping us love better? Someone who loves us may go to great lengths to hide certain truths from us, if they deem them hurtful or traumatic to us, even though some might also be helpful over the long haul. Someone who has no heart for us, on the other hand, might in brutal honesty reveal things we may prefer left hidden (and in some instances might be best left undisturbed), or may not have known were hidden. Sometimes such a revelation might do damage to us, but sometimes it might do us great good.

Can a heartless mirror at times serve a better purpose than a loving one? Perhaps. More often than not, though, the best ones lovingly and gently reveal aspects of ourselves that may be difficult to acknowledge, showing only as much as we can take in at any given time.

Drunk with Love

Fundamentalist Muslims claim that their faith has no room for sensuality. Rumi differed with them. He was considered an iconoclast at best, a pariah at worst, for writing of the joys of dance, of the beauty of sensuousness, the ecstasy of being "drunk" with God's grace. Though Rumi considered himself a conventional Muslim, his works were banned by the fundamentalists of his day, as they are now. His poems are celebrations of the everyday, of the potential and actual beauty and goodness and love in everything, if we only would take the time to develop the inner eye with which to see it.

Rumi scholar and devotee Andrew Harvey writes that the mystic-poet "combined the intellect of Plato, the vision and enlightened soul-force of a Buddha or Christ, and the extravagant literary gifts of a Shakespeare." Harvey might have noted that in many respects Rumi was much like Socrates, who, like him, "never claimed total enlightenment" and instead, with a combination of humility and unquenchable curiosity, searched relentlessly for new possibilities and manifestations of all that love could be. Harvey notes that one of Rumi's "most original contributions to the history of mystical thought" has proven over time to be his "intuition that evolution is an infinite process that never ends in any of the planes of any world . . . and that the journey embodying and living Love is as infinite and boundless as Love itself."

Love is evolutionary in nature, not something solely to be found in objects out there, but rather something capable of further creation and sculpting, if one knows how. What Rumi intuited might have led to even more profound insights if he had subjected his intuitive insights to rational scrutiny. But likely this is unfair; Rumi masterfully utilized poetic inquiry as his method for scrutinizing love from a wide variety of standpoints, and imagining love in new incarnations.

Rumi did not write about worlds of hate, of indifference or intolerance, not because he turned a blind eye to them but because he believed that the world we dwell on is the world we are inspired to realize. Rumi saw his poetry as a vehicle for showing us ways of loving that would lead us to more direct intimacy with God, whom he equated with universal love. To Rumi, anyone who has truly loved another, even once, regardless of whether it was requited, has moved forward along the path of the divine.

Rumi's most ethereal notions of love did not transcend sensuousness; they exuded it. To him, sex itself was a form of inquiry, a pathway to the divine. Sex with a beloved was a form of the sacred, one of mutual intimacy and exploration that put one more in touch with the divine, reflecting the love of one who has pushed further outward and inward the bounds of sensual and spiritual intimacy and epiphany, making one more connected with the immensity. To Rumi, the pinnacle is to be drunk with the ecstatic illumination that we are alive, loved, capable of more expansive loving.

Rumi shares the view of Diotima of Plato's *Symposium* that love is the quest for beauty, indeed that true love and sublime beauty are manifestations of the same thing. Further, love is Rumi's paramount religion, as it was Socrates'. They each had faith in the essential goodness of each human being, in each person's potential to make ours a more loving world, once each person is not only aware of this inherent goodness within, but is inspired to share it with the world. Each believed that one must explore love in ways that connect and transcend self, family, community, culture, faith, in ways that lend themselves to continually introduce one to new perspectives, experiences, dimensions of love.

To Rumi, in all instances, a lover's goal is the beloved's attraction, to feel the push and pull of love. Lovers who do not seek this, Rumi would say, reject true love, because they do not care to change. They refuse to leave themselves vulnerable to love, to lay themselves bare to its possibilities and so are missing out on life, missing out on the prospect of true love. Above all else, Rumi says, one must imbibe love with all one's heart and soul.

CHRISTIAN SCHOLARS ARE fond of pointing out that the early Greek versions of the Bible make no use at all of the word *eros*, typically considered a base form of love. It is conveniently overlooked that the Bible contains one of the most sexually explicit and sensual stories ever told: the Song of Songs, or Song of Solomon, a 117-verse piece of ecstatic poetry sandwiched between Ecclesiastes and Isaiah. It is a love poem about the sexual awakening and erotic longing of two young lovers. It even makes this exhortation: "Feast, friends, and drink till you are drunk with love!"

Scholar Robert Alter notes that the Song of Songs is one of the all-time great love poems, one "of commingling—of different realms, different senses, and of the male and female bodies." This biblical story is believed to be authored by Solomon, the son of David and Bathsheba, who was chosen to be David's heir to the throne even though he was not firstborn, because David loved Bathsheba so deeply. In a new translation, Ariel Bloch and Chana Bloch describe the Song of Songs as

> A poem about the sexual awakening of a young woman and her love . . . [who] meet in an idealized landscape of fertility and abundance—a kind of Eden—where they discover the pleasures of love. The passage from innocence to experience is a subject of the Eden story, too, but . . . [t]he Song looks at the same border-crossing and sees only the joy of discovery.

What really sets the poem apart from other love stories of its epoch is that passionate love, rather than being depicted as a quintessential type of suffering, as "a consuming disease," is something to revel in. The lovers "don't suffer love, they savor it." The Song of Songs celebrates *eros* as it was first conceived of centuries before in Greece, when *eros* was a celebration of interpersonal love, and an integral part (though by no means the only part) of most any journey of meaningful human discovery.

Beautiful Heart and Mind

Socrates was no good looker; in fact, by most aesthetic yardsticks, he was plain ugly. Socrates himself was the first to admit that his potbelly, snub nose, and craggy face were not ingredients for a fatal attraction. He didn't feel the least bit sorry for himself about his god-given bad looks, didn't see the least incongruity that a person so beyond homely should dwell in most of his philosophical meander-

men among those with whom he inquired didn't see any incongruity either; they were smitten with him. It wasn't just that they overlooked his physical appearance; rather it made even more evident what a beautiful mind and heart he had. It's not that their love for him was blind, but rather that they were incapable of seeing his physical aspects apart from the rest of the package; and the package in its entirety was to them a beautiful thing indeed. In fact, if you'd asked them, they likely would have insisted that, seen in the right light, Socrates' physical features were beautiful.

In Plato's *Charmides* and *Symposium*, Socrates parries his inquirers' unrelenting advances in ways that make them more masters of their domain, in control over determining when and how they incorporate their passionate side, and toward what form of inquiry—sexual, axiological, epistemological, or a bit of all at once—and whether they steer it away from baser compulsions, such as pure lust, avarice, power. *Eros* was at play here, but also what was at issue were the means and ends toward which it was aimed, and whether the objectives were base or noble. Moreover, *eros* did not operate in a vacuum but rather in tandem with other forms and dimensions of love—familial, communal, existential, and aesthetic, among others. It was an integral part of the contributing factors that prompted the transformations among those with whom Socrates inquired.

Alcibiades, the handsome general and politician, is feeling no pain when he speaks in the *Symposium* for all his fellow inquirers. He bares his heart to his mentor and waxes eloquent on Socrates' nonpareil ability to move a man's soul:

> The mere fragments of your words amaze and possess the souls of every man . . . my heart leaps within me . . . and my eyes rain tears. . . .

Then, turning away from Socrates and directing his gaze at the rest, Alcibiades goes on to say:

He makes me confess that I ought not to live as I do, neglecting the wants of my own soul. . . . You should know that beauty and wealth and honor are of no account with him.

But Alcibiades also speaks to how Socrates' way with words and his way of living "with serious purpose" affect how he sees this man. Alcibiades is not blinded; he is the first to admit that Socrates physically is a homely specimen to anyone who looked just at his physical features. Yet in Socrates' case, to know him is to know beauty; all those intimate with him come to see how his superficial ugliness just accentuates the fact that he reflects "golden and divine images of such fascinating beauty" that it moves a man to change his life and strive to live the beautiful life that Socrates modeled.

Ugliness Is in the Eye of the Beholder

Plato seems to show that Socrates' offputting outward features put to the ultimate test whether those whom he encountered and with whom he inquired could detect beauty in its more lasting forms. Most seemed to pass the test. Socrates, however, did not change the standards by which one gauged what was beautiful; he obviated them. When you fall in love with someone, you fall more in love with the world in such a way that beauty pervades even the most mundane and ostensibly ugly, or in such a way that you are inspired to make beauty out of what at present is its converse.

The type of inquiry itself in which Socrates engaged with others was a sort of love-in, but not primarily in an erotic sense. The nature of their exchanges altered the lenses through which the participants viewed and acted in their universe. Their passionate, intense, rigorous philosophic exchanges were themselves pivotal in transforming how they saw their world and their place in it. They came to see how much they needed one another if they were more fully to articulate and in fact discover their own perspectives, and become autonomous yet socially conscious thinkers and doers.

I'm Too Sexy for This Dialogue

Socrates turned all the erotic rules upside down. In his inquiries in the agora, it was the handsome young men who chased after a homely old man they nonetheless thought downright sexy. Frustrated though they were when he refused their overtures, they'd rather be in his company, engaging with him in intimate philosophical inquiry, than have nothing at all to do with him.

What if Socrates had given in to the advances of his handsome interlocutors? Would they have necessarily ceased their quest to inquire with him? Perhaps this would not have been so at all. Sating oneself sexually may make one *more*, rather than less, philosophically inquisitive, and may lead to greater illuminations on *eros*. For some, sexual inquiry may be a vital "precursor" for fruitful philosophical inquiry. For others, the more sex they get, the less interest they may have in just about everything else. If Socrates had given in to his fellow inquirers' desire to have him, would the spell he cast on them have been diminished, or become more bewitching than ever?

Love Potion Number Nine

Scholar Christopher Faraone writes in *Ancient Greek Love Magic* that the use of love potions was a common practice in Greece, and that women used love potions to engender or enhance tenderness and affection for the man they loved. Although Socrates is typically noted for his appeal to other men, according to Xenophon, he was equally appealing to women, who often directed their potions his way. Xenophon records Socrates saying: "I also have my girlfriends, who do not allow me to escape from them day or night," because of their expert use of "love potions and incantations."

Make Love If You Can

José Ortega y Gasset (1883–1956), a Spanish essayist and philosopher, in his elegant book *On Love* says that every human era and epoch and cultural age "has had some great theory of the sentiments"—except ours in the modern-day West. In his own effort to make up for this shortcoming and pick up where the love theorists of yesteryear left off, Ortega y Gasset asserts, in philosophizing on romantic love, that love is not just in the eye of the beholder, no more or less than what you choose to make of it. Rather, what you are made of determines what kind of love, if any, you can make.

> [S]ince love is the most delicate and total act of a soul, it will reflect the state and nature of the soul. The characteristics of the person in love must be attributed to love itself. If the individual is not sensitive, how can his love be sentient? If he is not profound, how can his love be deep? As one is, so is his love. For this reason, we can find in love the most decisive symptom of what a person is.

By this view, there is no inherently transformative nature to a loving relationship. To Ortega y Gasset, who we are at any given moment is . . . who we are. This is a pessimistic and rather loveless philosophy of love. Who among us is not in need of knowing a great deal more about love, of becoming a better lover, or of learning to become a lover in the first place? Only others who are more experienced in love's ways and take an abiding interest in us can help us learn more about the ways of love. We need others, and likely they need us—friends and strangers and dearly beloved others alike— every step of the way. In particular, though, a beloved can show us how to discover and deepen our love, reveal to us characteristics we did not know we possessed, and inspire us to cultivate them, to help us become a great deal more than we are in any given moment of our life.

Pretense

Incomparable Greek classicist and Socrates scholar Laszlo Versenyi, who wrote at length about Socrates and love, opines that Socrates showed in his discourses on *eros* that all love relationships

> are ironical because they are full of pretense. Each participant in the relationship pretends to the other that he loves him as he is, for what he is, when in truth each aims at transforming the other into something other, i.e., something better than he already is.

But this overlooks the inherently transformative nature of loving relationships—not necessarily because one person overtly aims at transforming the other, but because the relationship itself can kindle a burning desire to become more, or better, than one is at present, to open oneself to experiences that afford new possibilities for growth and discovery, for showing and sharing the love.

Versenyi also neglects all the great loves in which one comes to love another more, rather than less, with more intimate knowledge of another's faults and with more experience of the changes that grappling with life might provoke. As Shakespeare put it in sonnet 116:

> ... Love is not love
> Which alters when it alteration finds ...
> O no, it is an ever fixed mark
> That looks on tempests and is never shaken

What's wrong with someone wanting us to be better? Does it depend on what that "better" is? The best loving relationships help us clarify and understand our fondest hopes. Our beloved comes to take them for her own and does whatever she can to help us realize them. But she can also help us see aspects of ourselves, potential capacities and talents, that we did not realize we had, help steer our lives in unforeseen directions. Loving gadflies can help us see if we are selling ourselves short, settling for too little, help us come to grips with those feelings of inadequacy as well as clearcut faults and failings that keep us from being all we might.

Moreover, there are times in genuinely loving relationships when such pretensions to transform can be very much of the selfless sort. Someone who truly loves you may steer you in directions that may augur the end of your romantic involvement but are in your best interest nonetheless.

Versenyi, a romantic pessimist in the great Eastern European tradition, says also that the erotic relationship

> is by nature . . . full of doubt, questioning, examination, and inquiry with respect to the other, for the lover seeks in his beloved for what would complete and fulfill him. . . . [L]ove is by nature a quest for oneself and one's own fulfillment.

If this is so, then it is not purely based on the pretenses of one's expectations for transforming another, but also on one's pretenses for transforming oneself.

Love-in

When I started holding Socrates Café dialogues more than ten years ago, I had this idea of bringing people together, most of whom wouldn't know one another at the outset, to engage in Socratic philosophical discourse. My hypothesis was that by investigating questions dear to their hearts, a community of inquiry would fast gel, with the questions as the glue that bound participants together. Although I'm no longer surprised that strangers, in the course of a philosophical sharing, can develop an intimacy and camaraderie over a short time, the thrill of witnessing these bonds form never ceases.

The dialogue itself makes us both more and less strange to ourselves and one another—in ways that connect and make us more passionate about ourselves, our lives, and those with whom we interact. Most who attend such dialogues think at the outset that they know their own thinking quite well, only to discover, as the dialogue progresses, that in certain aspects they hardly know themselves at all. They articulate and discover thoughts and ideas they hadn't realized they possessed. Thus, they find they didn't know themselves so well after all—an epiphany and element of surprise that inspires them to continue with others their shared quest for philosophical discovery of the novel and unfamiliar as it pertains to matters close to their hearts. This can compel us to take a greater interest in ourselves and others, and in our world, whereas when we feel there are few surprises left, apathy or indifference might be the result.

A PHILOSOPHICAL DISCOURSE in the spirit of those held by Socrates ideally is a type of love-in. Participants help one another tease out and reveal those forms of uniqueness long hidden within that inspire them to do their part to seek unfamiliar paths of knowing that can contribute to greater *arête*.

Best of all, quite often people who would otherwise never have had the chance to meet, or who would otherwise never have had anything to do with one another, have become fast friends. On occasion, those attending Socrates Café have met the love of their lives.

Strange yet Familiar

"You were defying my idea of a gringo—which I'd gotten watching too many Hollywood movies," she says. "You talked with so much passion, the first time we met, about how you wanted to reach out to those who don't have a voice in society. But because of all the stereotypes I had about Americans, part of me almost thought you were putting me on."

And then: "It's easier to think of people in cultures you don't know as strange in an off-putting way. It's a ready-made excuse for never making the effort to get to know them."

"You were 'exotic' to me," I tell her. "I knew next to nothing of Mexico or Mexicans—yet I felt an immediate connection with you. You were so passionate in your own right, sharing with me all the projects you were involved in to help lift the indigenous people of your country out of poverty, and your experiences living in their communities and learning about their culture. Already I was beginning to think, 'I want to go there, engage in dialogues with them, and work alongside you.'"

"Well, I was already thinking, 'Wouldn't it be nice if this guy came down there and joined me for a while,'" she says in turn. "They've been holding Socratic-type inquiries, though they wouldn't call it by that name, for centuries. I also thought it would be the perfect way to get to know you better. I was already feeling something I couldn't believe I was feeling. . . ."

"I had this perfect storm of passions—from absolute lust to absolute love for you," I say.

"I posed to you the question, 'What is love?'" she then says, "though I had planned to ask an entirely different question. But that's the question that spontaneously came out after I looked in your eyes. There was this little voice saying, 'This is the one.' I kept saying to the voice, 'You must be out of your mind. Be quiet.' I was able to silence the voice a little bit. But my heart wouldn't listen to me when I said, 'Be still.'"

Time passes. We look into each other's eyes, comfortable in silence. "It's a miracle when passionate love evolves, becomes stronger and more passionate, as you become more intimate and familiar companions," she says.

"I love that there's still an 'intimacy of the strange' between us after all these years," I say. "Every morning when I wake up, I look at you and think, Who is this amazing person? I learn something new about you, and from you, every day."

"A friend of mine wrote me recently to say she and her husband of ten years were ending their marriage," she tells me. "She said, 'There's no surprises left in our relationship.' They know each other too well! There should always be more to know about your life partner. Through you, I discover more about me. Every day is a day of discovery, because of our love."

"I'm doing things with my life I'd never have even dreamed of if not for you," I say. "You give me not just a greater sense of possibility when it comes to expanding my horizons, but you make me believe I can dream it and do it."

Then I say after a while, "You'd just arrived in the United States when we met. That was brave of you to venture alone to the dialogue. Even braver when you showed up and I was the only other person on hand! From there on out, I wanted to be your caballero, your knight in shining armor. I wanted to do everything I could to make your stay in the U.S. hospitable—to make the country just familiar enough so you'd feel comfortable exploring more and more."

She takes my hand and caresses it, her finger brushing across the Kokopelli ring she gave me the day we married. "I bought this for you from an elderly woman in Old Oraibi on the Hopi reservation, the old-est continuous village in North America. She told me that Kokopelli means 'flute player,' and is the mythical symbol of replenishment and nourishment, love."

"Not to mention fertility," I add. I caress her abdomen and feel the life stirring within.

"I can still remember our first dialogue on love almost word for word," Cecilia says as she places her hand over mine. "We talked about my favorite of Plato's dialogues, the *Symposium*, and the myth of love's origin: how humans were once one being—not sexless, but made of both sexes, until they were separated by Zeus. Ever since, the two separated selves have searched for each other, longing to come together again as one. Our baby is that 'coming together,' the entwin-ing of our bodies and spirits. In her, our two hearts beat as one."

It is nearly ten years since the day Cecilia and I met. We are at the place we first met and engaged in dialogue together. Soon we will be parents, in wholly unfamiliar terrain. How will this little person react to me, to us, to this world? Will she love me like I already love her? Will she have enough moments of joy that she will be grateful that we brought her into this world? Will we love her in a way that gives her roots as well as wings?

Cecilia leans forward and kneads my furrowed brow. "She'll always know, in good and not-so-good times, that she was brought into this world out of pure love."

Just then, she kicks. "She's excited," Cecilia says. "She's saying, 'Mommy, Daddy, ready or not, here I come!'"

PART II

—

STORGE

Family Ties

Storge is familial love, a natural and spontaneous—what the Greeks of old would call instinctual—outpouring of warmth, tenderness, affection. It is first and foremost displayed with immediate family members, among whom there is a particularly intimate sense of mutual dependence for identity, nurturing, happiness. However, it is also a type of love that sometimes can be experienced by people related by tribe or mission or shared duty, such as among soldiers in the trenches. At its loftiest, *storge* moves some to relate to all humans as members of the family of humankind. But it typically starts with the love of family members toward one another, particularly of parents toward their children.

All in the Family

"No matter how badly your children err in judgment, or how far they stray from the values you try to instill in them, you never lose complete faith in them, and you always love them just as much," Jean says in reply to the question we're examining, "What is parent love?"

"If you don't," says the attorney and mother of three, "it's not real parent love. A parent's love is one of acceptance, understanding, and forgiveness without limits. You still punish, you still judge, you're firm and strict when need be, but you never give up on your child, even when he seems to be doing everything possible to get you to."

I'm at a chain coffee shop in an exurb of a major southern city, with a small group of moms, and one dad, who are taking part with me in a midday, midweek dialogue.

"When our twelve-year-old son was caught stealing at school, my first thought was 'not my Jeremy, this isn't the way he was raised,'" Jean tells us. "The second time he was accused of stealing there, I still had lingering doubts. But the third time, he was caught red-handed shoplifting at a store, and I had to accept what my Jeremy was doing. We go to family counseling now. We're much more involved in our children's lives than before. I now work from home as much as possible, so I can spend more time with the kids, and my husband has cut down on travel, though it'll mean he might not get promoted."

Jean's husband, Todd, says, "We gladly made these changes, and are grateful we're in a position that we can do so. Our kids were by no means 'latchkey kids,' but we still weren't spending enough time with them. I think now that our son Jeremy was crying out for attention, for that 'parent love' that we maybe assumed he was getting enough of but obviously wasn't."

Todd goes on. "From what we've heard from other parents with whom we've shared our experiences, our son's 'transgression' was rather minor in comparison. The thing is, though, no matter how well and no matter with how much love you raise your children, they can do some awful things—but no matter what, you love them just as much."

"But what happened with our Jeremy also made me question not just whether I was giving him enough parent love, but whether I was giving him the right kind," says Jean. "I think that at first, part of me didn't want to acknowledge what he'd done, because then I'd have to take a hard look at myself and ask if I was really raising my child properly. I came to realize that being overly permissive, coupled with being blind to your own shortcomings as a parent, can be a recipe for disaster for your child. Now I put much more thought and care into parenting, and sometimes, though it hurts me, I do show 'tough love' and read my son the riot act when need be. This is not easy for me, but who said raising a child was easy?"

We sit in silence for a while. "My teenage son injured someone in a drunk driving accident," says a woman who does not offer her name. "I had always preached to him 'don't drink and drive,' and he promised he never would. Yet he did just the same. He did terrible damage to another's life. But if my love for him lessened in any way, then another life would be irreparably harmed. I've cried my heart out over what my baby did to another, but I also know he suffers terribly. So I have to be there for him when he needs to cry. To find that balance between punishing your child and being there for him heart and soul is the most difficult and imperfect—and necessary—part of parent love."

Penelope, a stay-at-home mom and community activist, says to us, "What I'm about to say raises the category of 'terrible things your child can do' to another stratosphere. I've been thinking of Timothy McVeigh's parents."

McVeigh, a Gulf War veteran, was put to death by lethal injection in June 2001 for the April 19, 1995, bombing of the Alfred P. Murrah Federal Building in Oklahoma City that killed 168 people.

"His mother, in the penalty phase of his trial, told the sentencing judge how he 'was a loving son and a happy child' whom 'any mother would be proud of.' She went on to tell the judge, 'He's not a monster . . . he's a human being.' She was as horrified by his evil deed as anyone, yet her love for him was still strong. She could still see her boy behind all that anger and misguided hatred. She said she couldn't begin to imagine the pain and suffering of those who lost loved ones at the hands of her son. But she did ask, as any parent would, that her son's life be spared.

"I do wonder if anyone tried to imagine the pain and suffering of his parents," says Penelope. "Maybe his life should not have been spared for his sake—but for the sake of his parents and their love for him, just maybe it should have been."

"Eric Rudolph's mother said much the same thing as Timothy McVeigh's," says Jean. Rudolph was sentenced to life without parole for bombings at the 1996 Olympic Games, as well as blasts at a women's clinic that performed abortions and at a lesbian nightclub which killed one woman and wounded more than a hundred others.

"Rudolph's mother said in an interview, 'I don't see him as a monster. I don't think I could.' Of course she couldn't," says Jean. "Not, as some might think, because she's blinded by her love. She acknowledged forcefully that what he did was heinous. Even so, she said she'd love him 'no matter what happens.' That is parent love in a nutshell—loving your child no matter what."

"I have to admit, I just see monsters when I think of those two," says Caroline, who works at home as a tutor. "I like to think that there's no way a child of mine could ever do something even remotely as terrible. They're raised with too much love."

She sighs. "Yet part of me knows that no matter how good and loving a parent you are, things can go terribly wrong. I ask myself, 'If that were my child, would I want his life spared?' Of course I would. Yet because he's not my child, I do judge him unforgivingly. But . . . the minute I force myself to consider the 'what if this were my child' scenario, parent love enters the picture, and I become forgiving in spite of myself. I pray I'm never tested as the parents of Rudolph and McVeigh have been. How many could live up to this ultimate test of parent love?"

"I know of some parents who've disowned their children for committing *far* less serious 'offenses' than those we're talking about," says Penelope. "Yet because they did something that didn't conform with their parents' wishes, they were disowned. It can be something as innocuous or ludicrous as following a career path that your parent is opposed to, or being gay, or marrying someone your parents don't approve of, or getting pregnant out of wedlock. Any parent who treats her child that way doesn't practice parent love—which is about nurturing and guidance, but also acceptance."

She then says, "My husband is a union chief and I'm a liberal political activist. We are trying to raise our son in such a way that he doesn't think money is the value to end all values, that 'making a difference' in the world is what it's all about. But he still may choose to pursue a career that's mostly about money, and he may become a political conservative. No matter what choices our child makes, though, I know that some of the values we've raised him with will rub off. I know he'll be a good-hearted soul, even if he doesn't choose the path we might have hoped or expected."

"Is parent love simply accepting the values that one's child chooses, even if they conflict with yours?" I ask. "Or should a loving parent also be open to his conflicting or at least different values, and receptive to the possibility that they might be even 'better' ones?"

Penelope thinks long before replying, choosing her words carefully. "Obviously a parent raises a child according to those values she considers 'best.' But how do you become a better person if you're not open to new sets of values—especially if they're ones that your son embraces? I've always thought of my values as 'best'—and yet I didn't get them just from my own parents by any stretch. I got them from my friends, from the books we read and music we listened to, the classes we took and causes we took on. Why should I expect my child to be different? We should want him to search far and wide in developing his own values."

"That makes me think of John Walker Lindh, who was twenty when he joined the Taliban in Afghanistan," says Todd. "Since his capture there five years ago by U.S. forces, he's been demonized not just as a traitor but as a murderer, though there's no evidence he took up arms against U.S. troops. At a clemency hearing, his father tearfully described his son as 'a decent and honorable young man who embarked on a spiritual quest.' His son had been raised a Catholic, but after seeing the movie *Malcolm X* he became interested in Islam, and at age fifteen converted to the religion. Eventually, with his parents' blessing, he went to Yemen and Pakistan. There he learned the Quran by heart and became an Islamic scholar."

Continues Todd, "When his father was asked at the hearing what he thought of this, he replied, 'It's a wonderful thing for an American kid to . . . learn another language, to learn another religion; these are great things.' Of course his parents didn't know he then made his way to Afghanistan to train with the Taliban—which at one time had been fully supported by the United States—initially to fight against Northern Alliance troops backed by the Soviets. His father said if he'd known, he would have told his son that if he wanted to help, he should 'go work in a refugee camp.' His father ended by telling the judge, 'I feel very proud of my son. He acted with great integrity throughout this entire ordeal.'"

Todd then goes on to say, "I've asked myself if I'd have done anything differently than John Lindh's parents. I can't think of a thing. They raised their son with good values, to think for himself, to become his own person. They raised him to be a seeker and to try to make a difference in a world in which too many parents and corporations and countries switch alliances all the time—not because of a change in core values but because they have no core values—and in which so many kids his age are glued to the tube watching *Survivor* and *Temptation Island*. As misguided as what the young Lindh did was—and he may well spend the rest of his life behind bars—it seems to me his intentions were honorable, and that he was raised conscientiously by parents of good heart."

After a considerable silence, Teri, co-owner of a public relations company, who arrived after the dialogue began, says, "We adopted one of my sons at age four. He came from Eastern Europe, and had a difficult family history. He has some serious behavior problems. No matter what, I'm there for him. From the moment I met him and hugged him, a bond of parental love formed that is so strong it doesn't matter if he's my flesh and blood or not. He's my child. If I ever stray from my lifelong commitment to be there for him, I'll betray parent love.

"When he's old enough," she continues, "I'd like to return to his homeland with some frequency. I want him to know his language, his culture and those values unique to it. I want to know them too. They're part of his makeup, part of the two who made him. It'll help him, and me, better to know his heart."

Says Jean softly, "So far, I've only been thinking of parent love in terms of my own children. I've been estranged from my father for years, for his infidelity to my mom. I judge him harshly—more harshly even than I judge my first husband, who was the furthest thing from a saint. And I certainly judge my father much more harshly than I do my own children. Yet he was a good father in many respects. I've blocked out that goodness because of this one 'unforgivable thing' he did.

"Parent love," she then says, "isn't just about love of your children, but of your own parents—and ultimately of yourself, a reflection of how you want your own parents to love you, and how you will want your children still to love you when they're old enough to discover you're the furthest thing from perfect.

"I've let too much time go by already without letting my dad know how I love him. I'm going to remedy that right now."

Forgive Me Father

In his autobiography, Mohandas Gandhi says the pivotal experience of his life occurred when he confessed to his father that he'd stolen money for food and cigarettes:

> . . . pearl drops trickled down his cheeks. . . . I also cried. I could see my father's agony. Those pearl drops of love cleansed my heart. . . . Only he who has experienced such love can know what it is. . . . This was for me an object lesson in love. Then I could

see in it nothing more than a father's love, but today I know that it was pure love. When such love becomes all embracing, it transforms everything it touches.

This pure love shown to him by his father transformed Gandhi. He spent the rest of his life passing it on to others, trying to create a world that mirrored the type of love shown to him by his father on that fateful day of his youth.

All My Children

My maternal great-grandfather, William Ira McKinney, rose to the respected position of school principal in Raleigh County, West Virginia. From what I've been told, he had a knack for coaxing his students—almost all of whose fathers' work was tied to the coal mines—to expect high achievement from themselves. In the oppressive Appalachian environs, he inspired them to see beyond the high mountains, to envision carving out a life for themselves of their own choosing, if they would nurture their god-given talent with drive and discipline. Indeed, he considered drive and discipline the most important "talents" one could possess. To him, all of his students were family, like his own children. He brought out the best in his charges, and they endeavored to make him proud. He made the community itself, far from being separate and apart from the outside world, an extension of the school, a laboratory for practical and scholarly endeavors.

My great-grandfather would agree wholeheartedly with the educational philosophy of the renowned Japanese philosopher and social activist Tsunesaburo Makiguchi (1871–1944), born into extreme poverty in a rural hamlet in northern Japan, who asserted that formal education, even at the tenderest age, should never separate the world of learning from the world at large. Makiguchi believed that all children, regardless of their socioeconomic background and ethnicity, were deserving of the chance to realize their potential, and were equally capable of becoming exceptional learners. "They are all equally students . . . ," he wrote. "Even though they may be covered with dust or dirt, the brilliant light of life shines from their soiled clothes."

Makiguchi's example was a principal inspiration behind my desire to hold philosophical dialogues with children and youth, particularly those at society's margins, so that I could be exposed to and illuminated by the "brilliant light of life" of their minds and hearts.

Y Tu Papá También

"As the oldest child, I have to be the man in the family now," Javier—or Javi, as I've long called him—says to me. "That's what family love is, answering the call when it's your turn to step up."

The tall and disarmingly handsome nineteen year old absent-mindedly strokes his goatee as he talks in a deep and full voice. He is a far cry from the skinny towheaded youngster with whom I began philosophizing almost a decade ago at one of the first Philosophers' Clubs I started for children and youth in the Bay Area. Javi had lived here in a cramped, run-down apartment with his parents, who had come to the United States from Guatemala, and his four brothers and sisters. Javi still sports the same type of round spectacles he wore way back when—he says now he's partial to them because they're the kind John Lennon wore—and he is as thoughtful as ever. This is the first time we've seen each other in more than five years, since his family moved to East Los Angeles. We're sitting on the stoop of his girlfriend's bungalow home.

"My dad had a good trade here as a construction worker," Javi says. "As good as he was, he'd burned every bridge. His drinking had gotten too bad. It put us in a bad way. Then one night, after being out of work for months, he up and left us while we were sleeping.

"You can imagine how distraught Mama was. For a while, she wouldn't sleep. I'd watch over her all night. Like I said, I have to be the man now, so I'm taking care of everyone as best I can. But I do it also because I know it's what my dad would want me to do.

"I know why he drinks," he goes on, "because of problems in his own upbringing as a child that he tries to run away from. He could get hurtful when drunk. Every time he sobered up, he'd cry and apologize for what he said and did, tell us how much he loved us. We always forgave him. But finally, I guess he couldn't forgive himself.

"I wish I knew how to contact him," Javi tells me. "We're not mad at him, we're just worried. I'm sending out love waves to him. I hope he gets them." He brushes away a tear.

"My girlfriend is pregnant," he soon reveals. "We're getting married. I want to be the kind of dad all the time my dad is on his best days. My dad has never said, 'I love you,' but you can see the love in his eyes. I'm going to tell my baby in actions *and* words how much I love him.

"I've got a good-paying part-time construction job—those skills Dad taught me are going to good use—and I'm going to the community college," Javi says next. "I'll stay in school, persevere even more because of my baby."

After a while, Javi says to me, "Remember when you asked us what we wanted to call our group, and someone suggested 'The Philosophers' Gang'? I said, 'No way. Gang has the wrong kind of meaning. Let's call it the 'Philosophers' Club.'

"A gang and a club are both kinds of families. But one is a bad kind—you're looking out for one another like blood brothers, but you do bad things to everyone outside your group. A club, though, is a good kind of family, where you're all trying to do something good or positive for those inside and outside your group, out of love.

"Family love always has to be of the good, by the good, for the good, in order for it to do the good it's supposed to do."

In the Name of the Mother

Just then, a group of young teens makes a beeline our way. By the way they greet Javi, it's evident they worship the ground he walks on. They ignore my presence until he introduces me and makes it clear that I am a close friend. Javi, to my delight, tells me he has been holding Philosophers' Club dialogues with them, "so when they have to make fateful decisions, they'll do the right thing—and even when they do the wrong thing, they'll know better and eventually come around."

Javi tells them we're discussing "What is family love?"

"Did you see the latest Star Wars movie, *Revenge of the Sith*?" Emilio asks us in short order. When I first began philosophizing with kids, I might have wondered what in the world such a reply has to do with our question. I've long since learned it will fast come to light that it has everything to do with it.

"In the movie, Anakin Skywalker went over to the dark side, even though he didn't want to. It was the only way to save Senator Padmé, the mother-to-be of his child. See, he had foreseen that Padmé would die while giving birth. But Anakin couldn't bear that. The only way to prevent it was if he swore allegiance to the Dark Lord, who then would save Padmé, and so then she would be there for Anakin and their baby. So Anakin became evil out of family love."

"I don't think you can ever do evil out of love—family love or any other kind," Adalberto says firmly. "If he'd really loved Padmé, he'd never have put her in a compromising situation in the first place—never have seduced her and got her in a family way—so he wouldn't have had to do evil to get her out of such a jam.

"Anakin didn't have his priorities straight," Adalberto explains to me. "He wanted everything yesterday. Jedi Knights are supposed to be the most patient of all people, and he was the opposite. They're charged with looking out over all their people, who are their flock, their family. They vow to make every personal sacrifice on behalf of them.

"Yet Anakin Skywalker had sex with Padmé and got her pregnant, though it's forbidden by Jedi law for one of its knights to have such relations—because they can cloud your judgment, and put you in a situation like the one he got in, where you endanger those you've sworn to protect."

Precocious ten-year-old Saira now chimes in, "Anakin Skywalker was a typical macho, rash and brash, flirting with evil since the day he picked up a light saber, the Jedi sword. He wanted to be appointed to the Jedi Council even though he was too young and wet behind the ears. He wouldn't accept the council's explanation that someone his age was never appointed to the council. They'd nurtured and loved him like their own son, with his best interests at heart—which is what family love is all about. But like a stubborn son, the black sheep of the family, instead of understanding where they were coming from, he became jealous and resentful. He went over to the Dark Lord to learn the dark arts out of spite, *not* mainly to save Padmé and the baby."

Adalberto then informs me, "Well, whether he went to the dark side for Padmé or for spite, the bottom line is he began following its code: 'Peace is a lie, there is only passion. Through passion I gain strength. . . . I gain power. Through power I gain victory. . . .'

"The Jedi code, on the other hand," continues Adalberto, "is all about gaining the good kinds of knowledge, to overcome ignorance so you can deliver your flock from evil. Their passion was for peace. They didn't believe you gain strength and power through passion but that you use your passion to gain the knowledge you need to best use your strength and power to win peace for your people."

"I try not to flirt with the dark side," says Saira with all seriousness. "I try to make sure that because of the choices I make, it'd be impossible for me to get caught up in the wrong things, hurting myself and my family."

"My older brother 'knew better,' but joined a gang anyway—and now he's really learning about the dark side, in a juvenile detention center," says Paco, twelve, speaking for the first time. "The choice he made, to find out firsthand about gang life, would've been okay if it only affected him. But it's been a nightmare for my family, just like

Anakin's choices were a nightmare for all the people who were like family to him. For family love to be family love, you have to consider how your choices affect those you love the most, and act in ways that never hurt them on purpose. Anakin didn't do that any more than my brother did.

"Obi-Wan Kenobi, the Jedi Master who'd reared Anakin like his own son, did his best to save Anakin from the evil Sith lord," Paco goes on. "Yet Anakin allowed himself to be convinced by the Dark Lord to join him. Deep down, he knew he was betraying family love in doing so. He *knew* the Dark Lord needed him to join forces with him to win against the forces of good. How was Obi-Wan repaid for all his love to Anakin? Anakin killed him. He betrayed his father figure—not to mention his wife, his child, and everyone else he was supposed to have loved."

"*However*, in the end," points out Emilio, "Anakin's love for Padmé and his child conquered all. Anakin's son, Luke Skywalker, became the person Anakin should have been, and Luke did save his people."

"Luke's own dad—Darth Vader, the former Anakin Skywalker—had to die in order for that to happen," notes Adalberto.

"Luke's dad *wanted* to go down," insists Emilio. "Even with the dark side controlling 99.9 percent of him, that 0.1 percent of good still inside of him—that family love—conquered all. He died in the name of his love for Padmé and their child.

"As long as there's even the littlest bit of family love left in you, it can conquer a world that's almost entirely dark," continues Emilio. "As long as it doesn't die out all the way, there's always hope."

Family Affair

Like *eros*, the ties that bind people via *storge* start out with the most intimate or immediate, but do not always end there. As with *eros*, lower forms and higher forms can be at play at the same time, vying for primacy. At their best, feelings fostered by *storge* (pronounced stor-gay) can be the impetus for broadening one's scope and inclusivity, seeking a goal higher than just mutual support.

The rise and fall of ancient Athens in telling respects begin and end with family ties. At its zenith, Athenian *storge* was a key factor behind the cultivation of empathetic imagination, leading to timeless philosophical, aesthetic, cultural, spiritual, and political inroads and insights; at its nadir, it was a principal cause behind bitter factionalism.

I have yet to come across a work, scholarly or otherwise, that writes about Socrates in relation to *storge*, though this type of love undergirded his love of and search for redeeming truths and his subsequent decision to drink hemlock and die rather than quit his questioning pursuits. Socrates was driven to act as he did out of love for his family of fellow inquirers, his tribe, the family of his polis—perhaps even the family of mankind.

Family Feud

Storge, like all types of love, can be at the root of all sorts of conflict and tension, as well as harmony, growth, and discovery. What's more, other competing types of love may overshadow *storge*, or may make of it—by someone calculating enough—something to be exploited or distorted, in order to drive wedges between family members. For instance, certain political or spiritual ideologies may make *storge* a secondary value at best, a type of love to be nurtured only if it jibes with one's "higher" ideologies as one sees them—or a type of love to be discarded if it does not.

Socrates' own era, in the end, pitted family members against one another as rival polis factions and confederacies began to face off.

Blood Ties

"Blood should be thicker than everything . . . particularly water and politics, right? Yet for too much of my life, I put water and politics above family." Eighty-one-year-old Elequemedo looks out the picture window of his living room at a banner strewn the length of the street. It declares, "*Patria o Muerte*"—homeland or death.

"Family is the only real homeland," he says, "whether it's separated by an expanse of water, whether its members agree or disagree on everything or nothing. Today, I'd like to think that if put to the test, I'd put myself between my family and anyone who threatens their right to live and believe as they choose. Only family is worth dying for."

Those gathered with us are moved by the heartfelt remarks of this decorated war veteran. We are in Havana, Cuba, crammed into the living room of one of the former colonial mansions that were long ago abandoned by or appropriated from their original owners. The grandeur of these homes is still evident, even after nearly a half century of such severe neglect that they appear on the verge of crumbling before our eyes.

It is New Year's Day. I had first come upon several people with whom I am now gathered while visiting Lennon Park, where there is a life-size bronze sculpture of John Lennon, whom Cubans revere. These people had been at the park since early the previous evening, drinking very good rum and smoking fine cigars, distributed each New Year's Eve by the government so that ordinary Cubans can celebrate in fine fashion the anniversary of their successful *levantamiento*, or uprising, led by a young attorney named Fidel Castro. Cuba had officially garnered independence from Spain on May 20, 1902—the fruit of an uprising initially led by the revolutionary, pro-democracy activist and political philosopher José Martí, who died in battle— making it the last of Spain's colonies in the hemisphere to gain its freedom. But its long-standing tradition of authoritarian rule didn't come to an end; Cuba's homegrown leaders were as autocratic as their Spanish predecessors, exploiting, upon garnering independence, Cubans' pervasive "oppressed mentality," which kept them from forging a positive new collective identity.

On January 1, 1959, then-President Fulgencio Batista, Cuba's most ruthless and longest ruling of their homegrown dictators, fled Cuba for safe haven in the Dominican Republic. Castro and his fellow bearded insurgents had accomplished the seemingly impossible—their ragtag army had defeated Batista's superior forces. Along with Batista, most elites who had benefited from his autocratic rule, living in extraordinary privilege at the expense of the poor, escaped the country as well for safe haven in the United States and elsewhere. Castro and company entered Havana, where the jubilant throngs hailed them.

After I had thrust myself upon the contemporary celebrants of this anniversary, introducing myself and telling them about the dialogue I hoped to hold—on the question "What is worth dying for?"—they assented to take part. It turns out that few people anywhere enjoy conversing candidly and for hours on end, even or especially to strangers. They did insist on holding the dialogue in the home of Elequemedo, to avoid the possibility of eavesdropping by government undercover agents. As soon as we were indoors, about fifteen others materialized, along with folding chairs they'd brought with them. Somehow all of us wedged into the small quarters of a living room. No one seemed to mind in the least the cramped conditions.

Elequemedo has fallen silent. No one else speaks, out of deference to him, sure that their host, and patriarch to many here, has more to say. He continues to look out his window, now setting his gaze on the Florida Straits, across which, just ninety miles away, is Miami. On a clear day like this one, you can imagine you can almost see its shores.

The burly man squeezes the shoulder of the slight younger man beside him. Despite considerable differences in physical size and age, they bear a remarkable resemblance. "Richei here is my hero and role model. It took his visit to teach me that no sacrifice is too great to reconcile family. Without family, what else matters?"

Richei, who appears uncomfortable being in the limelight, says softly, "Some of my family in Miami, especially my dad—Uncle Elequemedo's brother—may disown me when one day I tell them I came here. They think I'm on a business trip in California."

He looks around at all of us and says with great feeling, "I'm thirty-eight years old, a man. How can I expect my parents or my siblings, or my relatives here, to come around, after decades of animosity and division, if I don't take the lead and make overtures myself?

"Most here," Richei says next, referring to those surrounding us, all touching him in some way, "are family members whom I hadn't met until I came here a week ago. This may sound like Latino melodramatics, but I am deliriously happy to be here. For the first time, I have such a strong sense of self and place and roots that if I die tomorrow, heaven forbid, I'll die a contented man. Anything was worth the risk of making the trip here. And if it doesn't kill us, it'll someday bring our entire family closer."

"Because of Richei's brave and loving gesture, our family as it existed for decades, divided by resentment and ill will, is dead and buried forever," says Magalys, thirty-two, a physician. "Now it's been reborn. We have a family worth dying for again.

"My Uncle Elequemedo here and Uncle Abelando, Richei's father, fought side by side in the *levantamiento* against the murderer Batista," she then says. "They were wounded when they were ambushed in a mortar attack by Batista henchmen, and later received medals of valor from Fidel himself.

"After the Bay of Pigs victory, Fidel banned all political parties except the Communist party. He prohibited freedom of speech and assembly, and had his opponents—really, anyone who disagreed with him on anything—jailed and in several instances executed. Fidel claimed it was to preserve *socialismo* against enemy infiltrators, but Abelando came to believe that was just a pretext for Fidel to become what he'd aspired to be all along, Cuba's latest dictator for life. Abelando decided to escape for America with his wife and Richei's older brothers, while Cubans were still permitted to leave. My dad tried to talk him into staying."

Elequemedo interjects, "At the time, I was convinced Fidel had only taken these extreme measures out of necessity, over the short term, for the long-term good of our homeland. I told Abelando that if he went to the U.S., which had propped up Batista all those years, he'd be a traitor to all we'd sacrificed in the name of our families, that he'd taint the supreme sacrifice Magalys' dad, our younger brother Teofilo, had made as a comrade in arms for the cause. Abelando said I was a stooge and apologist for Fidel, and that I was the one tainting our brother's good name. He said at least in the U.S., he'd have the freedom to speak his mind, and make a life of his choosing for his wife and children. He left the next day.

"We've been in touch from time to time over the years, but our exchanges are curt and impersonal, and we've never seen each other since. We're both too stubborn to back down and let bygones be bygones. Now, though, I have a mind to write him and apologize. I don't want to die without reconciling with my brother.

"We're from a family of illiterate peasants," Elequemedo goes on. "We lived hopeless lives. We'd tried for years, through peaceful means, to bring to an end our mistreatment by the Batista regime. Its response was to torture, humiliate, even kill us. So me and my brothers risked our lives willingly to be part of the uprising. We believed it was well worth dying for *por el amor de nuestros hijos*—out of love for our children."

He says to me, "You probably want to ask me, if I knew then what I know now, would I still feel it was worth dying for? Yes, and for the same reason—family—even if the outcome has been a mixed bag. I'd like to think that even my brother would agree that ordinary Cubans are far better off than they were in the days of Batista.

"Both of us can read because of the literacy brigades Fidel deployed after the uprising to all the poor communities," Elequemedo explains. "You cannot be fully human, fully know how or what to hope and dream for, without the gift of literacy. Our classes were held out in the open air, because we had no schools, and were led by well-educated people from well-to-do families who joined Castro in the *levantamiento*. They opted to stay here rather than escape for Miami. To them, risking their lives to be part of the new Cuban family was worth any sacrifice on their part. They knew they might die as a consequence—and many in fact were killed by Batista supporters who'd gone into hiding and now were snipers terrorizing us—but they felt the sacrifice was worth it, just as me and my brothers felt it was worth spilling our blood for the greater good of our country and of our immediate families."

"All our seven children have graduated from universities," says Elequemedo's wife, Laline. "Two have PhDs. What they've achieved would never have been possible for the poor before the revolution. Everyone in Cuba today has been brought up to a certain basic standard of living, despite severely limited resources. We all see one another as an extended family. None of us live in plenty, but none live in anything resembling the absolute poverty of before, when there were no decent homes, no schools, no paved roads, no electricity or proper sewage. We have exceptional medical care. We're a so-called Third World country, yet our average longevity rate equals yours."

Elequemedo sighs deeply, and his wife falls abruptly silent, as if on signal. "As wretched as our lives were, there was still a great deal to lose," he tells me. "There was always plenty of love in our families. We had many beautiful and tender moments. But every single one of us nonetheless believed we should risk it all out of hope for a better future for our loved ones.

"Fidel was the scion of a rich family, yet he took our plight for his own, saw us so much as his family that he put himself regularly in harm's way on the front lines. In 1953, upon being captured by Batista's troops and charged with treason—after storming the Batista army barracks on July 26, the opening salvo of the uprising—Fidel declared in his 'history shall absolve me' speech that it was 'inconceivable that children die for lack of medical attention,' and that 'the majority of our rural people are now living in worse circumstances than the Indians Columbus discovered.' To remedy this, he called for Cubans to come together to create a 'radically original culture,' one of 'democratizing access' and 'guided by thinking that is democratic, nationalist and dedicated to social justice.' I never dreamed he'd betray this vision. The Cuba we live in today is not the Cuba we revolutionaries envisioned was worth dying for."

"Will it be necessary to risk it all again, if you're going to have a Cuba that's worth dying for?" I ask.

At this, Elequemedo smiles cryptically and says, "It's definitely worth taking risks for." And then, "I'm going to tell you now what I haven't yet told my family. I signed the Varela petition." His family, particularly his wife, looks in disbelief. The Varela Project, led by Oswaldo Paya and Elizardo Sanchez, asks the Castro regime to allow a plebiscite on Cuba's future. If enacted, the plebiscite would give blanket amnesty to political prisoners, allow freedom of speech and assembly, and bring about electoral reforms. More than 25,000 signatures had been gathered by the time ex-President Jimmy Carter visited here in 2002, at Castro's invitation, and spoke in favor of Varela to a national TV audience. The signatures are more than enough needed to pass the petition.

"To render worthless the petition, Fidel pushed through this edict," he tells me, "after your ex-president Carter visited in 2002, that made *socialismo* the law of the land for eternity. But where is socialism? We have a paternalistic leader who treats us condescendingly, who demands we march in lockstep to his tune, because he 'knows better.' By signing the petition, I may well be punished someday, but so be it. I don't think I need fear dying for it, but it would be worth it, if it came to that. I won't go down alone. Since Fidel forced through the new law, more Cubans than ever have signed Varela."

"My dad would be proud of you," Richei says to his uncle. "Or he would be if he weren't so blinded by his hatred of Castro. My dad thinks that if Castro dies, then even if he is fated to die the following day, he'll die a happy man. But that kind of hate-filled obsession can never make life worth dying for. Only working towards positive, affirmative goals can do that. Rather than make out Castro as the root cause of all problems, we need to see if maybe we're part of the problem, too, rather than part of the solution."

Richei then says, "I first started thinking seriously about coming here after the Elian Gonzalez episode."

Elian Gonzalez was six years old when, in November 1999, his mother tried to cross the Florida Straits with him in an inner tube. She died in the attempt, but Elian was rescued by fishermen and brought to Miami, where he stayed for months with Cuban expatriate relatives. Then-U.S. Attorney General Janet Reno eventually had him returned to his father in Cuba, but only after a furious clash between Castro opponents and sympathizers.

"Instead of examining what would drive any mother to such desperation that she'd risk not only her life, but that of her young child, to make an ocean crossing that might lead to their deaths, the shouting between Castro and the U.S. hard-liners became more shrill than ever," Richei says. "They stooped to using this family tragedy as a pawn to support their shared view that their differences are too deep to bridge. Putting family first was the death knell for Janet Reno's political future, but she believed that that boy needed to be with his surviving parent, needed the love of his father more than anything. That's when it began to sink in with me that someone in each divided Cuban family had to put it on the line in the same spirit as Reno. Family members have to risk something to bring Cubans on both sides of the straits together. We can do this, one family at a time, and then demand that more political leaders take risks to do the same."

"I think if Elian's father loved his son properly, he would have stayed in the United States when Reno offered him the chance," says Richei's second cousin Ynilo.

Then Ynilo tells me, "My only brother and his family left in the Mariela boat lift. They tried to talk me into joining them. But my girlfriend, pregnant with our child, wouldn't go. So I stayed. My child has no future here, but I'd never risk her life in a dangerous crossing, and I'd never abandon her."

The Mariela exodus took place in the spring of 1980. After a number of Cubans rushed into the Peruvian Embassy in Havana, Castro abruptly announced that all Cubans who wanted to go were free to leave the island with impunity. About 125,000 Cubans took up Castro on his offer.

"All the *balseros* left because they considered the promise, and the promises, of the original revolution unfulfilled or broken," Ynilo continues. "They did so in the same spirit and for the same reasons many risked their lives for the 1959 uprising here."

He becomes angry. "What has Fidel done for us? Sure, we can read now, but only what Fidel says we can read. Sure, we can get a good education, but we can't get a job. My brother has a doctoral degree in sociology, yet he can only get a job working as an elevator operator in a hotel for rich tourists. Sure, the state pays for our burial, but what kind of life do we have before we get that free burial? The life we have is hardly worth dying for.

"If it wasn't for the dollars they [Ynilo's brother and his wife] send me, I'd hardly be able to survive since our 'special period' began, after the Soviet Union collapsed, and their financial support of Cuba dried up. I used to think my brother and his wife must be millionaires to send me all this money, but now I know they work seven days a week in order to help me out."

"Fidel keeps telling us that we Cubans have to be willing to sacrifice more than ever for the good of the country," says Ynilo's second wife, Yuriceima, who is expecting. "And we do. It wouldn't occur to us *not* to share what little we have with our neighbors, whom we consider extended family. While you can bet Fidel lives in plenty, I wouldn't trade the love we have here in this room for his material wealth. Without the love of family, nothing is worth living for *or* dying for."

There's a long silence before Elequemedo says, "When I first found out Richei was here, I'm ashamed to say I wasn't sure whether to welcome him into my home with open arms. But when I saw him, all the old resentments just melted away and were replaced by pure love."

I look at a large framed picture of Che Guevara hanging over the mantel. Scion of an upper class family in Rosario, Argentina, Guevara had nearly completed his medical studies when in 1952 he embarked on a life-changing journey, traversing more than 4,000 miles on a motorcycle through northern Argentina and other South American countries. Along the way, he came to know intimately the plight of the region's poor, particularly the indigenous groups whose land was being expropriated for its abundant resources by corporate interests, with the blessings of the government. Of this transformational experience, Guevara wrote that in coming "into close contact with poverty, with hunger, with disease, with the inability to cure a child because of a lack of resources," he "began to see there was something that . . . seemed to me . . . as important as being a famous researcher or making some substantial contribution to medical science, and this was helping people."

I remark now, "Che was willing to alienate himself from his immediate family, from their upper class values, to fight and die on behalf of the world's disenfranchised. Sometimes, do you have to be willing to sever ties with your family and the values they hold dear to have a life worth dying for?"

In due time, choosing his words with care, Elequemedo says, "I think Che felt you could never really love your immediate family if you didn't first learn to love all families, to see them all as precious and as equally deserving of all the best things life could offer. If a family just looks out for its own selfish interests, as too many rich

families do, theirs isn't true family love, because they have no concern for the greater family of man."

Elequemedo continues to look at Che's portrait, then says, "Che
was a great believer that love was the most revolutionary agent of all.
Listen to what he wrote, 'At the risk of sounding ridiculous, let me
just say that the true revolutionary is guided by a great feeling of
love,'" reads Elequemedo. "He said you cannot be 'an authentic revolutionary without this quality,' because it's what gives you the 'large
dose of humanity' you need in order to 'avoid falling into extremes,
into cold intellectualism, into isolation from the masses.'"

Richei says now, "Reasonable people can disagree over whether
Che lived—and died—by his philosophy of love, or whether his true
love was communism at the expense of everything else—Cubans, the
poor, even his own wife and children."

One might raise the same question about Castro, a man whose
ideological devotion seems to have mutated into an overpowering
self-love. Castro's estranged sister, Juanita, who fought alongside her
brother against Batista, fled Cuba in 1965 when it became clear that
Castro was installing his dictatorship under the guise of socialism.
Ever since, Juanita has denounced her brother. A Reuters article
quotes her as saying that Castro's "megalomania knows no limits."
Castro's out-of-wedlock daughter, Alina Fernandez, who fled the
country in 1993 to become one of her father's most mordant critics,
told the London *Observer* that she does "not refer to Mr. Castro as my
father . . . I am his exile."

After a while, Elequemedo says, "José Martí, the father of the
Cuban independence movement, warned against that kind of 'blind
love.' My brother and I, too, have been blinded by ideology. It distorted the passionate idealism for which we risked our lives. They say
charity begins at home, but I haven't been very charitable towards
him. I have to fix that.

"Richei's visit opened my eyes. No one can dispute that the path he
charted to my door was paved with the intent of building *el amor familiar*, family love. His visit has been just the 'dose of humanity' I needed."

Family Matters

In *Cuba Confidential: Love and Vengeance in Miami and Havana*, Ann Louise Bardach writes that although Fidel Castro has fulfilled a number of his original promises in the realm of health care, education, and athletics, in virtually every other regard, Cubans continue to live in great deprivation. The most pernicious impact of his policies is at the family level: "Most Cuban families have experienced a searingly tragic episode of separation and loss."

But times are changing. Bardach says that as reunions such as the one I witnessed become more commonplace, it may bode hope for eventually bridging the gulfs that exist between thousands of families. In Miami, she notes, increasingly "(h)ard-line exiles—*duros*—are being challenged . . . by their own offspring" as "U.S.-born Cuban-Americans, unfettered by their parents' rage, have sought to engage with Cuba" and, in signs of both defiance and reconciliation, venture to Cuba "without notifying their families." In this, she predicts, lies hope that Cuban-Americans and Cubans will come together. Bardach sees striking parallels with the Chinese who came to New York and San Francisco to escape the brutal rule of Mao Zedong, and vowed that they would have nothing further to do with mainland China until its Communist dictatorship was toppled. Yet their American-born progeny have not taken this vow for their own, and out of deep interest in their roots have, since the late 1970s, taken decided steps to forge not only new ties with mainland China but among long-estranged families.

Bridging Islands

Most today who, on their respective side of the straits, are most prominent in trying to bring about reconciliation were inspired by

philosopher-poet José Martí (1853–1895). Martí spent most of his
life in forced exile from his beloved homeland because of his political
activism, and received his PhD in Humanities and Philosophy in
Spain. Yet no one was more part of the main of Cuba than he. One of
Martí's biographers describes him as "the tortured lover of his own
land, and though his body remained in exile, his heart was true for
Cuba."

There he became known as a standout scholar, poet, journalist,
teacher, and social and political activist. Only recently has he been
given his due as an original political and social philosopher. Martí
believed that if Cuba was to win independence over the long term,
overthrowing the Spanish regime in Cuba was just the first step.
Another revolution had to take place as well: Cubans had to overcome
all the divides within, all the internal fractures, the understandable
scars of generations of oppressive rule, as well as all ethnic, class, and
political factionalism. A liberated people, upon ousting a colonial
power, could not get rid of colonialism itself, Martí believed, if a master-slave mentality still lingered. He thought that all those engaged in
liberation must also consciously seek to forge a new identity, and not
solely from their shared mission to liberate themselves. Rather, they
must carve a collective self from their traditional cultural, moral, and
indigenous heritage. If Cubans didn't achieve this, Martí feared that a
new leader could exploit their divisions and install himself as dictator
for life—an especially tragic outcome given that it would be one of
their own who undid all of the promise of the revolution.

To prevent this, Martí called for all Cubans to come together as a
family with the same kind of natural warmth he'd witnessed time and
again during his stays in exile in Latino countries that had been liberated by his hero, the Venezuela-born Simón Bolivar (1783–1830). If
Cuba was to become a member of this greater Latino family of
nations, Martí believed, Cubans first had to discover those attributes
unique to them that would inspire them to transcend pettier divisions
and strive to make broader connections with Hispanics elsewhere.
Such a scenario could come about only if Cubans on a broad scale

first inculcated *cubanidad*, which Martí scholar James Kirk equates with "pride of being Cuban." The objective was not to have this pride for the sake of it, or to build a type of jingoism that would set Cuba at odds with other nations, but that through the equal recognition and validation among Cubans inspired by *cubanidad*, they might become more unified with nations, particularly in the Hispanic world, that strive for a higher good based on shared values and histories. As a pioneer philosopher of identity, Martí believed that one could never become a vital part of *humanidad* if the route to get there did not pass through the heart of one's own culture—in this instance *cubanidad*—and the unique humanistic mores that rooted it to a particular place and transcended it.

Many ordinary Cubans, inspired by their hero Martí, still seek to practice *cubanidad*. The only place where they have not been able to make inroads is in the political realm. Haroldo Dilla, a prominent Cuban political sociologist now living in the Dominican Republic, was long associated with the Center for Studies of the Americas (CEA), an influential independent think tank for social research founded by the Cuban Communist Party. The CEA was dissolved in 1996 for "exceeding its mandate." Dilla observes that Cuba is becoming—in spite of all attempts by political leaders and hard-liners on both sides of the straits to thwart it—a "civil society" based on the ethos of *cubanidad*. Dilla stresses that this is not to be confused with the government apparatus, but rather is a close-knit society formed among everyday Cubans who "advocate greater autonomy in official political structures, greater democracy—greater freedom of action and discussion." Below the radar, they have formed an alternative society.

AT THE OUTSET, Che Guevara, like Martí, saw in Cuba the ideal laboratory to forge a particular identity among Cubans that would resonate among people everywhere, that held promise of serving as the impetus for a more expansive revolution that would create an evolved family of man. That Guevara "acted for the good of human-

ity as he interpreted that cause seems certain," asserts Henry Butter-
field Ryan in *The Fall of Che Guevara*. Ryan writes that Guevara without question was among those paradigmatic figures in human history
who "displayed . . . loyal adherence to an ideology," and "whose dedi-
cation to principle is inspirational, regardless of what one feels about
his belief." Ryan says Guevara "brings to mind early reformers of the
Christian church" what "with his extensive learning, his disregard for
worldly rewards, his devotion to an ideal . . . and his certainty that he
would someday become a martyr for the faith, as indeed he did."

In the end Guevara, made an official Cuban citizen by Castro, may
have put being a "martyr for the faith," a particular ideology, above
being a martyr for the faithful, the world's marginalized. If so, he
became smitten by the "blind love" that José Martí had warned against.

Tribal Family

Each "tribal nation" in the Hellenic world had a sophisticated form of
social organization, one of a comparatively inclusive and participatory
bent. It was a logical next step, under the visionary leadership of Athenian statesman Solon (630 B.C.–560 B.C.), that they join together to form
a greater intertribal confederacy, with Athens as the vortex. Over time,
they came to develop a sense of what might be called "Athenness,"
which transcended their loyalties and identities to particular tribes.
Solon instituted his sweeping democratic reforms. The seats in the various democratic councils of Athens were apportioned so that each tribe
was represented equally, ensuring that no single group could monop-
olize, preventing a resurgence of civil strife of times past.

As the Greek confederacy expanded, it did not do so in hierarchi-
cal fashion, but rather in the mode of a widening circle, in which all
the tribes that came aboard were given equal value and recognition.
They shared a common, higher goal: the cultivation of *arête*, or all-

around excellence. Yet *arête* did not mean excellence in the individualistic sense in which we use it today. It was a kind of excellence that
could not be realized unless every member strove for it, each developing talents and capacities that would contribute to greater actualiza-
tion of self and society. The tribal democracy that strove for *arête* was
inspired and driven by a higher form of *storge*.

Today, another tribally based democratic nation is showing the way
to broaden and deepen the concept of familial love at a time when
many of even the most open societies find such a goal elusive at best.

In the Name of Ubuntu

"The most valuable value is *ubuntu*," says forty-three-year-old Mae.
"It means in Zulu, 'I'm who I am because of who we all are'—for good
and for ill. If one member of my tribe does harm, we all do harm, just
as when one does good, it is a reflection on us all. But because *ubuntu*
is meant to be a positive striving, it should mean: I can't be all I am
unless I do everything I can to make sure you can become all you are.
It's this striving for goodness that makes it the most valuable value. It
requires that all of us show great love, warmth, compassion."

I'm in Pretoria, South Africa, the nation's administrative capital.
The insular city, founded in 1855, about fifty miles from the industrial center of Johannesburg, was named after the leader of the Boer
settlers, known as Voortrekkers—Afrikaans for "pioneers"—who
vanquished the indigenous Zulu kingdom. It is inauguration day,
marking the commencement of the second term of Thabo Mbeki, the
one-time anti-apartheid activist and leader of the African National
Congress (ANC), who was reelected by a landslide. Mbeki is the son
of prominent African National Congress activists. His father, sentenced to life in prison for his activism, was incarcerated along with
Nelson Mandela in Robbens Island. Mbeki was forced into exile in

1962 to Britain, where he organized and spearheaded the ANC movement among other exiles, until he returned at apartheid's dissolution.
Today's events take place on the nation's tenth National Freedom Day,
marking a full decade since the dissolution of South Africa's racist and
segregationist apartheid system.

Prior to the 1870s, South Africa was an amalgam of autonomous
polis-like groupings, each with a diverse yet harmonious populace
comprising of an array of ethnic groups and languages. When gold
and diamonds were discovered by prospectors, the British empire
invaded, conquered, and colonized the country. As Anthony Butler
writes, the result was the rapid decimation of the autonomous societies, which were supplanted by English rule and the subsequent
"forging of the migrant working class" of virtual slave labor among
the indigenous peoples, who worked the mines for the colonizers.
Subsequently, the apartheid system—"organized around enforced
classification of a historically complex and diverse South African
population"—was formally established.

Well over a million people are on hand for the inauguration. South
Africans have converged here, using any and every form of transportation imaginable, from the most remote provinces of this nation
of 45 million to be part of this special day. There isn't nearly enough
room for all celebrants to congregate in the main plaza, and eventually event organizers steer well over 100,000 of us to a large soccer
field nearby, where we will be able to watch the inauguration proceed-
ings on a big screen. This is where, for the first time all day, I
encounter a group of blacks and whites sitting in close proximity.
Most seem receptive to sharing their perspectives on the question
"What value do you value most?"

Mae, the first to offer her thoughts on the question, appears
unfazed that her response draws looks ranging from undisguised
bemusement to downright skepticism. She addresses the matter
squarely. "It must sound strange that a white person, of Afrikaaner
ancestry no less, talks about *ubuntu* as the most valuable value," she
says, looking at each participant one by one.

Then, looking my way, she says, "I'd always thought of myself as a liberal, even in the worst days of apartheid. I'd actually thought that just by saying that I believed whites and blacks were equals, that was sufficient for me to have a clear conscience over what was going on. I was so ignorant, and so sheltered, about the reality for the oppressed. One day, after I was married and pregnant with my only child, I saw a white police officer brutally beat a young black man, for no other reason than that he would not step off the sidewalk as he passed by. That was my 'consciousness raising.'

"I began to ask myself, 'Will my child come to look at those with different skin color from his the same way as that policeman?' Heaven forbid. Soon after, I took part in a massive anti-apartheid protest. One of the organizers read a letter from Nelson Mandela that he'd composed in his prison cell. It wasn't a call to violence, but to togetherness. He said whites and blacks must come together as a tribe, because that's in fact what we are, with a shared story and shared roots. He said each must do her part to dismantle apartheid by breaking down the divides between us, and within us. Mandela was 'inciting' us to overthrow a political and social system based on pure division with one of pure togetherness.

"I went on to join the African National Congress, though it was still outlawed. After my husband found out, he moved out of our home. He wasn't even at the hospital for my child's birth. By the time my son came into this world, it was becoming pretty clear that the days of apartheid—Afrikaans for 'separateness'—were numbered. [My son] would be part of a brave, new and loving world. And for having at least contributed a little bit towards this myself, I experienced a kind of happiness and contentment I'd never experienced in my life. I began reading more about my history, about all the African people and the tribal tradition of *ubuntu*. I began learning Zulu, and I started to gain an even clearer understanding of what I had to do to deserve to be part of the new South African family."

Her moving words win converts among the initial disbelievers in the room. One man, Moeketsi, in his late forties, who works as an itinerant laborer and is on hand with his wife and his baby girls—identical twins—takes Mae's hand and squeezes it. Then he says, "I had long been an anti-apartheid activist, motivated out of anger and hatred for our oppressors. These were the values I valued most, but they're negative values. They were not the values of my ancestors. My Zulu forebears didn't believe that when someone slaps you, you turn the other cheek. They believed, when someone slaps you, you hug him. That is *ubuntu* in action. We have a sage proverb, 'Never turn your back on the culture of your forefathers and -mothers,' because you are turning your back on yourself. They believed it was each person's moral duty always to take into consideration the interests and welfare of everyone else with whom you interact—not just your tribe, but everyone. By showing compassion and hospitality, you widen the circle of your tribe by bringing all of humanity into your fold.

"But I rejected that value system. Even after apartheid ended, my negative values colored my world. But then I too had a turning-point moment. I heard Thabo Mbeki speak, after apartheid's end, when we were at a critical crossroads, that if we are to honor the values of our ancestors, we must strive 'never to hate people because of their colour or race, always to value all human beings, and never to turn their backs on the deeply entrenched sentiment informed by the spirit of *ubuntu*—to forgive, understanding that the harm done yesterday cannot be undone today by a resolve to harm another.' Mbeki said the formerly oppressed and oppressor alike are all part of the same story, of heartbreak and hope, and that we need one another more than ever if we are to enter this new chapter and have an unforgettable story that will be inspiring around the world. He also said we must be united, see ourselves as a single tribe, so that 'those who were disadvantaged can assume their place in society as equals with their fellow human beings'. His 'I am an African' speech changed the way I viewed whites, myself, my tribe, and my place in it. I couldn't value myself fully without valuing everyone else fully. That is what *ubuntu* is about."

"I was also moved to change my way of living and sense of myself by President Mbeki's speech," says Rose, Mae's best friend. "To do my part to give the historically disadvantaged the chance they deserved to assume their place in society, I voluntarily am giving up my job with the federal government several years earlier than I would have been required to, and am training a black South African to replace me.

"When she's thoroughly trained, I'll be among the record 40 percent unemployed. But I'll stay put right here in South Africa, because I value these people, this place, and myself among these people and this place—though I'm sure this value will be put to the test when my financial coffers run dry."

"The 'white flight' from South Africa has been for the worst reasons," Mae says next. "Those who flee value 'me, myself, and I.' They don't want to sacrifice, not even for the short term, for the long-term good of their homeland. The result is a terrible brain drain. Professionals like doctors, lawyers, engineers, accountants left by the thousands. Like Rose, I'm staying on, even after I'm unemployed from my federal job. I want my son to have his roots here, rooted in what Mbeki called a new tribe with the shared identity of 'Africanness'. To flee would be to teach [my son] the 'worst valuable value': that when the going gets tough after you've had it made for so long, you get going someplace else."

"My dad is an investment banker," Mae's seventeen-year-old son, Blaine, tells us. "He left for London after apartheid ended. I had a choice to go or stay. Like Mom, I wanted to be part of my country's future." Then he adds a bit sheepishly, "And I didn't want to leave my girlfriend."

His girlfriend, Samora, says to me, "*Ubuntu* also means 'humanity towards others.' It means you consider all people your equal—of no greater, but no lesser, importance. Many white *and* black South Africans don't practice *ubuntu* towards me, because I have a white boyfriend."

"Does this influence how or whether you practice this most valuable value toward them?" I ask.

"No," she says flatly. And then: "Well, I'd *like* my answer to be 'no.' Sometimes they do get to me, though. But if I respond by stooping to their level, I feel horrible. That's not being who I am or want to be—but who they want me to be. They win."

"I've seen Samora subjected to terrible racial taunts and epithets," her mom, Venda, tells us. "You know how she responds? She approaches these people and calmly asks them why they'd say such hurtful things. I want to pull her back and protect her. They might hurt my precious girl. Most of the time, they back down or walk away. But on rare occasions, they apologize. Samora is my personal role model when it comes to *ubuntu*."

"Mine too," says Blaine. Looking askance at his mom, he says, "As much as my mom considers *ubuntu* the most valuable value, she's not completely comfortable that I'm with a black woman."

"I love Samora like my own daughter," Mae replies. "I feared, though, they were both in for so much hurt. But they've taught me that some types of hurt are worth enduring—obviously, foremost in the name of their love for one another, but also in the name of making our society the color-blind place it needs to be. Well, not color-blind, but one where all colors are valued equally."

"I'm sorry to rain on the *ubuntu* parade," says Moeketsi's friend Khoe, "but it's hard to feel equal when you still don't have the privileges and advantages the whites have. How can I treat others as equals when we're not on a level playing field?"

To which Samora replies, "Father Mandela was imprisoned for almost three decades. They tried everything they could to demean and humiliate him. He showed them how puny they were, and how great he was—not because he put himself above them, but because he didn't put himself below them. You can't let your circumstances determine whether or how you value yourself or others."

"It's only because of those in South Africa who *didn't* wait for circumstances to be ideal that we're now a decade removed from the poison of apartheid," says Samora's mom. "We got to this point because of the shared belief among anti-apartheid activists that they were every bit the equals of their oppressors, and their decision to act on that belief, for the greater good of the South African tribe."

"How does one square or reconcile the violent tactics of some anti-apartheid revolutionaries with the 'most valuable value' of *ubuntu*?" I ask. "Does it mean that in an imperfect world, sometimes—in order to create the conditions for a society based on 'humanity toward others'—you have to act violently?"

"The overwhelming majority of activists employed violence as a last resort when it was the only recourse to prevent the continuing wholesale slaughter of blacks," remarks Venda. "But a few did go over the line and stoop to the level of the oppressors. After the days of upheaval were behind us, Nelson Mandela and Bishop Desmond Tutu established the Truth and Reconciliation Commission in the name of *ubuntu*. To come together as one, they knew you and your former enemies have to confront one another, and you have to confront yourself, about your shared past. You have to remember and repent before you can forgive and reconcile. The idea and ideal was for everyone who'd committed egregious acts of violence to own up to them without fear of retribution, and seek forgiveness, so we could move forward as one tribe. The commission finished its work in 1998, issuing a report based on over 20,000 cases of mistreatment and violence by both Afrikaaners and ANC activists. But the reality was that an exponentially greater number of former ANC warriors testified, even though in most cases theirs were not gratuitous or unprovoked acts of violence, like those of the Afrikaner police, and even though in any event the oppressors committed far more atrocities by any measure than the oppressed."

"The truth is there's still too many whites who do not want reconciliation," says Mae. "Too many who committed the most inhumane acts got off scot-free, and still feel no remorse. They don't value others outside their small group, and in fact wish our society would return to 'the good old days.' The difference now is that people of all races present a united front of *ubuntu*."

"There's a Zulu term, *simunye*, which means both 'unity through strength' and 'we are one,'" says Venda. "As we become one, we become stronger, so we can more effectively drown out the fractured forces and voices of hate with a unified voice of love. We have another coinage, *umuntu ngumuntu ngabantu,* that means we can only become a human being through others—the more humans we bring into our lives, the more we make them part of our world, our family, our tribe, the more human we become."

Moeketsi remarks, "Novelist Nadine Gordimer said in her Pulitzer acceptance speech that it was the critical task of writers of the South Africa experience to explore deeply and honestly enemy and friend alike 'warts and all.' She quoted our country's revered poet and freedom fighter Mongane Serote, who exhorts us to 'page through each other's faces' and 'read each looking eye.' I think that to really belong, we must first page through our own faces and read our own looking eye, to make sure we've confronted and overcome our own dispositions toward intolerance and prejudice, so we deserve to be members of this new tribe.

"Apartheid didn't just mean we were separated physically," he continues. "There was apartheid in our hearts too. *Ubuntu* is the language of love in action, bridging all our hearts."

Reconciliation and Forgiveness

Nelson Mandela says that "the spirit of *ubuntu*—that profound African sense that we are human only through the humanity of other human beings—is not a parochial phenomenon but has added globally to our common search for a better world." Rather, it is a parochial phenomenon that, if practiced in a wide range of cultures around the world, can become more and more global in scope.

DISTINGUISHED NIGERIAN PLAYWRIGHT Wole Soyinka—who in 1967 was arrested and jailed, then forced into exile, for trying to arrange a cease-fire at the apex of his country's fierce civil war—said in his Nobel acceptance speech that the world has a great deal to learn from indigenous Africans'"capacity to forgive," which is based on a "largeness of spirit" that can be attributed directly to the ethical precepts of their heritage. The centerpiece of their heritage in virtually all tribes is *ubuntu*—a value that even generations of colonial oppression could never efface. This was reflected prominently in South Africa's interim constitution as it made the transition from apartheid to a full-fledged democracy. The constitution itself called for the "need for understanding but not for vengeance, a need for reparations but not for retaliation, a need for *ubuntu* but not for victimization."

I Am Because We Are

I encountered a person in a Paris suburb who held a philosophy of family love strikingly similar to that of *ubuntu*. I had ventured into an area where, a year later, rioting would erupt after two youths were electrocuted at a power substation, and then unsubstantiated rumors spread that they had died attempting to escape the police. An Associated Press article that came out during the riots said that in this area's dreary projects, "Families break down in the pressure-cooker of crime, poverty and unemployment." One woman who resides there is quoted as saying that "the absence of fathers causes some boys to become apathetic, while girls often rush into unsuitable marriages that often lead to divorce, and some turn to drugs and prostitution." She added, "There's so much of this in this community. Death of love has destroyed a whole generation." She was referring specifically to the death of family love, without which there cannot be the other vital sorts of love—of self, of community, and of others.

The woman running the café at which I stopped for lunch had immigrated to France from West Africa. The single mother of two boys, abandoned by her husband, had come to Paris to work in a garment factory. She told me that owning the café, made possible by a

government program offering grants and no-interest loans to immigrants to start microbusinesses, was the fulfillment of a longtime
dream. Still, it was a struggle, what with juggling the responsibility of
running her café—which often entailed twelve-hour workdays, seven
days a week—and trying to raise her sons on her own. "My kids feel
like they're in a twilight zone," she told me. "They don't feel French,
though they are French citizens, but they are also removed from their
African heritage, even though I try to tell them all about it. But I'll tell
you one thing they're not removed from—me. They never lack in
love. No matter how bone tired, I make ample time for them.
Extended family and friends help me care for them, spoil them as
much as possible, remonstrate them when they misbehave, take them
to and pick them up from school and soccer practice.

"According to our traditional beliefs," she goes on, "there is no 'I'
without 'you,' and there are no 'others,' only 'us.' Only by taking care of
one another do we exist as individuals. So we look out for one
another, pick one another up when we fall, praise and criticize when
we deserve it, always with loving purpose. In even the poorest villages,
we never let go of this tradition—caring for one another's children,
considering one another extended family. There's no good reason why
this tradition has to fall by the wayside here.

"If you bring a child into the world," she continues, "you've
accepted the responsibility of teaching them right from wrong, teaching them their heritage, nurturing them in ways that will help them
overcome life's hardships. We adults have to quit making excuses, and
again start looking out for one another, and one another's children."

Military Family Love

The troops of ancient Greeks were citizen-soldiers, freemen and
equals, superbly equipped, trained, and motivated. As Edith Hamil-

ton writes in *The Greek Way*: "Each man . . . had a share in the responsibility," though there were commanders, considered the most expert at military strategy and engagement. Because of his special status, a commander knew and expected that he "must be ready to suffer more hardships than he asks of his soldiers." Troops in Greece, Hamilton points out, had been known, when push came to shove, to "throw stones at a general whose order they did not approve," to "put down incompetent leaders and [act] for themselves." But this was typically averted, because when most critical military decisions were made in emergencies, deliberative gatherings with all the troops were held; all were invited to offer their two cents' worth and encouraged to differ even with generals to ensure their "willing co-operation" rather than enforced duty. Greeks had long ago learned that troops fight hardest and troop morale is greatest when they feel like they are their own men, equal brothers in arms, fighting to defend hearth and home of their own free will, in keeping with the shared Greek ideal and ethos of "free individuals unified by a spontaneous service to the common life." A special form of brotherly affection made them fierce and instinctive protectors of one another in time of battle.

Band of Brothers and Sisters

Diane, private first class in an engineering battalion in the Army National Reserve, says: "When you're in the field of battle, all you think about is carrying your part of the load for your team, doing right by them. That's a soldier's duty in a nutshell. You don't think about whether this is a just or unjust war, whether Americans back home support us. While I think it's the duty of every American to be behind us, regardless of whether they support the war, all I can do is do all in my power to make sure all my team members return home alive and well."

Diane has recently returned from a yearlong tour of duty in Iraq, as have the twelve other servicewomen and -men in U.S. armed forces Guard or reserve units gathered with me to hold a dialogue on the question "What is your duty?" Diane is among the nearly 185,000 National Guard and reserve troops—citizen-soldiers—on active duty. Of the nearly 150,000 U.S. troops stationed in Iraq, about 40 percent are Guard or reserve members. As this dialogue takes place, nearly 1,500 U.S. troops have lost their lives in Iraq, and well over 10,000 have been injured. To date, at least sixteen members of the National Guard, forty of the Army Reserve, and forty of the Marine Reserve have died. Earlier today, two more U.S. reserve troops were killed when their Humvee, which was not fitted with armor, tripped a bomb planted in its path that was detonated by remote control.

"Is risking your own life to save others in your troop above and beyond the call of duty?" I ask.

"Not in my view," says Diane. "Because they're family. And I don't mean just 'military family,' like we're trained to think, but 'family family.' Who is family if not those with whom you laugh and cry, with whom you confide everything and share everything? So of course I'd put myself between them and a bullet."

"So duty is not just obligation, but a willing obligation?" I ask.

Says Jacquie, a sergeant major who'd been deployed with a battalion of mechanics, "Well, in this case, the willing obligation sprang out of the formal obligation I made after I enlisted and gave my oath to protect and defend my country. But it's one thing to defend your country in the abstract; it's another when you're with your troops in the line of fire in a faraway place. They become the personal embodiment of your country, of all that you hold dear, to put it in highfalutin terms—mom, dad, sis, apple pie, all of that. The bond we develop is way beyond 'fraternal.' When you're on assignment together for months on end, 24-7, they're like your Siamese twin. I never even think about 'duty' when we're in the thick of it. It's instinctive to us to look out for and protect one another, just like a mamma and papa bear do for their cubs."

Diane now interjects: "I know many would like to ask our president, 'Would you be willing to send your own children to fight and maybe die in places like Iraq?' My *own* answer is: I wouldn't be willing to send my own or anyone else's children there, *unless* they aspired, like me, to be a professional soldier. But I wouldn't be willing to send *anyone* into war unless I'd first done everything in my power to resolve conflict through peaceful means. That should be a commander in chief's foremost duty.

"I don't want the commander in chief, in debating whether to go to war, to think of those of us he's putting in harm's way *as if* we were his siblings or children," Diane continues. "I want him to see us *as* his siblings and children. Because that's what we are: the few and the proud willing to risk it all for love of family and country, in an era when so little is asked of so many, and so much is asked of us [the armed forces]."

"I'll be honest, I first joined the reserve for the benefits," says Jacquie. "I'm a single mom who's an assistant manager at a chain store in the civilian world. I needed the extra income and the benefits for education, retirement, and health. But I was also aware there could come a time when I'd be called on to serve, though as a reserve member I thought it'd be to help out in a community near home, in a dire emergency in Louisiana, not in a preemptive war thousands of miles away. But I'll go wherever my commander in chief thinks I can best be of service, and just pray he sees it as his God-given duty to make sure he never puts us in the shit for any other reason than he thinks it's so vital to the defense of our beloved homeland, he'd risk his own life, his own sibling's or child's life."

Cutler is a corporal in an Army Guard infantry unit who was called to serve in Iraq with just one semester to go before completing his pre-law studies in law school; he is engaged and set to be married in less than a month. He says, "The political leaders of old who were also chief military commanders would always be at the head of the battle, the first in the fray. They felt it was their duty, based on a higher, unwritten code. They'd never ask their fellow troops to do anything they wouldn't do themselves. They loved their troops more than they loved any blood kin who shied from fighting alongside them. Those who didn't make it home again could die at peace, knowing that those who survived would take their families under their wing and provide for them as if they were their own, and they'd make sure their companions' heroic deeds and example always burned bright in their memories."

"Socrates himself answered the call and fought in wars for Athens whenever his country asked him to," says Cora, a recently divorced mother of three who is a major in a helicopter unit and an inveterate philosophy buff. "He was a foot soldier in a number of engagements in the Peloponnesian War, and he was decorated for his valor on the field. Socrates said that in all the campaigns he fought, 'I never left my post,' and, like everyone else, 'I ran the risk of dying.' He's the ideal citizen-soldier. He exercised his right to free speech at home, criticizing his country sometimes—but out of a loving sense of duty, when that was the best way to defend Athenian democracy from domestic enemies. But he was also the first person to put his life on the line for his country against outside aggressors."

"Here in America, we citizen-soldiers have far fewer rights and privileges than ordinary citizens, rather than more, which is pretty disgraceful in my book," says Cutler. "In one of my favorite movies, *Starship Troopers*, in the civilization that exists there, the laws that are on the books give you a choice of being either a civilian or a citizen. A citizen, unlike a civilian, is one who volunteers to go to war to defend her country. Personally, I don't think you should have to go to *war* war to be a citizen. There's lots of other ways to do your patriotic duty: fighting the war against poverty, homelessness, illiteracy, or the war against bad health care or hunger. But you should *have* to do something like this to enjoy the rights and privileges of a citizen."

The movie *Starship Troopers* was adapted from a science fiction novel of the same name written by Robert A. Heinlein, a naval reserve officer. It tells the story of young Johnnie Rico who, against the wishes of his upper-crust parents, joins the military to go to war against invading bugs and, as a reward for carrying out his duties as a soldier, gains citizenship. In the book, Rico's mentor, Colonel Dubois, instructs him that "it wasn't the voting process that made a citizen"; rather, "(c)itizenship is an attitude, a state of mind, an emotional conviction that the whole is greater than the part . . . and that the part should be humbly proud to sacrifice itself that the whole may live."

Says Jacquie, "In our country's last four elections, we've twice elected and reelected presidents, and one vice president, who pulled strings, shirking their duty, so they never had to be in harm's way. We elected these people, who all the time are talking about 'duty this' and 'duty that,' over authentic war heroes, who instead of just talking the talk answered the call to duty. They still get choked up when they recall those among their military brothers and sisters who didn't make it back. As a troop leader, I know that if one of my team members died, I'd feel personally responsible, like I failed, losing someone I consider both a beloved brother and son. It's beyond me how people can ballyhoo duty and cloak themselves in the flag who've never put it on the line and done their duty to God and country.

"Our own revolutionary philosopher Thomas Paine said, 'the times that try men's souls' are when, in time of crisis, 'the summer soldier and the sunshine patriot shrink from the services of their country,' whereas the one who does his duty 'deserves the love and thanks of man and woman.' I have to say our task can seem pretty thankless, but once in a blue moon, some civilian, a stranger, will come up to me and shake my hand, even hug me, out of thanks for the duty I'm carrying out on behalf of our country. I accept their thanks, but on behalf of all my military brothers and sisters. When I tell them I hope they go to a cemetery where veterans are buried and pay their respects to those who made the ultimate sacrifice, they just sort of nod dumbly."

Says Cora, "The thing is, you want to think you're being asked to sacrifice your life for a cause that's so sublime, anyone who is able to serve would be willing to do the same, but even those who thank us don't seem to have any inkling of what our duty really amounts to.

Our own president, when asked what sacrifices our citizens are making that compare with those of the soldiers, replied, 'They have to wait in longer lines at the airport.' So even at the top, there's a disconnect when it comes to duty.

"You want to think your leaders made every effort to properly train you for as many contingencies, foreseen and unforeseen, as possible. You want to think they did all they could to know the enemy, so the enemy could be defeated with as few casualties as possible—on *both* sides, because the death of a loved one in battle destroys so many others who are waiting for them back home. You want to think that citizens of your own country would consider it their duty to pay more in taxes so you can have body armor and armor on your vehicles. You want to think your employers and colleagues welcome back citizen-soldiers with open arms rather than grudgingly. And you want to think that your life means so much to your leaders and fellow citizens that they'd shed as many tears over your death in battle as they would over one of their own. But that means they'd have to think of us as their own siblings or children. It should be their solemn duty and honor to consider us so, but how can they when they are never made to feel any ties to us, never have to step up and sacrifice anything themselves? But we carry on, because no matter what, we do feel a deep sense of duty to country and to one another."

Cora murmurs, after a thoughtful silence, "Shakespeare's King Henry said: 'We few, we happy few, we band of brothers. For he today that sheds his blood with me shall be my brother . . . .'"

"Do you think that's true?" I ask. "Someone in the field of battle who sheds her blood with you, no matter the cause, is a brother?"

"Back then, I think they shed blood too easily, that they saw too much glory in doing so," Cora says, after thinking about it long and hard. "The rest of that passage goes: 'And gentlemen in England abed shall . . . hold their manhoods cheap while any speaks that fought with us upon Saint Crispin's Day.'"

She looks at me and says, "I don't think anyone's manhood or womanhood is cheap. You should never glorify war. It's never a good day to die on the field of battle if there was any possibility that war could have been averted."

A long silence is broken when Diane says, "I'll tell you straight up, these people here mean more to me than life itself. I love them that much. And I know they feel the same about me. If you die so they can live and go back home to their loved ones, then it really is 'mission accomplished,' and your death has been worthwhile."

The Art of Peace and Love

Premier Chinese military strategist and expert in diplomacy Sun Tzu (544–496 B.C.), like Socrates and Confucius, lived in the fifth century B.C., a time when societies were amalgams of clans. In his aphorisms, he stressed the importance that a commander in chief must nurture kinship ties if he is to have the best fighting force possible. Sun Tzu wrote that it is imperative that a commander "look upon the troops as his children," that he consider them "his beloved sons," taking on their tasks to get a firsthand sense of their trials and tribulations. In Sun Tzu's world, commander and troops were likely related in any event by immediate or extended clan or tribe, growing up in the same communities, sharing the same values, knowing one another's families.

According to Sun Tzu, the supreme leader of troops must above all else strive to be a "sage commander," and as such will never fall prey to the "five fatal qualities," those of being "reckless," "cowardly," "quick-tempered," have "too delicate a sense of honor," or falling easy prey to harassment and so react in a careless or precipitous way. Sun Tzu said these character defects are "fatal," even "calamitous," in military affairs. Sun Tzu, who had witnessed many times the horrors of war, and had served under good and awful commanders, was keenly aware that even under the best of circumstances, many would die in war, some nobly, some not so. But he also knew that the decisions a commander made, based in large measure on his personal temperament, informed by his regard (or lack thereof) for his troops, would determine whether countless soldiers lived or died. He sought to elaborate pragmatic strategies for winning wars that would minimize the number of deaths and injuries on both sides. His works show how cognizant he was that soldiers were someone's child or spouse or parent or grandparent or sibling who wanted above all else to return to their loved ones; consequently, he thought deeply about how to avoid violent conflict altogether.

SCHOLAR KIDDER SMITH writes that Sun Tzu's *Art of War* in effect shows "how to conquer without aggression, whether our conflict is large or small," for to Sun Tzu "(s)ubduing the other's military without battle is the most skillful" victory of all. Sun Tzu recognized that although you "live in a world where aggression cannot be avoided," such aggression does not have to lead to violent conflict. If you take the time to "know the other," you can gain greater self-understanding, confronting and coming to terms with your own inner conflicts and aggressive tendencies. Once you have a greater grasp of your own strengths and flaws, you are better equipped to "skillfully engage" your opponent. One of Sun Tzu's most critical insights is:

> If you know the enemy and yourself, you'll never be in danger, even in a hundred battles. If you know yourself but don't know your enemy, you'll win sometimes and you'll lose sometimes. And if you don't know your enemy or yourself, you're in grave danger of losing every battle.

Like Socrates, Sun Tzu believed that one's guiding tenet in life must be "know thyself," and that this must hold even more so for those whose decisions determine the fate of so many others. Sun Tzu's *Art of War* principally deals with the art of knowing oneself, of cultivating those virtues that enable one to see conflict as an opportunity to wage peace, even love, within and without. Sun Tzu scholar Ralph Sawyer observes that Sun Tzu's book "repeatedly emphasizes the need for rationality and self-control" in all a leader's dealings that involve conflict, so a sage commander must cultivate the "ideal traits" of wisdom, knowledge, credibility, benevolence, discipline, courage, and skillful analysis, so that those passions that might impel him to fight first and think later are kept in check, for the sake of all in his military family who serve under him, and the long-term sake of the nation he is charged to protect and preserve.

THE WAR THAT led to the downfall of ancient Athens, the second Peloponnesian War, which ran from 420–405 B.C., was at its foundation an interfamilial dispute, a conflict between two sides that became inevitable rather than guarding themselves against Sun Tzu's five fatal qualities. They failed to confront the seeds of their aggression, which in this case was to note that theirs was a sibling rivalry. Edith Hamilton observes that these "two little Greek states . . . fought not because they were different . . . but because they were alike." A mere five decades earlier, Athens and Sparta had been on the same side, defending the Greek territories from the Persian Empire, which they successfully repelled. But over time, after the defeat of the Persians, though the two sides continued with the shared goal of developing a more advanced civilization, they increasingly deviated over how to get there. Sparta became an aristocracy, Athens a democracy (though Spartan women enjoyed more rights than their Athenian counterparts). And although the citizens of the two states were still part of the same Greek family, now they saw themselves as rival brothers, each trying to outdo the other in extending their particular confederation among other Greek entities. In most instances, Athens outdid its rival, because, as Edith Hamilton notes, they were widely seen as "defender of the defenseless," not out to take people's land or resources but to widen their confederacy to bring more under the umbrella of their democracy.

But Athens' forays were perhaps too successful. At some point it lost sight of why it was expanding, yet it continued to expand anyway, developing, Hamilton writes, a "passion for power and possession which no power and no possession satisfy." The Peloponnesian War was an amoral war, one that "had nothing to do with differences in ideas or with considerations of right and wrong." With the sudden and "rising tide of power and money," Athens began to covet land and resources rather than the spread of Athenian values (though it might have made specious claims to be attempting this still). Then it set its sights on Syracuse, a people and a land that no one could assume, even charitably, that Athens desired for anything but to sate its avaricious passion for power. Sparta allied itself with Syracuse, but still Athens' army had all the advantage. However, it committed a cascade of unprecedented blunders, based on a new approach by military leaders who fell prey to Sun Tzu's five fatal qualities. They lost all semblance of all-important "rationality and self-control." As classical historian Donald Kagan writes in *The Peloponnesian War*, the troops themselves were no longer heeded, and the Athenian practice of restraint and moderation was now "held to be a cloak of unmanliness."

Edward Shepherd Creasy writes that Athens, in "staking the flower of her forces, and the accumulated fruits of seventy years of glory, on one bold throw for the dominion of the Western world," lost everything. The great virtues that had brought a wide array of Hellenic tribes together in a spirit of harmony and collective endeavor and exploration, that had inspired them to transcend particularisms and dissensions in the name of a greater good, now devolved into infighting, factionalism, and parochialism, reversing all the good that had been cultivated. They were a confederacy no more, no longer a united family. "Even the powerful ties of family . . . succumbed to the pressures of the long war," writes Kagan. The sad consequence, according to Hamilton, is that a "great power brought about its own destruction." But sadder still, "[t]he cause of humanity was defeated. Greece's contribution to the world was checked and soon ceased."

Norman F. Cantor writes in *Antiquity* that with the war's end there was "a new atmosphere in which the ideals of rational debate, of mod-

eration and humanity, could hardly flourish." The city was "demoral-
ized by fear," there were "chaotic factional disputes among the Athenian citizenry," and eventually there was a veritable "reign of terror,"
making their fall complete.

It wasn't the end of the war that brought this to pass, however, but
the beginning of the war, the launching of a conflict that was avoidable. Athens ceased to be the place it had been for so long, as described
by Pericles (460–429 B.C.), the prominent Athenian political leader
who said rightly that "we alone do good to our neighbors not out of
calculation of interest, but in the confidence of freedom and in a
frank and fearless and generous spirit."

Xenophon, himself an Athenian general, lauded Socrates as an
exemplary soldier with innate leadership ability, and records him saying that it is "incumbent" that a commander in chief be like a shepherd who cares for his flock in such a way that they are "well and want
for nothing." To this end, he must

> furnish the soldiers with necessary ammunition and provisions;
> he must be inventive, laborious, diligent, patient, quick of
> apprehension; he must be mild and rigorous together; . . . he
> must know to preserve his own . . .

According to Socrates, any military leader who fails to learn how to
command in this fashion "ought to be severely punished."

The Greatest Generation

In *Generation Kill*, journalist Evan Wright, who was embedded in Iraq
for two months with twenty-three Marines from the elite First Recon
group, writes that "these Marines are virtually unrecognizable from
their forebears," namely the "Greatest Generation," who fought in

World War II. He said the soldiers he was with ranged from "tough guys . . . who pray to Buddha and quote Eastern philosophies and New Age precepts" to "gangbangers" to "born-again Christians." But this does not make them different from the Greatest Generation. They gave the same oaths of enlistment, have put themselves just as much in harm's way, have been just as expendable. In Wright's own words, today's soldiers, like those of World War II, "face death every day," "struggle with fear, confusion," and many "kill a lot of people" and likely in some cases "will no doubt think about and perhaps regret for the rest of their lives" some of their actions. One soldier in the book says he simply hopes that "the American people . . . know the price we pay to maintain their standard of living."

What *does* distinguish today's soldiers is that rather than being conscripted, they volunteered for military service. The greatest difference between today's soldiers and those of World War II is that most of the American people of that generation were well aware of the sacrifices being made by their troops; indeed, soldier and civilian alike sacrificed together for the greater war effort, most undergoing some degree of hardship and deprivation, with a sense of common purpose and shared mission. A generation arguably can't be characterized as "great" unless there is some shared code, some keen sense that everyone is in this together out of a sense of shared duty and sacrifice, whether contributing to the war effort at home or abroad. If the disconnect is so great that most Americans have no sense of the sacrifice being made by their soldiers, it is a clear indication that ours has become a dysfunctional family.

Socrates Family Values

Where "family love" is concerned, should unconditional acceptance be the norm? Should children and parents accept one another with-

out qualification, even though children never asked to be brought into the world (by most belief systems, at least)? Parents, once children themselves, also never asked to be brought into the world, yet here they are, and now—expected or not, married or not, ready or not—they have children of their own. Children may not turn out as their parents hoped, but at least, in some way, parents had a hand in deciding their coming-to-be, or their coming to be part of their family. Does this give kids the right to be less accepting of their parents' shortcomings than the other way around?

Socrates' son Lamprocles certainly thought so.

Xenophon (427–355 B.C.), soldier, scribe, and student of Socrates, was the other contemporary of his mentor besides Plato who wrote at length about him; he was forced into exile for his admiration of the philosopher. Xenophon relates this vignette in his *Memorabilia*: Once, when Socrates' son Lamprocles complained about how strict his oft-irascible mother was with him, Socrates fast came to his wife's defense.

Socrates was unusually devoted to his wife, even though his fellow inquirers were rather merciless in deriding him over his relationship with Xanthippe. In Xenophon's *Symposium*, the chauvinistic males criticize Socrates for failing to put his wife in her place, for "permitting" her to be so spirited. Socrates counters, Why would he want a submissive wife? What in the world would he be able to learn, how would he be able to grow from the experience of being a husband if, like his friends, he had a doormat for a wife? At the time, his perspective on husbandhood was quite radical. But Socrates held women in comparatively higher esteem than his fellow free men. Eva Cantarella writes that Socrates, "unlike the majority of his fellow citizens," "had a certain regard for women, and, in particular, did not believe them inferior by nature." He even recognized women's superiority "at least in certain fields." To Socrates, what made anyone inferior in anything was not gender but lack of education and experience, and he was an early booster for women receiving educational opportunities.

Even though he was more enlightened than most, Lamprocles had every expectation that his father would side with him. Like his father and unlike his mother, he was automatically a citizen of the polis, endowed by his gender and age with all the rights his dad enjoyed. Yet when he berated his mother, his father instead jumped to her defense. Socrates tells Lamprocles that he should know full well that if his mom remonstrates him, it is with the best of intentions: "She wishes you more good than any other human being." In true Socratic fashion, he then presents his son with compelling evidence to support his view. He points out how Xanthippe is "so benevolent to you when you are ill, takes care of you to the utmost of her power," sees to it that he "wants nothing," "entreats the gods for many blessings on your head," and even "pays vows for you." Given this, Socrates is bemused that Lamprocles lambasts his mother so.

Lamprocles, just as spirited as his mom, insists that she still has no right to berate him, and is of the mind that parents bring children into the world in order to have someone to torment. Socrates tells Lamprocles that he should thank his lucky stars for having such a mother, and calls him ungrateful. Not only that, he says that parents who have devoted as much time to their children's upbringing as Xanthippe have every right to remonstrate them when they are not comporting themselves well. In Socrates' view, gratitude is largely a one-way street—children for their parents, but not the other way around—for "father and mother brought them out of nothingness into being," made it possible for them to "look upon all these fair sights and take part in all those blessings which the gods bestow on man, things so priceless . . . that we shudder at the thought of leaving them" when our time is up.

Lamprocles still is not convinced, so Socrates, in the same fashion with which he would engage anyone in interrogation, asks Lamprocles to whom he owes his allegiance. Would he owe his allegiance to a stranger who assists him in need? Lamprocles replies that indeed he would. In that case, Socrates responds, how is it that his son professes no allegiance whatsoever to his mother, "who loves you more than all else"? Lamprocles at last seems to see the error of his ways. He is instructed to "earnestly entreat" his mother for forgiveness. To ensure against any further recalcitrance on his son's part, Socrates adds that if any of his fellow citizens knew Lamprocles had such a disdainful attitude toward one of his parents, he would find himself fast "devoid of friends," for they would take it that someone like him would scorn any kindness, and so not be deserving of their friendship.

Father Knows Best

What kind of father was Socrates? Was his love for his children conditional? Was he telling Lamprocles that parental love hinges on whether their children do as they say, and live up to their expectations? We have no way of telling whether he might have been as authoritarian a parent as he was democratic a philosopher, but it is clear he wants to channel his son's energies and spirit away from what he perceives as avoidable conflicts with parents and toward more productive ends, such as his own self-development.

Socrates goes on, in this account by Xenophon, to tell Lamprocles that parents, more than anything, set the bar highest for themselves. He tells his son that it is a father's role to provide his children "with all those things he believes will contribute to their well-being—and, of these things, to provide them with as large a store as possible." He is not talking about material possessions. Socrates did not reject material things, but he did not worship them and did not expect any child of his to. He cherished his middle class roots and values, and was content to be a person of modest means—even as his fellow middle class citizens were on the fast track to ever greater wealth in a new era of rampant commercialism, abandoning values they'd long held dear. For most, the accumulation of money and the material goods it provides had become an end in itself, and this was the new value that most parents were now passionate about passing on to their offspring. There were plenty of well-paid sophists on hand to validate their parental philosophy and assure them it took great courage to pursue material wealth without apology and to equate love with showering their children with worldly goods.

Socrates, meanwhile, continued to model for his children and other youth another set of values. The difference was that now he was seen as a corrupter of youth for doing so. Parents worried their children might become tainted by his example, question their own way of living, and rebel against them. Athens' leaders, in great need of a scapegoat for all their failed foreign and domestic policies, exploited this chasm in Athenian values. So effective was their propaganda demonizing Socrates that they managed to convince many that he was trying to replace old Athenian values and upend the pantheon of long-revered gods with new ones—that he was a heretic.

Before long, Socrates found himself sentenced to death for committing the crime of living as he had always lived. On his last opportunity to defend himself, to plea for a lenient sentence, even to recant his way of living, which is what most expected he would do to save himself (if not for himself, for the sake of his family), he told his fellow freemen,

> I love you and respect you, but I will obey God rather than you. As long as I have life and strength in me, I will never abstain from exhorting anyone whom I meet and telling him . . . : "You, my friend—a citizen of the great and mighty and wise city of Athens—aren't you ashamed of yourself for heaping up great amounts of money . . . , and caring so little about wisdom and truth and the greatest improvement of your soul?". . . I tell you that virtue is not given by money, but that from virtue comes money and every other good, public and private. . . . [I]f this is the doctrine that corrupts the youth, I am indeed a mischievous person.

Socrates' apology, as it has become known, wasn't an apology at all; rather, it was a defense of classical Athenian values. Yet it so angered those deciding his fate that the Council of Five Hundred, as they were known, voted to sentence him to death *by a larger margin* than they voted to find him guilty.

Socrates' moving speech also likely incurred their great ire because it was an explication of his philosophy of parenthood, which put their own to shame. The only reason one brought children into the world, in his view, was to inspire and equip and guide them in their own quest for "wisdom and truth and the greatest improvement of their soul."

From the vantage point of a number of centuries after the fact, the outcome of Socrates' trial might seem fantastic; yet it was not at all.

Greek historian Thucydides (460–400 B.C.), whose masterful accounts of Athenian history during that period are considered to this day the objective benchmark, described Athens' unraveling after its loss of the Peloponnesian War:

> Practically the whole of the Hellenic world was convulsed . . .
> Fanatical enthusiasm was [now] the mark of a real man . . . any-
> one who held violent opinions could always be trusted, and any-
> one who objected to them became a suspect . . . Consequently
> . . . there was a general deterioration of character throughout the
> Greek world. The honest and straightforward way of looking at
> things, which is such the mark of the noble nature, was regarded
> as a ridiculous quality and soon ceased to exist.

Socrates' children soon would be adults, and out on their own. If he gave in to his persecutors' demands that he abandon his values, what message would this send to his offspring? What were a few more years of life in comparison to that? He'd had a good long life, prepared his children for the vagaries of the world, had had a long and fruitful relationship with his wife. To live longer for the wrong reasons would taint his achievements up till then, and lessen the likelihood that his children would be inspired to live with the values with which they'd been raised.

SOCRATES DIDN'T WANT his wife, much less his children, at his sentencing. Eva Cantarella scolds him for being annoyed with his wife when she visits him in his cell and weeps over his impending death. Instead of consoling her, he says to a fellow inquirer, "Crito, let somebody take her home." Cantarella concludes from this episode that "Socrates had not put his theories into practice," didn't love Xanthippe the way he claimed. It doesn't occur to Cantarella that it upset Socrates to see his beloved wife weeping, that his putative annoyance was his way of dealing with his own emotional turmoil—or that he was accustomed to his wife being spirited and combative, and preferred her to remain "in character," now more so than ever.

BEFORE HE DRANK the hemlock and died, Socrates exacted a promise from his friends gathered with him—namely, to punish his sons if they ever followed the herd and came to covet material riches more than the continual quest to cultivate greater virtue. And just as he secured their assurance, he got them to promise that they themselves would "follow that path of life," which they'd discovered together—a life that not only makes life more worth living on an individual scale, but is one "of most service" to polis and to humanity.

Chip Off the Old Block

Socrates' father, Sophroniscus, was a sculptor; his mother, Phaenarete, was a midwife. They were people of modest means who led a creative, rewarding existence. Clearly his parents encouraged him to follow his own drummer and develop his innate questioning nature—to ask "Why? Why? Why?"—in ways that would help him discover what his unique station in life should be.

Socrates tried his own hand at sculpting, but he didn't have his father's talent. Yet he remained fascinated that an amorphous piece of stone could be shaped in lifelike detail. He saw each human being, in a sense, like a piece of stone, each a sculpture in the making, a work in progress capable, until the final moment, of dramatic reshaping.

He must have witnessed many births that his mother attended to. Socrates was fond of saying that his version of philosophy was akin to that of a midwife, but in his case it was to give birth to new ideas, new possibilities for being human.

Motherland, Fatherland

Crito, one of Socrates' young protégés, urged him to escape prison and go into exile. Crito was so sure Socrates would accede that he had already arranged an elaborate escape. Yet to Socrates, escape was out of the question. He said it would be the height of ingratitude for him to keep Athens' judicial system from carrying out the verdict rendered against him, no matter how unjust.

Athens as an entity, he told Crito, was like a parent. Upon meting out its punishment to him, it had every right to say to him, if he protested: "We brought you into the world, we raised you, educated you, gave you and every other citizen a share of all the bountiful things we had to offer." Socrates said that Athens, as a parent might set straight a recalcitrant son, had every right to say to him, "What complaint can you have against us and the state that you would try to undo us? Aren't we, first and foremost, your parents? It was, after all, through us that your father married your mother and then brought you into the world."

Socrates stressed that he'd had his day in court, and, try as he might, he had not been able to persuade his fellow freemen of his innocence.

Xenophon, who devoted himself to rehabilitating Socrates' good name after he drank the hemlock and died, records that Socrates accepted his fate not with resignation but with a sense of long-term optimism that all would come out right in the end. All in all, Socrates said, it was a good day to die:

> If I were to live longer, perhaps I should fall into the inconveniences of old age. . . . Past experience lets us see that those who suffer injustice, and those who commit it, do not leave a similar reputation behind them after their death. And so, if I die on this occasion, I am certain that posterity will honor my memory more than that of those who condemn me. For it will be said of me that I never did any wrong, never gave any ill advice to any man; but that I labored all my life to excite to virtue those who spent time with me.

Friedrich Nietzsche believed that Socrates was a romantic, that he had *amor fati*, or "love of fate," and wouldn't change a thing about the way he lived or died: "That he was sentenced to death. . . . Socrates himself seems to have brought about with perfect awareness. . . ."

Socrates didn't resign himself to his fate; he created it, willed it, loved it.

PART III

XENIA

Stranger Love

Xenia is "stranger love," a type of love shown for and to strangers or guests—and featuring a solicitous warmth, hospitality, and compassion for those with whom one typically docs not have ready familiarity or a close association. *Xenia* was a longtime, pervasive practice among Greeks until Socrates' adulthood. On the one hand, they cultivated *xenia* because they believed that it was pleasing to the gods. The negative spin on this would be that if they did not, they'd incur the wrath of Zeus, ruler of the Greek gods, who demanded the practice of *xenia* among his mortal subjects. The Greeks believed that they never quite knew the stranger knocking on their door: Even if he appeared in rags, he might be someone important or well-to-do disguised as a beggar at the behest of Zeus to test whether he would still be feted as royalty. Consequently, no matter how abject or beggarly the appearance of a stranger, the Greeks extended effusive hospitality.

They also practiced *xenia* to a fault out of genuine conviction and passion, as well as for pragmatic reasons. By being such attentive hosts to strangers who knocked on their door, they could be assured that when it was their turn to travel far from hearth and home, they would be shown similar hospitality. Though wherever they made forays they were likely to encounter someone of shared ancestry, the region was vast, and they would seldom if ever know someone personally once they ventured far. With *xenia* widespread throughout Hellenic and Dorian societies, they knew they'd be showered with hospitality at day's end.

Borders

In the Socratic dialogue *Phaedrus*, Phaedrus says to Socrates, "When you are in the country, you're like a stranger led about by a guide. Do you ever cross the border? I rather think that you never venture even outside the gates."

To which the historical Socrates might have replied, "Why venture outside the gates when all the world comes here to Athens?" Athens was the vortex of the world. He didn't need to go past the bounds of his own agora to encounter diverse people and be exposed to a world of new ideas.

In the dialogues that Socrates held in the agora, he invited any and all comers, strangers passing by as well as friends and acquaintances, to take part. He did so not just out of obeisance to the gods but because he believed that one of the best ways to know himself was to get to know strangers, whose novel and unfamiliar views would provide him with a bracing variety of perspectives to consider and compare with his own, leading to further articulation and discovery of his own views.

No Strangers Here

My grandfather on my father's side, after whom I was named, immigrated to the United States in 1922 with his wife, Calliope. He came to

a strange new world to make a home for his family, of which my dad
soon would be a member. The moment he arrived on U.S. soil, my
grandfather made himself at home—and made others feel at home
with him. He was the newcomer, yet he turned the tables and went
out of his way to put others at ease. Though he spoke English halt-
ingly with a thick Greek accent, he made this a vehicle for breaking
the ice. People who were ornery or downright hateful in anyone else's
presence couldn't help but break into a smile in his company. His wit,
effusive warmth, and seeming desire to know everyone with whom he
crossed paths—coupled with the fact that he'd literally give the shirt
off his back to someone in need—was a throwback to the *xenia* practiced by Greeks of old.

LIKE MOST OF my Greek relatives, my grandfather settled in the
South. The rituals of Southern hospitality—of opening one's door to
friend and stranger alike, and treating them like family—were nothing foreign to my relatives. Many went to considerable lengths to help
new arrivals from the old country to become situated and acclimated
to their surroundings. It wasn't expected of them; they expected it of
themselves.

A variation of *xenia* seems pervasive among all immigrant groups
in the United States with which I am familiar. They help out one
another in ways large and small, connected by culture and language,
by shared hopes and dreams.

Be My Guest

"When a stranger knocks at your door, you don't want to have to
scramble to show him a little hospitality," says Joel, after I tell of my
interest in exploring the question "What is love of strangers?"

Joel and his wife, Emma, have a farm near the Arizona-Mexico border. They are among the many Socrates Café-goers who have invited me and Cecilia to stay at their home during our tours.

"That's the philosophy of 'love of strangers' my parents raised me with: that there's always room at the table for one more," he tells us now. "At every supper, they'd set an extra plate at the table. Once in a blue moon, sure enough, a stranger would join us—a door-to-door salesman down on his luck, a Mexican man who'd crossed the desert with his pregnant wife on their way to Chicago for the promise of a job. What a difference a good meal and conversation made. It can be like a new lease on life. We're just continuing the tradition they started."

He goes on, "It was rare back then when a Mexican crossed over the desert to come to the U.S. Nobody loves their land more than they do. They'll do anything before they quit their land short of starve. That's a sign of how desperate times are, that so many are risking their lives to come to the U.S. Our president calls them 'guest workers.' Since they are our guests, we're showing a few of them a little hospitality, thanking them for coming over and being the driving engine behind our economy."

"Leviticus tells us to love strangers as thyself," Emma comments. "So we're carrying out this commandment of the Bible. Stranger love is a kind of neighbor love. The moment you show this love, they become like a neighbor to you. They never will forget your act of kindness, and odds are that someday they'll pass it on to someone else in need.

"One of the few who has come to our door—a man asking for water—is from Chiapas, Mexico," she says next. "He told us that the North American Free Trade Agreement, or NAFTA, has creamed them. He was a fourth generation coffee farmer, but now American businesses can sell their product retail in Mexico cheaper than he can sell it wholesale in his own country. He plans to earn enough to buy a taxi, and then he'll go back and make a living as a taxi driver to support his wife and four children. He said he doesn't want to get accustomed to life here. He just wants to go back home to the land and the family he loves and be able to live decently. So if helping him a little bit can get him further on his way to achieving his dream, we'll do it."

Joel tells us, "Thousands of Mexicans have passed through this way on their way to somewhere else over the last decade. Of all those, only a few have ever knocked on our door. Most people don't realize that it's easier to offer help to a stranger than it is for a stranger to ask for help.

"I'm an American citizen five generations removed," he goes on. "Those on my dad's side are German, but my ancestors on my mom's side are Mexican. Some lived not too far from our property when this part of the country was theirs. Thanks to my maternal grandmother, who insisted I learn some Spanish, I speak passably enough to make a go of communicating with those I meet.

"Their stories would break any feeling person's heart. They leave behind everything—hearth, children, all possessions but those they can tote hundreds of miles—for a chance to come here and work their hearts out to send money home. They send back over a billion dollars a year to extended family back home. No one even remotely related to them is a stranger to their generosity."

"You can look in their eyes and see into their hearts, see that they're good, decent people," says Emma. "That's reason enough to help them out."

"Do you show 'stranger love' with the hope that the stranger will one day return the favor if you or someone else is in need?" I ask.

"Well, the fact is that one day we might be the ones wanting to cross the border to their side, and asking them for help," Emma replies. "Some say that's an impossibility, but they lack a sense of history, and also humility. We're using up all our natural resources in this country. And you never know when there'll be a natural disaster. My parents grew up during the Great Depression, and had to go from one place to another looking for work and food. If it weren't for the decency and generosity of complete strangers, they wouldn't have survived. While they saw the worst in human nature, they also saw the best, and usually from those they'd have least expected it. Most Americans today can't imagine that someday the tables might be turned, so they can't imagine why they should show love of and to strangers."

"Now, some are legitimately concerned about the integrity of our borders," Joel says. "In that vein, governments here and in Mexico should work together to create policies and treaties that give the poor real opportunities to raise their families decently back home. A wall sure isn't the answer."

"You don't show love of strangers by building a wall," says Emma. "America's great poet Robert Frost had this philosophy of walls: 'Before I built a wall I'd ask to know / What I was walling in or walling out, / And to whom I was like to give offence.' Too many walls today give offense: they wall people out, while those walling themselves in hide behind defensive righteousness. That is not a loving act from a nation that's supposed to be the humanitarian beacon of the free world.

"One of the founders of the Minuteman Project characterized its members as 'a bunch of predominantly white Martin Luther Kings,'" Emma says next, "implying, I would think, that theirs is in fact a loving act towards strangers."

The Minuteman Project, whose stated mission is to stave off attempts at entering the United States through a twenty-mile stretch of the Arizona border in Cochise County, was launched on April Fool's Day 2005.

"Dr. King would turn over in his grave," says Joel. "He believed Americans should go out of their way to care for people everywhere. He worried about the type of people Americans were becoming. 'If an American is concerned only about his nation,' he said, 'he will not be concerned about the peoples of Asia, Africa, or South America'—not to mention Mexico. Dr. King believed an American should never be allowed to live so far removed from the pain and suffering of the rest of the world that he can't relate to it.

"Too many these days can't relate, because they're strangers to need and pain and suffering—and so the idea of stranger love is alien to them. If the borders of your heart are sealed shut, showing love of strangers is an impossibility."

Stranger in a Strange Land

Xenia is a central theme of Homer's *Odyssey* and also figures in his *Iliad*, epics on which Socrates was brought up. Odysseus, the wily and resourceful hero of the battle of Troy, had the idea of sending a Trojan horse as an offering to the citizens of Troy—sort of a reverse *xenia*, with the invading visitors playing the role of host, presenting a (seeming) gift to the besieged—a gesture that turned the tide of the war and led to the downfall of Troy. Troy paid dearly for violating the sacrosanct conventions of *xenia* by one of its own: the war started when the Trojan prince Paris abducted Helen, the former queen of Sparta, while he was her husband's guest.

The god Poseidon, upset that his side lost, and particularly peeved with the decisive role played by Odysseus in Troy's defeat, cast him off to sea, where he was doomed to wander for more than a decade. In his misadventures, Odysseus encountered lotus eaters, Cyclops, sirens, princesses, and goddesses, and even ventured into Hades. In his journeys, he was often totally reliant on the kindness of strangers—from the succor of a swineherd on whose shores he drifted to that of the nymph goddess Calypso, who extended him hospitality (albeit as a quasi prisoner) for seven years. Calypso would have liked Odysseus to stay on forever, and she tried to tempt him into doing so by offering to make him an immortal if he would remain. Odysseus turned her down. All he longed for was a homecoming to his native Ithaca, to return to his beloved wife and son.

At last, Odysseus is allowed to go home, but only as an unrecognizable stranger. Upon arriving, he is unknown to his son, Telemachus, and wife, Penelope, who think he is long dead (only his dog recognizes him). They are unusually preoccupied, in the throes of fending off Penelope's relentless suitors, who have committed egregious transgressions against *xenia*, long since overstaying their welcome and refusing to leave when requested.

Penelope and her son had provided her suitors with every creature comfort. In return, as guests, they were expected to be respectful and grateful, and never to take advantage of the hospitality proffered—for there is a spelled-out protocol for guests as well as hosts to adhere to when it comes to *xenia*. By abrogating their own responsibilities, the visitors paid with their lives, at the hand of Odysseus.

City of Strangerly Love

"Somewhere along the way, someone has to teach you, or you have to teach yourself, the lesson of 'there but for the grace of God go I,'" says Russell in response to my question "Can compassion be taught?"

"I was taught compassion by those who lacked it," he goes on between sips from a huge mug of coffee. "I grew up in the other Philly—Philadelphia, Mississippi—during the civil rights struggle. I saw how horribly some whites treated blacks, and I decided that if I were ever in a position of power or pull over the poor and vulnerable, I'd be the opposite of these whites—a force for good and compassion."

We're at a coffee house within sight of the Liberty Bell in Philadelphia, Pennsylvania. Russell and I had been corresponding ever since I visited Philadelphia to hold a dialogue several years earlier.

"Philadelphia is Greek for 'City of Brotherly Love,'" says his friend Harold. "While the Philadelphia of the Deep South didn't live up to its name, this one sure does, thanks to people like Russell. I thought I knew all there was to know about compassion. But it wasn't until Hurricane Katrina that, at the ripe old age of forty-nine, I *really* learned about it.

"Russell and his family didn't know us from Adam, yet they took in me and my wife and three kids, no questions asked. They've showered us with the kind of hospitality we might expect from our closest relatives on Thanksgiving. They've given a whole new meaning to the saying *Mi casa es tu casa*."

Russell shrugs off the compliment, seeming uncomfortable with such high praise. "This could have been us," he says simply. "To learn compassion, you have to have humility. I know that tomorrow, or the next day, it might be Harold's or someone else's turn to extend to me and my family a helping hand.

"When I saw the images on TV, in the aftermath of Katrina, saw how so many, especially blacks, were left to fend for themselves, I had to do something. I was shocked that the richest nation on Earth was treating its own like second-class citizens. I notified one of the relief agencies that my home was available. I got no response. So I began calling friends, then friends of friends, who might know of someone in need. Finally, I got a call from a man—Harold here—who said he was about to be bussed to the Houston Astrodome, and that they might separate his family. The relief in his voice when I told him there was plenty of room at our home oozed through the phone."

"We were shy about accepting," says Harold, "but you overcome shyness real quick when you're in straits like ours. Just the thought of having a real roof over our heads, a real bed to sleep in, a real bath-room . . . paradise."

"My kids were excited," Russell tells me. "They missed having someone in those vacant rooms to play with and take care of since their grandmomma passed.

"For me," he soon goes on, "it was the easiest thing in the world to be compassionate the first days. It's when you realize the strangers you've welcomed into your home are here for a good while that you're put to the test. My kids have shown *more* caring and hospitality as time passes. They've taught me more about compassion as a long-term gesture."

"We haven't once been made to feel unwelcome, that they wish they could take back their generous invitation," says Harold. "Com-passion to me is understanding, empathy, grace, love, all put together. That's what the Kelly family is made of. It's like, every day when they wake up, they imagine what it's like to be in our shoes, and they treat us accordingly."

He squeezes Russell's shoulder. The genuine affection between the two is palpable. Russell says, "Never again will I think that compassion is just a one-way street. It's a many-way street. The Andrewses have been so considerate of us and our own needs."

"We treat their home like we would ours—better, really, since we don't leave any dirty clothes lying around," Harold tells me. "We try to give them their space. As their guests, we also have to imagine what it's like to be in their shoes, what it's like for them to have opened their home to strangers, and so be extra considerate towards them."

"So compassion has to have a give-and-take reciprocity to it?" I ask.

"Absolutely," says Russell. "But not the quid pro quo type, where if someone does something for you, you have to do something of equal measure for them. It requires that all involved in the 'compassion transaction' be considerate of the needs of one another."

"Does someone have to have suffered to some degree like you have to show you the type of compassion you need?" I ask.

"Abolitionists helped my ancestors gain freedom," Harold says. "They hid them from slave owners and trackers and helped them escape in the underground railroad, even though they had no direct sense of slaves' experience, of the brutality and torture. What they *did* have was that sense of 'there but for the grace of God go I.' It takes 'compassionate imagination' for them to realize that but for the accident of birth, that could just as well have been them."

"That's lacking in Bill Bennett, the former secretary of education," Russell says now. "He said on a radio program that even though it'd be morally reprehensible, if you wanted to dramatically curb or even eliminate crime, just abort black babies. That statement betrays an absolute lack of ability to imagine in a way that'd give you an inkling of the black experience in the U.S. since our slave days.

"Being black isn't the reason for so much crime; being born into a world where the odds are so stacked against you is. If he really wants to eliminate crime, people like him would have to give up willingly a large chunk of what they have to create a more level playing field."

After a while, Harold says, "Compassion may be about trying to put yourself in another's shoes, but the shoes never fit perfectly. No matter how compassionate you try to be, you'll never be perfectly compassionate, because you can never completely know what another person is going through, even if you've had a similar experience. It's the heartfelt attempt that matters."

"I used to think I could judge how much, or whether, people were compassionate by how they treat their dogs," Russell says. "But I've seen too many people treat their dogs better than they treat people."

"I, on the other hand, treated this dog pretty badly once upon a time. I used to give this little fella here the cold shoulder," he says as he caresses what has to be one of the scrawniest and most pathetic-looking—not to mention deliriously happy—dogs I've ever seen. "Buddy here waited patiently at my doorstep, as if he knew I'd come around eventually.

"He was on the verge of starving. I actually thought the most 'compassionate' thing to do would be to have him put to sleep. Buddy seemed to think I was made of better, more loving stuff than I realized. Why would I take this scraggly little thing into my life? This was not my idea of a dog. But I was his idea of a dog owner. He wore me down and won me over.

"He's my best friend. He knows my moods before I know them, and knows how to act accordingly. This dog is all about compassion. If, before I die, I can be half as compassionate as he is innately, I'll be all right. He may be a tiny fellow, but he has the biggest heart of anyone I know."

City of Strangers

When given the choice between exile and staying in Athens to face a death sentence, Socrates likely tried to imagine what it would be like to leave the city in which he was born and raised, whose every nook and cranny he knew so well, and enter wholly unfamiliar terrain.

But in another respect, he no longer recognized it; he'd become a stranger in his own land. Most of his own people were as unrecognizable to him as he to them, so different now were the values they had come to honor.

THE PRACTICE OF *xenia* was based on a sense of egalitarianism—that other people even in far-off places were deserving of the same respect and concern as one would afford one's nearest and dearest. But Athenians in Socrates' final years, to his dismay, came to see themselves as above others elsewhere—to the point that they came to believe it their right and even their manifest destiny to take whatever they desired from whomever they desired.

Stranger in a Familiar Land

"This land is part of me," the woman says, more to herself than to me and Cecilia. "Shouldn't this be the place where I'm most at home?"

We are at the Wounded Knee Memorial on the Pine Ridge Sioux Reservation in South Dakota. I first came here in the mid-1980s, when writing an article for *Parade* Magazine on Dennis Banks, cofounder of the American Indian Movement, the radical social and political activist group that in 1978 sparked an uprising here. Ever since, I have found myself drawn to this hauntingly beautiful land. Cecilia and I are driving across country, and when we realized it would be only a three-hour detour to visit here, we turned off.

The woman, who looks to be in her late thirties, is in a mix of modern and traditional wear. She seems unmindful of her long raven hair blowing every which way in the strong wind. She had approached the cemetery soon after we arrived. When she saw us, she hesitated. We got up and made to leave so she could have the place to herself. She approached us and said softly, "Don't go on my account." She came and stood beside us. Then she knelt and began tending to the ground around the grave markers.

She eventually gets up and looks into the distance, at the buttes and mesas given dazzling colors by the setting sun. Then she studies the gravestones, one by one. A while later, she says, "I was born and raised on this land. After my parents died, I moved away. But I never stay away for too long. Coming back puts me back in touch with myself.

"But it also makes me realize what a stranger I am wherever I go. Even here in my ancestral homeland, I'm not completely comfortable in my own skin. It's like a war within—one between wanting to be like everyone else in the 'outside world,' and wanting to live like a traditional person. I want both and can have neither."

She directs her gaze at the simple memorial commemorating the Wounded Knee massacre. What happened here on December 15, 1893, is typically described as the last major clash between Native Americans and U.S. troops. But a "clash" implies that two sides went at each other with equal and opposing force. In this case, 500 U.S. troops were pitted against 350 Native Americans, 230 of whom were women and children. When the U.S. troops opened fire with Hotchkiss machine guns, the Indians did fight back, but they were vastly outgunned. All told, 150 Lakota Sioux were killed and 50 wounded; 25 U.S. troops were killed and 39 wounded. The U.S. commander was charged with killing unarmed innocents, but he was exonerated in court.

"My ancestors were dancing—something so unfamiliar to the U.S. troops, so out of sync with their view of how a 'defeated' and 'despairing' people should behave, that they decided their only recourse was to slaughter them," she tells us.

"They were dancing because their spiritual leader had told them that the only way they could be defeated is if they quit being who they were. He told them to return to a life of prayer—and dancing to them *was* prayer, their form of expressing their spirituality. He said if they lived as they should, they'd be invulnerable to the enemy's weapons. What I believe he meant was that as long as they practiced true Sioux ways, they would live on in eternity."

She goes on in due time, "My forebears welcomed the settlers with open arms, showed them nothing but hospitality, provided them aid when they were sick and starving, because that is the Sioux tradition of how you act when a stranger in need is encountered."

The nineteenth-century American artist George Catlin, whose paintings of American Indians are renowned and who spent long periods of time living among the Sioux during their final years as a free people, wrote that they were

> a people who have always made me welcome to the best they had . . . who are honest without laws, who have no jails and no poorhouse . . . who worship God without a Bible . . . who don't live for the love of money.

"To the Sioux," she says to us, "there really isn't such a thing as a stranger, since we all have the same creator. Humankind itself, and all other living creatures, were conceived in Mother Earth's womb, out of *techihhila*, of love. That makes all humans, no matter our race, part of *wakan tanka*, the spiritual essence."

She then says to us, "I come here every Columbus Day to mourn, while most in American culture celebrate. I mourn how, since Columbus' arrival, the indigenous tradition of loving hospitality was used against us by the settlers. Once they overcame all their crises that my ancestors rescued them from, and they got their feet firmly planted here, they turned against the indigenous and tried to exterminate them. Having all our land wasn't enough; they wanted to be rid of the people who occupied it."

Strangers of Kindness

"Not only *should* we care for one another, we should *have* to," says Lelia, a high school guidance counselor. "Well, no, we shouldn't have to care, we should want to. The 'have to' should come from the 'wanting to.'"

We're in Café du Monde in the heart of New Orleans' French Quarter, drinking their famous chicory coffee while holding a dialogue on the question "Should we care for one another?" Several months have passed since more than 80 percent of New Orleans was leveled by category four Hurricane Katrina, which caused parts of two levees to break, flooding most of the city. More than 1,100 died, and more than 400,000 of the city's residents had to flee and were now scattered all over the country. As this dialogue takes place, only about 20 percent of the city's population has returned—some only to salvage those belongings they can and move on again. But some, such as those with me now, are determined never to leave again.

"I live near the Algiers section of the city, which is black and low income," says Lelia's friend Ethel, eighty-nine. "It's one of the few poor communities that wasn't totally destroyed by the hurricane. Many with intact homes opened their doors to those, like me, in need of shelter. They didn't have electricity and had almost no food or water, but they had a safe roof over their heads, and they gave that to others, out of the belief that, yes, we should care."

"I was in the convention center the first night," says Samuel, a casino employee. "Horrors happened in there of which I will not speak. There was a breakdown of caring. Yet even there, a handful denied themselves food and water, all the while passing out what little they had to others. They put the rest of us to shame. They didn't care for others because it was in their 'enlightened self-interest'—they didn't do it to gain personally in any way—but did it because they knew it was the right thing to do, period."

"Some of us in the immediate aftermath formed a tribe," says Taylor, a hot dog vendor, who stayed put in New Orleans. "At first, we didn't so much as ask one another's names. We came together out of an instinctive sense that we couldn't care for ourselves alone. One of us would stay behind at our makeshift shelter to keep an eye out so looters wouldn't take our stuff, another foraged for food, another mended wounds, another got water, another dry goods. We made a compact to care for one another."

"To me, the question isn't 'Should we care?' but '*How* should we care?,'" Ethel says eventually. "The reason this tragedy happened in the first place wasn't the breakdown of care per se, but the breakdown of caring in the right way.

"We have to do away with 'crony care.' We have to quit putting our small circle of friends and loved ones first. If there'd been a decent FEMA [Federal Emergency Management Agency] director instead of an unqualified crony, many lives might've been saved, and the level of hardship for everyone would've been lessened in a big way. Even in the aftermath, too much of the money allotted to restoring our city seems to be going to a small group of cronies who are getting no-bid contracts, just like in Iraq. The money rarely trickles down to those truly in need. That is a form of caring, but it isn't a good form.

"Look," she says, "nobody's more familiar with patronage politics than the people of Louisiana. But in a democracy, all of us should equally be considered cronies, so we can all get a decent part of the caring pie that's distributed. Just before the hurricane struck, Congress passed a gazillion dollar federal transportation bill. It was all about boondoggling—representatives caring more about their constituents, and their constituents caring more about themselves and what their representatives could do for them than caring about Americans as a whole. Congress said it didn't have a dime to fortify our levee system, but they had millions to build a bridge from nowhere to nowhere in Alaska. That is crony care at its worst."

"In a democracy, caring has to be all about putting the common good first," says Samuel. "It's about putting the country's citizens' needs as a whole above those of any individual. We need a 'caring index' to measure how well we're doing in taking care of one another. We need an Office of Homeland Caring, dedicated to all forms of caring for Americans: health care, child care, educational care, environmental care, housing care, elderly care.

"What we need to be doing is working towards holistic caring," Samuel goes on. "If we'd done that all along, we wouldn't have destroyed our marshlands and wetlands, which would have been a natural protective buffer against a hurricane. We've treated nature like it's an alien with no rights instead of caring for it like it is an extension of us."

"What is caring?" I ask eventually.

"*Proper* caring is reaching out and touching someone in a way they want and need to be touched," says Taylor. "That has to be preceded by 'caring thinking,' where you're trying to figure out what a person you intend to reach out to wants and needs. If a person is living in a rickety home, his kids going to terrible schools, his land surrounded by levees that could break at any moment, then it doesn't help much if you give him an all-expenses-paid trip to Disney World. He'll be just as bad off as ever when he gets back home. What he needs is help that'll put him in a safe place with good schools."

"Caring is when you put yourself on the line for the good of others," says Lelia. "Regular citizens of New Orleans risked their lives, and in some cases died, to try to rescue people who were total strangers to them. And doctors and other professional caregivers from other parts of the U.S. came here to volunteer their services, though they were told by relief officials not to come, lest they be sued if they dispensed care without bureaucratic authorization. They came anyway. One of them dispensing medicine and bandaging the wounded told me the least he could do was come here and do his bit to help his fellow Americans in distress."

After some hesitation, Ethel says, "I hope this doesn't make you think me a bad person, but some of the things I care for most don't have minds or hearts. I care for my photos, for my furniture that's been in the family for generations, for my books, for my other keepsakes, because they remind me of people and places and memories I hold dear. I've lost most of these things, and I've been grieving their loss terribly."

"That's not bad caring, because those things are connected to people you hold most dear," Samuel tells her.

"Too often today," says Lelia after a while, "the philosophy is 'let others do the caring for us.' If I give money to a charity, I want them to do the caring for me. But we all need to spend at least some of our time caring directly. I do give to charities, but I also devote several hours a week to visiting elderly shut-ins."

"Caring is all about recognizing there's always someone worse off, and then, even in your downest times, reaching out to them," says Taylor. "As bad off as I was, there were people far worse off than me elsewhere—in faraway places like Guatemala, where hundreds of towns were wiped out by mudslides, or the tsunami and earthquake in Asia, but also in the devastated outlying towns and parishes in Mississippi and Louisiana and Alabama. If you don't recognize this, you'll just have a 'woe is me' attitude, and be so caught up in your own problems it'd never occur to you to lift a finger for anyone else.

"Like, Samuel here lost his home," Taylor goes on, "but because he's Red Cross trained, as soon as the Red Cross got here he went to work helping others as part of a mobile disaster relief unit."

"Some came out of that convention center and Superdome, got on a bus, and vowed never to return to New Orleans," Samuel then says. "They thought they knew their city, thought it was a caring place, but the catastrophe showed it was a lie, what with most having an 'every man for himself attitude,' the government missing in action, police abandoning their posts. But I decided just the opposite—to help make this city the caring place it should be."

"I always thought that in order to care, you have to have basics—decent supplies of food, water, shelter, decent education and health care," Taylor remarks. "But people in poor countries have sent us money and supplies. They deprive themselves in order to help people in a rich country, even though on their best day they're far worse off than we are on our worst. Now that is caring."

"When former first lady Barbara Bush came to the shelter in Houston to get a glimpse of how the other half—other nine-tenths, really—lives, she said that we were being treated so well, we'd never want to go back home," Lelia relates. "We were treated well—and by strangers at that, people who felt our pain and went out of their way to make us feel at home. But believe me, there's no place like home. All those people caring for us got to go home after their shift ended, and Mrs. Bush got to fly back to her mansion after her hour with us.

"Like everyone else at the Astrodome, I got angry when I heard such an insensitive remark from the mother who instilled our president with his own values. But what it also did was inspire a lot of us to be the kind of caring people we wish everyone in the country, especially our leaders, would be. I for one am trying to be a one-person welcome wagon, doing anything I can to help a fellow resident of the Big Easy in need. I pick up trash, help people salvage items from their homes. You name it, I do it."

Just then, we hear soul-stirring blues music waft our way. A funeral procession is approaching. Everyone gets up without saying a word. It is a longtime New Orleans tradition that strangers join in passing funeral processions and march along. Samuel and I go along with them.

Care and Care Alike

German philosopher Martin Heidegger (1889–1976), who was devoted to the question of being and the implications of human existence, maintained that "care is the basic state of human existence." Because ours is a finite existence, Heidegger asserted that it follows that we are incapable of being indifferent to our situation, that we *must* care. In the act of caring for others and for ourselves, he said we necessarily discover how human existence interrelates with existence in general, so we come to expand our scope of caring to include the entire orbit in which we find ourselves. In the process of making this investment of caring, Heidegger believed that we make this world into which we are "thrown" less alien and more "authentic," more of our own making.

Heidegger's notion of caring continues to resonate with people from many walks of life—from environmentalists to politicians, salesmen to health care workers to engineers. In his presidential campaign, even consumer advocate Ralph Nader reportedly quoted Heidegger, saying at a rally that the essence of being human is the fact that we care for one another.

Yet Heidegger himself did not practice his own profound philosophy of caring. As a member of the National Socialist Party in Nazi Germany, he defended its fascist ideals, antithetical in every respect to his notion of caring, betraying in the process his many stellar students, most of them Jews.

Whereas Heidegger, and his legions of apologists since, have invented an array of rationales for why he betrayed his own ethic, his former student Hans Jonas, for one, made it his life's commitment to live by it. Jonas (1903–1993), a German Jew exiled from Nazi Germany, whose mother died at Auschwitz, volunteered as a soldier in the Jewish Brigade of the British 8th Army, fighting for five years in World War II against the Nazis. In his landmark book *The Imperative of Responsibility*, Jonas writes that although "[m]odern technology, informed by an ever-deeper penetration of nature and propelled by the forces of market and politics, has enhanced human power beyond anything known or dreamt of before," we are wielding that power in pernicious ways. When we aren't depleting our natural resources or polluting the environment, he says we are harnessing nature in ways that could lead to our and our planet's destruction. If we're going to arrest this, Jonas believes, we must create "a new solidarity of the whole of humanity," thus coming together in a way in which all of us consider "care for the future of all nature on this planet as a necessary condition of man's own."

Jonas asserts that the necessity for environmental caring is so pressing that it renders all other ethical matters obsolete. I would say instead that environmental caring should be considered among the critical facets of human caring. After all, it is the same amoral sensibility that drives some to wantonly exploit nature in ways that could lead to our, and its, downfall that impels still others to treat some groups of humans in inhuman ways. Only when we come to care for one another as equals, and see nature itself as a type of equal, can headway be made in preserving our planet and human civilization.

Enlightened Selfish Interest

Philosopher Ayn Rand (1905–1982), via her "Objectivist" philosophy, aimed to upend the traditional, somewhat pejorative connotation associated with selfishness. To Rand, not only must each individual exist for his own sake, but doing so is his most noble undertaking and the only true path to human happiness. In counterpoint to altruists, as Rand conceives of them, not only does man have the right to exist for his own sake, but acting in his enlightened self-interest is his reason for being. If we do not exist for our own sake, in her view we negate ourselves—and this would be irrational. Any person who considers this matter rationally, Rand believes, will objectively arrive at the same conclusion she has.

In Rand's worldview, it isn't that compassion and caring for others can't exist, only that it would never be for altruistic reasons or some greater good beyond oneself. Rather, one would show caring and compassion only toward those objects—people, places, things—that one most covets personally.

Rand's views are tenable if one accepts her notions of self and of altruism. To Rand, the unequivocal answer to the question "Which came first, the self or society?" would be: the self. According to her, we can never dispense with the self, but we can dispense with society, because to her its sole function is to serve our self-interests—to settle squabbles among individuals, particularly ones in matters of commerce.

To the Greeks of old, the answer to the question would be: society. To them, there is no such thing as a self without society. They believed it takes social agreement to determine what constitutes a self, what its function and ends should be. To them, both self and society—indeed, to them, society is a *type* of self—must be united in service to *arête*. To the Greeks, a self was not just, or even principally—a physical-corporeal entity, but one's works and deeds, and one measured the worth of self by how it contributed to the evolution of *arête* in the context of one's society. To this end, it may well be that a particular individual deed, undertaken in the name of *arête*, might lead to the loss of one's physical life, yet nonetheless be the best means to perpetuate one's self.

This was Socrates' view. What gave his self value was doing what he could to perpetuate the way of life that he valued. To the extent that that way of life continued, whether in his own or in another epoch, he believed that his self would continue to live. If giving up his mortal life was the best way to achieve this end, so be it.

To Rand, such altruism is irrational and untenable, tantamount to "a moral system which holds that man has no right to exist for his own sake, that service to others is the sole justification of his existence, and that self-sacrifice is his highest moral duty, value and virtue." Rand's view would be alien and puny to the likes of Socrates, to whom service to polis *was* a form of service to self, in fact the highest affirmation of self. He did not place a great premium on physical longevity but in living a certain way, no matter how long or little, with contributing to the advancement of *arête* his most sublime and noble moral calling. It is because he lived and died this way that his self lives on.

JOHN MCCAIN, U.S. SENATOR from Arizona, writes in *Faith of My Fathers* that the most important lesson he learned while a member of the armed services—a naval aviator in Vietnam, he was a POW for five and a half years—was that "I was dependent on others to a greater extent than I ever realized," and yet that dependence was of a type that "gave me a larger sense of myself." Such a dependence is not at one end of a continuum, with autonomy at the other; rather, the two go together. In his years in military service, McCain witnessed "human virtue affirmed in the conduct of men who were ennobled by their suffering." To him, such ennobling suffering serves both self and societal growth at once. It is what one might call altruistic selfishness.

Failure to Care

Australian ethicist Peter Singer, one of the founders of the animal rights movement, asserts in *Rethinking Life and Death* that it is the duty of all people in the developed world to be "doing much more to help those in poorer countries achieve a standard of living that can meet their basic needs." In seeking to quantify precisely how much more each of us in the developed world should be obligated to do, Singer asks:

> If we are as responsible for what we fail to do as for what we do,
> is it wrong to buy fashionable clothes . . . when the money could
> have saved the life of a stranger dying for want of enough to eat?

What if there were no such thing as a complete stranger? How might those of us in the developed world act, so that we come to feel that those living in lesser developed regions are not so far removed from us after all? We might, as one for-instance, mainly purchase fair trade products. In doing so, we'd be directly contributing to a more dignified and equitable living situation for those who produce our goods. Conscientiously devoting the bulk of our purchasing power in ways that help create sustainable communities around the world might make us feel more closely connected with those far away. We may come to see them as neighbors of a sort. As a result, we may be inspired to continually seek ways to do more and more to help them with the resources we have.

THE UNITED NATIONS has long requested that each developed country contribute 0.7 percent of its gross national product (GNP) to economic development efforts in Third World countries. Only Denmark, Norway, the Netherlands, and Sweden have met or exceeded this "0.7 percent solution." The United States, the world's wealthiest nation, contributes 0.08 percent of its GNP to these efforts. Perhaps if its individual citizens more pervasively adopted practices in their everyday lives that made inroads toward forging the ethos that there is no such thing as a complete stranger, we might insist that our leaders increase our contribution to 0.7 percent, and so become less—as Peter Singer puts it—"responsible for what we fail to do."

Heart-Shaped World Redux

Is it possible to measure whether a society has much heart? Collaborating with Nobel Prize–winning economist Amartya Sen, philosopher Martha Nussbaum was instrumental in helping change the criteria by which the United Nations measured progress in developing countries. Sen and Nussbaum in effect measured a country's heart. Rather than gauging a country's progress by strictly economic criteria, they took into account such quantifiable factors as freedom of affiliation, good health care (including reproductive health care), adequate nutrition and shelter, the sex ratio of women to men, and literacy rates. What they have discovered as a result is that many developing countries (or specific regions, groups, or castes within them, such as in India) that otherwise would have been overlooked merited singling out for being of comparatively great heart. Sen and Nussbaum's approach, if implemented on a broad scale, might revolutionize the way we gauge whether our world is advancing.

The Human Team

"The Olympics date back to the eleventh century B.C., when they were held to pay homage to Zeus, the 'immortal father of *xenia*,'" Alexandros tells me during our latest rendezvous in Athens Square Park in Queens, New York. He's returned from a three-week visit to Athens, Greece, where he attended the Summer Olympic games—and where friends and extended family in Athens had vied so insistently for him to be their guest that he ended up spending two nights with each, lest he offend any of them.

"At a time when rival Greek factions were warring endlessly against one another, out of obeisance to Zeus, they started the Olympic games—which turned fierce combatants into fierce competitors in sporting events," Alexandros instructs me. "Greek tribes from all over that were normally at each other's throats laid down their weapons when they came to Athens to take part in the games. They obeyed the ancient Greek tradition of *ekecheiria*—the Olympic Truce. This guaranteed all participants and visitors safe passage to and from the Olympic site, which was a sanctuary of peace."

He sighs. "Look at the shape the world's in now. More than ever, we all should adhere to the codes of *xenia* and *ekecheiria* if we're to have any hope for peace."

Then Alexandros perks up and says, "Modern-day Athens hasn't forgotten how to practice impeccable *xenia*. It rolled out the red carpet in a way that made people from everywhere feel welcome.

"I wish you could have seen how the athletes treated one another, walking around the Olympic Village arm in arm, using gestures to communicate, exchanging gifts, laughing and hugging. I saw American athletes carrying on with the French as if they were fast friends—none of that 'freedom fries' nonsense. I saw Arabs with Jews, Iranians with Iraqis, Taiwanese with Chinese, Russians with Afghanis, North Koreans with South Koreans. They treated one another as each other's *xenoi*, or guests. That's the magic of such *xenia*.

"What I witnessed made me wish I could extend the Olympics sports complex to cover the entire globe, so people everywhere would treat one another the way those athletes did. Then we could form one big team, the Human Team, and the only thing we'd be in fierce competition over is which path among all those suggested would be the best one for achieving a lasting peace.

"Those athletes at the games showed that once you come together in warm camaraderie, it's almost impossible ever again to see that person as an enemy or antagonist. You've smoothed your surface differences over with your heart, and found that deep down, you're much the same."

Alexandros sighs yet again, then says, "There's always someone to rain on the *xenia* parade, though. As you can imagine, security was very tight. One morning, while I was in line to pass into the Olympic stadium, the man in front of me, as he was being searched, screamed at the Greek soldier, 'This is my ninth time passing through here. You must know by now I'm not a terrorist. Why do you keep putting me through these humiliating searches? Can't you show me enough humanity to just let me pass by?'

"To his credit, the soldier didn't get the least ruffled. In fact, the more livid the man became, the more gentleness the soldier showed him. When the man wouldn't relent, I said to him, 'The poor guy is just doing his job. He'd have to search his own mother if she came through.'

"He blew his top at me. He was deaf to what I was saying. I was so embarrassed that when it was my turn to be searched, I apologized in

Greek to the soldier on behalf of my countryman. The soldier, bless his heart, replied, 'There's nothing to apologize for. Your country has been through so much. At least that man had the courage to fly here and be a spectator at the games when, from what I read, many Americans seem too afraid to leave their homes. Give him another week of Greek hospitality and he'll be okay.'

"In those three weeks," Alexandros says, "that soldier must have encountered people from almost every corner of the world. I'm sure a little bit of his *xenia* rubbed off on everyone he met, even that man who yelled at him. If all of us would show each other the 'put myself in your shoes' kind of understanding of that very kind soldier, the possibility of a Human Team wouldn't be so pie in the sky."

Alexandros consults his watch and abruptly gets up. "I have to go to the airport. I became friends with these two guys from Turkey who had seats beside mine at the Olympic games. I told them if they ever came here, I'd gladly be their host. Little did I think they'd take me up on my offer so quickly!

"When I was a child, Greeks and Turks were constantly at loggerheads, if not outright war. We despised each other. Now Turks will be staying under my roof, and I will be the picture of *xenia*. One small step for lasting peace . . ."

Connected

About once a month, I facilitate a real-time online Socrates Café dialogue with participants from around the world. As attest their initial correspondences with me—after learning about our nonprofit mission, or happening upon one of my books—all have an abiding passion for Socratic inquiry. It's given me an opportunity to regularly encounter people, many of them in faraway places, with whom I'd otherwise never have the chance to philosophize. Just as with ongoing Socrates Cafés in which we engage one another face-to-face, each of us participating in the online discourse takes turns proposing questions.

CP: What, if anything, is your duty?

Afina: It's my duty to risk my well-being, maybe even my life, for what I cherish. Such as for my artwork. If I were told I could never paint again, because the government made it illegal—that the "crime" of painting was punishable by death—I'd like to think I'd continue, until discovered and executed. My artwork gives me my passion for living.

In the 1970s, the "art police" here in Romania regularly would confiscate and destroy my paintings if they remotely smacked of the political. They always threatened to jail me if I continued making such works. But as soon as they left, I'd start re-creating the same paintings, and try even harder to see that they made their way through the underground network to be viewed as widely as possible. The police were right to worry about them, because these works of mine, even more so than most, were intended to liberate viewers' minds and spirits in ways that might inspire them to seek physical and political liberation as well.

Let me also say that if anyone ever threatened the life of a family member, then I'd like to think I'd put my life on the line. I don't know if you'd call this duty, though, because I'd do it out of instinct—out of my love for them, and the fact that I wouldn't want to go on living if there was anything I could have done to save them, no matter how bleak the odds, and I didn't. To me, duty is something that implies premeditated thought and action.

Shep (a civil engineer in London): To me, your duty, at least ideally, should be a willing, rather than a grudging, obligation that you carry out—something you believe with all your heart that you must do, come what may. It can sometimes be undertaken instinctively, or it may be something that you do only after you've put in a great deal of time and thought.

CP: What would be the difference between "good" and "bad," or "good" and "not-so-good," duties one might want to carry out with all his heart?

Shep: I might say that Adolf Hitler and his minions, who knowingly orchestrated the Holocaust, or those Muslims who committed mass murder on London soil recently, had no heart. But they put their hearts completely into what they were doing—out of a heartfelt, albeit evil and sick, sense of duty—to perpetuate their sick ideals. In the cases of the London bombers, they willingly committed suicide in the process of carrying out what to them was this heartfelt obligation. So, we have to learn somehow what we should have a "heartfelt duty" towards accomplishing, and what we shouldn't.

CP: How do we do that?

Shep: Let me answer it this way: Even us normal folks without the artistic talent that Afina has should consider it our duty to "live artfully" *and* "heartfully." By that I mean that no matter your station in life, those of us fortunate enough to be in a position to do so should feel duty-bound to discover and apply those talents we have that can contribute to making this world a better place for the less fortunate. How did I come to this view? My father. He raised me to believe the reason we're put on this Earth is to "leave more wood on the woodpile"—to leave this world in better condition than it was before we got here. My workaday life is pretty mundane, but I'm involved in a number of efforts in my free time to live by this injunction—from giving 20 percent of my earnings to Oxfam [Oxford Committee for Famine Relief] UK to spending all vacations living in communities in the developing world, where as a volunteer I help them build up their infrastructure.

Tarah: Even if you're in prison for a long time, you can try to carry out this kind of duty that Shep is speaking of. I'm a literacy instructor here in prison. When I show someone how to read, you should see how they light up—they're exposed to a whole new world. That makes *my* world brighter.

I also feel a sense of duty—to me and my family, and my society—to pick myself up when I make a huge mistake, and still try to make something of myself. Now, this is something I had to teach myself. When I first was incarcerated, my mentality was "woe is me." But then I came to realize, one night when I was feeling despair, that I had to get busy living, or get busy dying. I've always been a whiz at reading, so when my counselor suggested that I might teach illiterates here, I realized that this was maybe a talent I had to make others' lives more meaningful—not to mention mine. These days, because of this work, I sometimes actually bounce out of bed in the morning, even in this forlorn place. Without some sense of heartfelt duty—both to others and to yourself at the same time—I don't know how you can make it through the day.

Joo-Chan: As a Buddhist, whenever I speak of duty, I always use this concept in combination with the Korean words *han* and *shinbaram*, which mean "sacrifice" and "loving-kindness." Because to me, one's duty is to make whatever sacrifice necessary, out of loving-kindness, to put our world more in harmonious balance—what we call *mot*.

CP: Can you give an example of how you might achieve this?

Joo-Chan: As do all young men in South Korea, I had to serve two years of mandatory military service. I was a soldier stationed at the Demilitarized Zone. At first, I resented this mandatory duty. But in time, what I experienced and observed made me see how out of balance we are, and how close we are to the brink of nuclear catastrophe. People say the North Koreans would never use such weapons, but do you really think a dictator who willfully allows millions of his own people to starve would hesitate to use such a weapon? And now, it's been revealed, my own government has been secretly planning to build these weapons—only adding to the looniness of a policy of mutually assured destruction. Today, I'm an activist for a radical peace group dedicated to bringing the North and South back to the negotiating table, while there's still time to achieve *mot*. It was out of carrying out my grudging obligation to serve my mandatory military duty that I discovered my calling, my willing and heartfelt obligation.

My father spent much of his life involved in pro-democracy activities during the dictatorship of Chun Doo Hwan, and he spent periods of time in jail. As a child, I resented him for neglecting his family, for which he reluctantly sacrificed quality time out of a greater obligation to see that my generation had a life of freedom and opportunity that he could only dream of. At the time, though, I thought his foremost duty should be to be with us. Now, because of my own beliefs, I spend much less time with my own children than I'd like—out of loving duty to them, so they'll possibly have a future in a world of genuine *mot*. Of course, my five-year-old daughter is too young to understand that, and she resents me just as I did my father. But in a world on the brink, you have to make painful sacrifices, out of a duty foremost to those you love most, but also for humanity as a whole.

Eleanor: Hopefully this is following onto what Joo-Chan said: I think it should be our duty to make beauty out of ruin. I'm working to rebuild a village outside of Kabul, Afghanistan, that was leveled by U.S. bombs. The U.S. *did* remove the Taliban from power, as promised, and women now have rights they couldn't have dreamt of a short while ago. But because they have almost no resources, they can't do much with these rights. The reality is the rubble all around us. The promised help from the U.S. government to rebuild what their bombs destroyed hasn't come. Those policymakers who believed it their "duty" to wage war here should have to come here and witness how they reduced this area to a wasteland, rather than only boast about how they acted out of what they claimed was their duty towards freedom, liberty, democracy. Hopefully then they'd feel duty-bound to fulfill their promise to rebuild. Everyone here asks why the U.S. doesn't rebuild their homes, doesn't build decent roads, schools, and hospitals. These projects would be genuine works of beauty—of love, of hope, and of heart—to the people here. There's many others who've come to Afghanistan from the West who are devoting their lives to making this a place of beauty, so Afghanis will know that not all Westerners shirk their greater duty towards them.

Terence (a civil liberties activist based in Maine): I believe it's the duty of each of us to live without fear of death, or we'll always play it safe.

We need to throw all caution to the wind if we're really to impact the world. Now, unlike the terrorists and homicide bombers who some might say operate out of such a duty, I believe this duty must only be carried out in ways, as Eleanor put it, to make ours a world of more beauty— the opposite of the havoc and chaos they're trying to achieve. We should be willing to risk it all, out of a sense of duty—but with a sense of the preciousness and precariousness of life, the fragility of human life and human civilization, and the desire to nurture and perpetuate it, even if it means I sacrifice my life in the process.

Jihan (works for a pro-democracy group in Egypt): Epictetus, the second century A.D. Stoic philosopher, said that we should live "as one seeking to be a Socrates."

CP: What did he mean?

Jihan: I presume he meant we should see it as our duty to live with a sim- ilar sense of purpose as he did—to do what we can to make sure this precarious experiment called human civilization continues.

I live in a closed, sexist, and autocratic society, and am risking much to carry out my duty in this regard. I pray I never have to risk my life, and am never incarcerated, since I am a single mother of two girls, and I have to consider how their well-being will be impacted if I'm not here, heaven forbid, to care for them. I believe it my duty to do whatever I can to see that they can grow up in a country where they have real opportuni- ties—where they can vote, drive a car, study at the university. So I can't play it too safe if this is going to happen before they become young adults. So, if push came to shove, I might end up having to risk my free- dom, perhaps my life, in order to see that my children have this better future that I yearn for them to have.

Azekel (a high school student in Angola): Socrates' hypothesis—that once people *knew* the good, they would *do* it—has turned out to be wrong. As he himself discovered, most who "do bad" know they are doing so, and do it anyway. It makes me admire him more, in a way, that he kept living by this hypothesis even when person after person proved him wrong. I think his message was: if we lose total faith in humans to do the good, then the "handwriting is on the wall." Even if you can only change one person in a thousand—even if you can only change yourself—it might make all the difference in the long run. He believed it his duty to be the change he wanted to see in the world at large, and risked it all so that others, even long after his era, might be inspired to do the same.

Tarah: Socrates tried to do the right thing at a time when everyone else was doing the wrong thing. And you *know* they were all doing the wrong thing in retrospect, because their civilization crashed and burned. As long as just one person is willing to do the right thing amid a sea of badness, there's reason to hope. Socrates' life and death, from what I've been reading, were modeled on a sense of duty that was "faith-based"—he had faith in people to do the right thing, at least over the long haul, even if over the short term most are acting foolishly. If we don't all act out of a similar faith, how can we ever hope to see light again in dark times?

PART IV

PHILIA

Friendship Love

Philia, to the Greeks of antiquity, was tantamount to "friendship love," but of a sort with a broader and deeper meaning than how it typically is construed today. As envisioned and practiced by the Greeks, *philia* is the type of loving sentiment that should undergird social relationships, even if the people involved do not know one another directly, but their lives intersect in some way because of common ends or some shared pursuit. In particular, *philia* was what principally comprised the tie that bound people together within a village, community, state, nation, organization, movement. However, first and foremost, then as now, it begins with the affectionate bond between friends.

My Friend Socrates

When I was thirteen, on a winter day in which blizzard conditions kept me from venturing outdoors, out of sheer boredom I pulled from a bookshelf a dog-eared, mildewed copy of one of my mom's high school textbooks. It happened to contain a number of Plato's dialogues featuring Socrates. Though raised in a coal-mining camp, my mom had received a strong education in the classics, and had studied these dialogues, translated in simple engaging English from the simple engaging Greek. I soon was immersed in reading them. I began to take a great interest in Socrates. I soon became smitten by his message that we each were capable of becoming our own best expert questioners and autonomous thinkers and doers, in service to humanity. I read the dialogues again and again, and began to join in on them, communing with Socrates. He became my friend.

At the time, I was a junior high school student in a city divided by race and class. It was the start of the public school desegregation era. Instead of walking to the new school less than a mile from my home, I was bussed to the other side of town, to a school in decrepit condition, with equally decrepit textbooks. I arrived well before dawn. While waiting for the homeroom bell to ring, I'd gather with other early arrivers in the cafeteria, where we could purchase a hot breakfast. Usually black students and white students sat apart from one another, each on opposite ends of the long row of benches; but there was a zone in the middle where, when the rest of the benches were full, we somewhat reluctantly mingled.

I usually sat by myself. Short, awkward, and self-conscious, I wasn't much for socializing. But after rereading Socrates' *Apology* on the bus ride to school one morning, I had the inexplicable gumption to park myself right in the middle of the students gathered in the cafeteria, and before I could stop myself, I blurted out, "What makes life worth living?"

Roy, a black student twice my size and star fullback on our football team, at first studied me, as did everyone else around, as if I or my question had landed from another planet. I was afraid to make eye contact, and was sure, in fact was hoping, that no one would say a word and that my experiment with Socratic dialogue would come to a quick and uneventful end. After a while, Roy said, "I ask myself that every day. Why do I get up before the roosters crow to arrive at this miserable excuse for a school to go through the motions of learning? What good's it going to do? Once, I told my mom I wasn't going to come. She slapped me upside the head and said, 'You are going to school because you are going to make something of yourself. You are going to become a doctor or dentist and make our community proud, show them nothing's impossible if you set your mind to it. You're going to show everyone that what should matter most isn't the color of your skin but the content of your character.' That to her is how I'm going to make my life, her life, and everyone else's life more worth living."

We looked at Roy, dumbfounded. We'd never heard the taciturn student string together more than a couple sentences at any one time. One of his best friends, Raymond, was about to laugh, certain that Roy was putting us on. But when he saw how serious Roy remained, he thought better of it, and instead said, "Man, I hear that."

Then Evan, who lived a few miles from me, looked at Roy and then at Raymond, and said, "I thought I was the only one whose parents told them stuff like that. My mom and dad both work two jobs so me and my five brothers and sisters can go on to college someday. My dad doesn't even get home from work until after the roosters crow. Yet today, like most days, I complain loud and long that I have to come to this godforsaken place. But once I get here, I'm glad, usually.

"The teachers are great, even if the classrooms themselves and the textbooks aren't. I never hear my teachers complain, any more than I do my parents, about the long hours and low pay. They act like it's a privilege to be here, and they treat me like they're privileged to have the chance to put some sense into my brain—as if that makes *their* life worth living. My astronomy teacher even has gone to the trouble of making our classroom into a mini-planetarium. When he turns out the lights, I forget where I am. I feel I can reach out and almost touch the stars."

Then he said, "I'm going to become an astronomer. That'll make my life worth living. It'll show my teacher, and my parents, that all their hard work on my behalf paid off."

Then Raymond, out of whose mouth I'd never heard a serious

word, said, "Well, for life to *really* be worth living, you have to be proud of what you're doing, even when all those who should be proud of you, and should be in your corner with you, aren't. If you can stand up to their disapproval and still be proud of yourself—if you know that what you're doing is something good and helpful, even if they don't get it—then you know you have a life worth living."

I am floored. I hadn't known Raymond had such thoughts within him.

I never said another word as they continued their exchange, revealing thoughts they probably never imagined they'd share in our school cafeteria at the crack of dawn. From then on, from time to time we'd consider another question together. It cleared the early morning cobwebs from our noggins and, best of all, brought us closer together.

I didn't figure out my own calling till my mid-thirties, when it struck me at a dark moment that it had been staring me in the face for decades, and the problem was I wouldn't stare back at it. What I really wanted to do was what I did that seemingly inauspicious day way back when in junior high school: ponder philosophical questions with people of all walks of life, all over the world. It all began the day I picked up my mom's old textbook and became fast friends with Socrates, and from there went on to discover how asking a heartfelt question can work magic in expanding one's horizons and, best of all, in forging friendships.

Eros *and* Philia

Benjamin Jowett, the classics scholar and premier translator of Plato's dialogues, asserts that the *Symposium* and its bedfellow *Phaedrus* "contain the whole philosophy . . . on the nature of love" as set forth by Plato's Socrates. Yet the fairly historically faithful dialogue *Lysis* is one of the most revelatory of all on matters of love—not just on *philia*, ostensibly its principal topic, but *eros* as well. This dialogue does particular justice to the beautiful complexity of friendship love.

Likes and Dislikes

At one thematic juncture of *Lysis*, Socrates and company explore how it is that that which draws together two or more people can be the fact that they are opposites, and so have *dis*similar "likes and dislikes." They determine that "mutual dislikes" can strengthen a friendship, whereas similar tastes and interests can attenuate it or even repel two people if each feels there is nothing new to learn from the other who shares his interests. Conversely, encountering someone with passions alien to your own sometimes can generate great interest and excitement.

Someone with interests similar to yours, who has knowledge on the matter that you don't, or has approaches to gaining enlightenment that are novel to you, can spur *philia*. To be sure, some types of likenesses may lead to relationships in which there are few surprises, and thus do nothing to contribute to *philia*, whereas others—shared curiosity in epistemological areas, shared passionate pursuits in politics or spirituality or hobbies—may contribute to the mutual expansion of the horizons of those in the relationship, and so further cement friendship ties.

LYSIS ALSO REVEALS how dialogue itself can promote *philia*. It is clear that the bond between Socrates and his fellow inquirers becomes more tightly knit in the course of their inquiry. Even though they emerge from their discourse on friendship love in a state of *aporia*, or uncertainty—they have more questions at the end than at the out- set—they each value the journey they have taken together, the plurality of perspectives offered, and the worth of the dialogue itself and of each participant's input, and they look forward to delving deeper into the subject together. In the process, they develop an even more intimate regard for one another.

Reunion

"For there to be friendship love—or *philia*, as the Greeks called it—there first has to be 'friendship like,'" Chinh says to me. "By that, I mean there has to be grounds for two people to like each other in ways that build a friendship. If there isn't, how can they ever love one another?"

I'm at my twenty-fifth college reunion, at a watering hole where as an undergraduate at the College of William and Mary I sometimes carried on discourses on political philosophy with friends and strangers into the wee hours. Sitting opposite me in a booth is the one person I'd hoped would come to the reunion, though he isn't a fellow alumnus.

I met Chinh, whose youthful looks belie that he is five years older than I am, in my sophomore year, when I volunteered to teach English to one of the growing numbers of immigrants living in the area. Chinh had escaped the killing fields of Cambodia during the mid-70s, when the Marxist Pol Pot regime undertook a ruthless "purge," putatively to rid the country of all Western capitalist influence. The campaign led to the deaths—by execution or starvation—of more than 1.5 million Cambodians, including Chinh's parents, brother, and sister. After his harrowing escape, Chinh eventually made his way from a refugee camp in Thailand to the United States. In Williamsburg, he worked as a cook in a restaurant. When we rendezvoused for our first formal English lesson, I realized I'd seen him before: he sat in on one of my philosophy classes. I'd thought he was a student, though I couldn't figure out why he wasn't scribbling notes furiously with the rest of us, and why he always left class several minutes before it was officially over. (It turns out he did so in order to get to work on time.)

It seems that he just wanted to listen and learn. And I found out that he knew English pretty well, though I'd been told by the nonprofit agency that paired us that he spoke the bare rudiments.

"It never occurred to me that my tutor might be a male," Chinh recalls. "I'd hoped to meet a co-ed. I didn't try to mask my disappointment when I saw you. Still, there was a chemistry between us from the beginning, part of which was our shared passion for philosophy—good grounds for 'friendship like.'"

Chinh was a voracious autodidact. When he slept, I'll never know. He worked seven evenings a week, and when he wasn't attending class or hanging out with me in daytime hours, he was reading. When I realized he resided in an abandoned trailer in the woods, so he could save every penny, I found him a cozier and safer shelter nearby at a dirt-cheap price.

"You introduced me to a lot of Western philosophy, and I opened up to you the world of Eastern philosophy," he then says. "It turns out my favorite Eastern philosopher—Mozi, from China—was a contemporary of Socrates. Mozi coined the term *ai*, or universal love. He believed that only if each of us is concerned about the well-being of all humans could there ever be genuine love in the world. He said we should show benevolence to everyone, love each person as if he were our best friend. To him, that was the only path towards greater *ren*, or humanity—the equivalent of the Greek term *arête*."

"Does universal love have to begin with 'particular like'?" I ask. "If I don't know you, how can I come to like, much less love, you? Should I love the stranger I pass on the street before knowing his politics or how he treats his family or his pet? Can I be concerned about another person's well-being without knowing something particular about him?"

Chinh considers this. "Too many times since I've arrived in the U.S., complete strangers passing me by, who don't know a thing about me, have given me looks of pure hatred—and a few times made derogatory comments just loud enough so I can hear them—just because I'm Asian. It makes me sad that they've bought into such mindless racism. I wish

I could stop them and talk some sense into them—out of a desire for a world of 'friendship like'—but know it would just make things worse.

"What I do try to do, just like you, is to give people the benefit of the doubt, and assume, unless and until I know otherwise, that they are good and decent. Even those who make a racist comment, as long as they aren't physically violent, I try to assume that they are just twisted, and that with the right education, they can be untwisted.

"But if I *do* know otherwise—that someone is truly bad, even evil—then heaven help him. I detest the likes of Pol Pot and his disciples as much as ever. How could I ever like, much less love, people like that? Every fiber of me, for the well-being of society, would like to 'do away with the being' of such people responsible for genocide. When they are in power, they make the attainment of a loving world impossible. I wish there were some way to eradicate the sadism within such people without stooping to their level and committing an act of violence against them.

"Deep down, though, I believe I should *want* to try to treat even a sadist as I would like to be treated," Chinh says next. "A sadist may treat others sadistically because maybe that's how he thinks—in his sick mind—he would want others to treat him. But by my ideals, if I am in a position to do so, I should try to show him some kindness. If I act in a way that mirrors how he would act—if I derived pleasure from hurting or killing him—then I'd only contribute to making this a world of sociopaths. So while I would want him to be punished, likely to spend his life behind bars, for his and for society's well-being, I would not want to go further than that if humanly possible."

Then Chinh says to me, "Sometimes I dream that Pol Pot is alive and behind bars, and I visit him regularly. I try to find out what makes him tick. I mean, he came into the world a helpless baby just like the rest of us, but somehow he grew into a brutal sadist. I'd like to know why, to understand how this is possible. Sometimes in my dreams, we even end up becoming friends of a sort, as I learn his story and he learns mine. When I wake up, I hate him as much as ever for what he did to my family and countless others.

"But my ideal in my waking life is nonetheless to try to take an interest in the well-being of even the most wretched bastard—out of a sincere desire to create a world of 'friendship like,' so maybe one day conditions will be such that we can work towards *ren*."

We sit for a long while in silence, nursing our drinks. "Confucius said that you should 'have no friends who are not as good as yourself,'" I eventually say, pleasing Chinh that I remember what he told me about the sixth century B.C. Chinese social philosopher whose singular moral thinking, as set forth in his comprehensive *Analects*, continues to be influential. "He also said there were three beneficial kinds of friendship: 'with the upright, the truthful, and the well-informed.'"

"I agree that those are necessary conditions, but not sufficient ones," Chinh says. "Confucius' criteria leave out the warmth and affection of 'friendship like,' which there has to be if there's ever to be friendship love in particular and in general universal love among people."

"And that means taking that interest in others," I say. "They may be 'informed' about things I have no clue about, and vice versa, but out of our friendship, we take an interest in things we'd otherwise never have looked into—and sometimes it becomes a passionate interest of ours too. And what we have more than anything is love for one another, despite and because of our different interests, and maybe our different ways of being upright and truthful and informed. There's also this: My friends see qualities and potentials in me that I don't see—and that I likewise see in them."

"You sure saw something in me I didn't see," Chinh says. "I thought you gave me way too much credit—your shortcoming, my gain. At first, though, I was mad at you, because I became dissatisfied with the goals I'd set for myself. You kept telling me I was meant to be a scholar. I thought you were full of bunk, mostly because I was afraid to agree with you, to take you up on the challenge. I could imagine myself as a restaurant cook, nothing more. I found myself wishing you didn't take such an interest in me. If I let you convince me of what you were saying, I'd have to sign up for classes, write papers, and get judged on my work. But I gave in to your vision of me."

He then muses, "Look at us: two people from opposite sides of the world, one from a middle class family in Virginia, one from a classless upbringing in Cambodia, best of friends. Even Chairman Mao Zedong—great hypocrite and sadist though he was—was right on the money when he said, 'The differences between friends cannot help but reinforce their friendship.' I think Mozi and Socrates would be proud. I've helped you find *ren* and you've helped me find *arête*."

Call to Service

Xenophon records the historical Socrates saying that one's greatest desire should be

> to have good friends . . . take great care of them [so] that you behold their good actions with as much joy as if you yourself had performed them, and that you rejoice at their good fortune as much as at your own: that you are never weary when you are serving them.

To be a friend is a call to a special sort of service. When you serve a friend, you serve yourself, sharing wholly in each other's joys and sorrows, successes and failures, being there for each other in bright and dark times.

Bridge of Love

I'd known Sara since I was fifteen, when she joined the bowling league of which I was a longtime member and was placed on my team. She was one of the league's few girls. I and the other guys on my team had low expectations—until after our first game. Sara reminded me of my mom in many ways; though painfully shy, her eyes revealed a vivaciousness lurking just beneath the surface, and she was very competitive.

When it turned out, as we chatted between bowling frames, that Sara shared my passion for another sport, soccer, and for my sport's hero, the Brazilian soccer star Pele, we unknowingly embarked on what would become a deep and abiding friendship. In a town that universally worshipped football, Sara was the only person with whom I could passionately talk nonstop about soccer, and who really wanted to listen, then talk back with equal passion. We began to get together to play soccer. As we passed the ball back and forth, I learned bits and pieces about her. Her father, with whom she'd been extremely close, had died of leukemia when she was nine; an only child, she lived with her mom and stepdad. She had developed a lisp after her mom remarried, and she still had not overcome it altogether. She said one day she was going to become a doctor or nurse and work with cancer patients. Once, Sara called to tell me she wouldn't be able to bowl that coming Saturday; she would be taking part in a leukemia walk, to raise funds for medical research. I offered to go with her. I didn't realize until long afterward how much it meant to her that I accompanied her on that walk.

Even at our fairly tender age, she took friendship more seriously than anyone else I knew. Once you were her friend, that was that. I suppose I shouldn't have been surprised that after my family moved from the area, Sara still stayed in close touch. Though I'd often let months lapse in my own correspondence, she'd write to me at least once a week, like clockwork, year in and year out, true-blue in a way that should have put me to shame.

Upon graduating from college, I moved to Maine to become a literature teacher at a six-room schoolhouse and begin what I hoped would be a successful writing career. Not long afterward, Sara moved to a nearby state to attend nursing school. Soon afterward, we got together for the first time in years, and picked up right where we left off. During one of our get-togethers, seemingly out of the blue she proposed that we share with each other the worst thing we'd ever done, and the worst thing ever done to us. After she finished, I couldn't help but cry. No one, and certainly no one as special as she was, deserved to be a victim of abuse. Our friendship deepened that day. We revealed our innermost secrets, and cherished each other all the more. From then on, whenever one of us was having a difficult time making it through the night, we'd call the other and talk for hours on end. Then everything would be okay. When I moved to southwest Virginia, and after that to the Mississippi delta, we continued to make the effort to rendezvous at least once a year, determined never to let too much time pass without seeing each other.

The last time we got together, she was happier than I'd ever seen her. She'd had to drop out of college because of issues in her personal life, but she had returned after a long hiatus and was on the threshold of graduating. Soon she would be on her way to completing her dream of becoming a full-fledged nurse on an oncology ward in a hospital. On top of that, she had a serious "love interest," as she put it. "I feel like I finally have my life totally together," she said to me.

A week later, I received a call from a mutual friend. The previous evening, Sara had committed suicide.

More than a hundred people attended her funeral. I'd thought she had only a handful of close friends. Yet all those present said they were close to her, cared about her, loved her, as she had loved them. However, almost none of us knew of one another. It turned out she'd had a large network of friends, and had preferred to keep most of us to herself. Only a couple of people there said they knew of me. One woman told me that Sara had mentioned me frequently, and told her once that she wouldn't have been able to endure for so long if not for me.

I, like everyone on hand, had been immeasurably changed for the better by Sara's friendship. Her funeral was a celebration of her life. When it was my turn to share, I mentioned that one of her favorite books was *The Bridge of San Luis Rey*, by Pulitzer Prize–winning playwright and novelist Thornton Wilder. During our walk long ago to raise money for leukemia—the walk that sealed our friendship—Sara confided to me that whenever she got upset that she could no long picture her dad in her mind as vividly as she'd like, she pictured all the love and caring concern her father had showered on her as a child, and she'd quickly feel better. I told those gathered that she then recited to me a passage from the book that she knew by heart:

> soon we shall die and all memory of those [we loved] will have left earth, and we ourselves shall be loved for a while and forgotten. But the love will have been enough; all those impulses of love return to the love that made them. Even memory is not necessary for love. There is a land of the living and a land of the dead and the bridge is love, the only survival, the only meaning.

Sara's death exploded many self-imposed barriers. I did away with all the mesmerizing excuses I'd concocted for not living precisely the type of off-the-beaten-path life I envisioned. Once long ago I'd shared with her my most cherished dream—to become a philosopher in the mold of Socrates—and she was the first to tell me without hesitation that I should do it, that she had no doubt it was what this world needed from me. I wanted to show Sara that her faith in me was warranted.

I do still wonder if I could have been there for her even more, if I had given her all the friendship love I had to give. Most of all, though, I'm blessed to have been her friend. Sara's impulses of love continue to thrive in all of us she touched.

Befriending

In *Lysis*, considered one of the more historically faithful of Plato's dialogues, Socrates holds that *philia* at its core entails the act of "befriending." We take such an interest, develop such an intimacy, and see such value and potential in those who are part of our interpersonal relations, of our community or principality, that we are moved to make a great investment of our time and energy and heart in their development. We do what we can to see that they have an optimal chance to realize their aspirations, just as they are driven by the same desire on our behalf, in a common pursuit of the "good and beautiful." Greeks widely believed they had come up with the perfect social organization for this to come to pass: the polis. Unlike most views on the foundational reason for why humans come together to form collectives—for example, to create a physically secure city—the Greeks saw it as one of the last reasons, not the first, to do so. Rather, the primary purpose for social organization was to make it possible for each individual to be more secure in himself, and to seek his maximum potential; this required the communal, compassionate love of *philia*.

Loving to Learn

In Plato's *Phaedo*, Socrates says that only those who devote their mortal moment to being "lovers of learning" will be invited to "join the company of the gods" when they die. However, they weren't lovers of learning just for the sake of it. Rather, the point of learning was to know how best to carry out the mandates of the gods. They believed that gleaning such knowledge was not an individual pursuit but one that could bear fruit only if they came together in communities of inquiry with a shared method and ethos, not to mention shared goals.

To Socrates, it was precisely those truths one valued the most that should be regularly scrutinized in the marketplace of ideas. One should use doubt as an opportunity to discover further whether one's passionately held truths are worth holding—and this is best done by inquiring with friends. Xenophon records Socrates as saying that undertaking such investigations with a community of inquirers who share *philia* creates "a soil the most glorious and fertile where we are sure to gather the fairest and best of fruit."

Inquiring Minds

"We should seek to know . . . everything! Every day, we should seek knowledge, talk knowledge, live knowledge," says Chitra. The soft-spoken but animated undergraduate biophysics major, dressed in traditional Islamic garb, goes on to say, "The very first verse, or *sura*, of the Quran exhorts us, '*Iqra'a!*'—'Read!' It tells us to seek knowledge to the far reaches of the universe 'in the name of Allah.'"

I'm gathered with about two dozen students at an art deco café in Toronto, Ontario, Canada's financial and cultural center, with a population of well over 4 million. Most are from Iran, but several are from Saudi Arabia, Libya, and Lebanon. There are now 600,000 Muslims alone living in Canada, half of them twenty-four or younger. Toronto itself is home to more than 40 percent of the nation's non-European population. Upon learning I'd be in Toronto for a book event, Chitra had written me, asking if I'd be interested in holding a dialogue with her and a group of fellow students.

The students bring to mind those about whom Azar Nafisi wrote in *Reading Lolita in Tehran*. Now a professor at Johns Hopkins, Nafisi lost her job at the University of Tehran for refusing to wear a veil. One can imagine the punishment she would have faced if her superiors had discovered she clandestinely gathered on a regular basis with a group of students to read forbidden novels so they could discover together "how these great works of imagination could help us in our present trapped situation." Nafisi and her students "were not looking for blueprints" but rather "a link between the open spaces the novels provided and the closed ones we were confined to." Like Scheherazade in *One*

Thousand and One Nights, they sculpted and expanded their universe, "not through physical force" any more than through verbal intimidation, but rather "through imagination and reflection"—and also through "fragility and courage" born of a shared love.

The students with whom I'm gathering are enthused about exploring the question "What should we seek to know?"

"Why does Allah exhort you to seek to know everything?" I ask.

"In doing so, you come to know best how to carry out His mandate to create *umma*—a just, harmonious, and compassionate world community. One of the Quran's central commands to Muslims is for us to go far afield in our seeking as the principal way for coming to deeper revelations about the *suras*. The Prophet Muhammad also tells us that the best way to cross-pollinate knowledge, and to come to know the part each should play in making ours a more loving universe, is to inquire with diverse people."

Saeed, with a double major in political science and applied ethics, then says, "Since all knowledge is from God, God wants us to know all we can, from everyone and everything we can. This is the way we seek to know how best to carry out his vision of realizing *umma*."

"*All* knowledge advances you toward this objective?" I query.

"All *true* knowledge. Any knowledge you gain which, when applied, creates discord, is false knowledge. It steers you away from *umma*, and so distances you from God. Seeking knowledge by the way of the Prophet implies constant scrutiny and assessment. The reward is the balanced frame of mind needed to cultivate *umma*. Extremists claim to have *umma* as their goal, but an extremist by his very nature is out of balance with Islam's 'Middle Path,' so his 'knowledge' is superficial, always exaggerated and rigid at the same time, and so he could never bring—never know how to bring about—harmonious *umma*."

"Islamic societies were intended to be laboratories of applied scholarship, gaining kinds of knowledge that lead to more fruitful experimentation for realizing *umma*," says Fereshteh, a graduate student specializing in women's literature, with plans to go to law school. "Muslim communities were meant to be 'seeking communities,' at the forefront of trying out new, creative ways of living in harmony and compassion. Our scholars were supposed to be at the vanguard of this, guiding ordinary Muslims along this path. A famous Quran *sura* stresses that the ink of scholars is more valuable than the blood of martyrs. Bombs and missiles, and all other instruments of indiscriminate violence and hate, can never pave the way to *umma*. Only visionary knowledge applied in compassionate ways can do this."

"The Prophet tells us to seek to be so sensitive to the hurts in the world that when someone else is suffering, not only do we feel their pain, but we're *in* pain ourselves," says Layly, Chitra's roommate, a philosophy and religion major. "You gain this kind of human knowledge by coming into intimate contact with the poorest, the most hungry, the most neglected, so you're moved to do all you can to ease their pain.

"The central tenet of *umma* is 'one body': if one suffers, all suffer," Layly goes on. "Muslim extremists, and fanatics of all faiths, put an impenetrable veil between themselves and the hurts of the world. They live in an intellectual and moral and feeling vacuum—and an unreasonable vacuum at that. The Quran berates 'those who do not use their reason' as the foundation for gaining knowledge. Yet rather than use reason, these are people who make up reasons as they go along to justify the unjustifiable."

"Our holy book encourages what in Arabic is called *itjihad*, or 'self-jihad,' which means 'independent reasoning,'" Chitra says now. "You have to 'go to war' with yourself, seeking to know how to overcome the ignorance and intolerance and conflict within that keeps you from doing all you can to achieve *umma*."

"I eventually hope to go back home to Iran to do my part to make it the first Islamic nation that actually is a model of *umma*," Fereshteh then says. "That's not possible right now. I take great inspiration, though, from Shirin Ebadi, who epitomizes *umma*'s principle of 'one body.'"

Fifty-six-year-old Nobel Peace Prize winner Shirin Ebadi is a pro-reform human rights defense lawyer who represents those persecuted by the hard-line government and whom no other lawyers dare represent. In particular, she is an outspoken advocate for Iranian women and children. The Associated Press notes that Ebadi—who had been appointed Iran's first female judge, only to be ousted from this post after the 1979 Islamic revolution, then jailed for a period for her outspoken views—"has challenged fundamental articles of Iranian law which maintain that a woman's life is worth half that of a man's."

"More than anything, we should seek to know how the Prophet lived, so we too can be God's direct messenger of love and compassion," Saeed then says. "The path of the Prophet is one paved with balance, moderation, tolerance, empathy for all human beings. It was his gentle and loving nature as much as his specific faith that moved people to seek to be like him. It was his way of seeing everyone as his brother and sister that inspired others to transform themselves and join him in a life of service to humanity."

"I'm the only one here who is a Sufi Muslim," says Mahasti, a physical therapy student from Saudi Arabia, after a thoughtful lull. She'd seemed on the verge of commenting on several occasions, only to apparently change her mind at the last instant. The Islamic sect of Sufism dates back to the times of the Prophet. "According to Sufism, all religions at their noblest are attempts to understand the mind and heart of God, in order better to carry out God's mandate on Earth. Sufism, a mystical version of Islam, emphasizes discovering the inner meaning of the Quran via direct communion with God rather than by learned inquiry.

"I'm deeply opposed to the approach of extremists of all faiths," she then tells us. "They're kindred in that they all have closed their minds and hearts. But Sufis don't dwell on how best to interpret the holy Quran's *suras*. You don't need a book or a text to tell you how to be just and compassionate, to tell you whether someone is a person of *wadud*, Arabic for 'divine love,' who lives out of *ta'aboud*, 'for love of God.'"

She falls silent for a moment, then says to us, "You seek to know what's in a person's heart by communing with her. The Prophet says that 'a person who knows himself knows his Lord.' By constant communing with others, you discover more both about your own heart and the heart of God, and so you experience *ishq*, also Arabic for 'divine love.' You discover how connected they are. The scholarly disciplines can help me learn how to use concrete knowledge in ways that contribute to *umma*, but only by communing with others can my heart become more pure, and so become more as one with God."

"People of other faiths may have different names for *umma*, but they all share the same goal," says Layly. "My boyfriend, Efrain, is Buddhist. We've found that the core values and objectives of our faiths, as we practice them, are very similar—something I'd never have known if I hadn't discovered 'the book of his heart.'"

Efrain, a fine arts student who works part-time at the café, says, "The objective of Buddhists is to seek to know how best to achieve *noble sangha*, or 'world civilized community.' The Buddha says we must do this 'for the good of the many . . . out of compassion for the world.' Both the Islamic and Buddhistic notions of communal compassion aspire to create spiritually, politically, socially blessed communities. A person's highest expressions of love for the Almighty come in seeking to know how to bring the sacred into being right here and now, in the communities we live in."

Chitra, turning to Mahasti, says, "I agree that you can read thousands of books, yet never learn anything of value in terms of how to help humans who are hurting. If your nose is always behind a book, you're never reaching out to others in need, never touching their souls and never letting theirs touch yours. Scholarship has to be marinated with loving intent if it is to be the platform for seeking to build blessed *umma*."

Umma

No one demonstrated practical compassion for the ends of creating more egalitarian community in the name of his God than Abu'l-Walid Ibn Rushd (1126–1198), or Averroes, as the twelfth-century legal scholar was known. Whereas extremists use the "method" of autocratic intimidation to sway others in their speculations on the rule of law, Averroes maintained that the charge of Muslims, as they further "unlock" or "unveil" Shariah law and the Quranic *suras* on which it is based, is to achieve a more just and equitable world. The only way to do this, in his estimation, was by using a rational method of inquiry to investigate their religious codes, determining how the principles of their faith can best be utilized as instruments for realizing *umma*. In *Faith and Reason in Islam*, Ibrahim Najjar writes how Averroes, as the foremost Islamist philosopher, exhaustively scrutinized "one argument after another in support of a different position." He examined a range of objections and compelling alternatives. Najjar points out that Averroes did this to demonstrate that without systematic reasoning, not only will "the understanding of religious texts remain incomplete," but inquiry into any area will fall short of illumination.

Averroes used rational argument to demonstrate why this form of logic should be a principal means for all those engaging in theological speculation. He reasoned that because man has proven himself adept at studying "the kingdom of the heavens and the earth and all things God has created," it is clear that God made man for man to reflect on and understand all that He made, in order to visualize how to utilize all His creations to make human communities more heavenly—more compassionate and just. Averroes' views infuriated religious zealots, who believed that no inquiry was necessary, lest anyone dispute their demagogic notions of God's will.

Averroes came by his approach honestly. Born in Cordova, Spain, he followed in the footsteps of his father and grandfather, becoming, like them, a *qadi*, or judge, so he could continue the tradition of evolving a compassionate Islam, because in his view this contravened God's will. His progressive judicial rulings contributed to a golden age of Islamic culture. Yet he was exiled by fanatics, his books burned by the new caliph, even as his ideals of *umma* seemed achievable. With his exile, with its rejection of all Averroes represented, Islamic society went into a downward spiral from which it has not recuperated to this day.

SEYYED HOSSAIN NASR, who is from Tehran and is professor of Islamic studies at George Washington University, writes in *The Heart of Islam* that *umma* is God's call, issued specifically to Muslims, "to the good." For the Quran charged Muslims

> to strike a balance between this world and the next. Another interpretation . . . is that "middle community" means that God chose for Muslims the golden mean, the avoidance of extremes in ethical and religious actions. Yet another meaning of this verse, with global implications, is that Muslims constitute "the middle community," because they have been chosen by God to create a balance between various communities and nations.

These interpretations, taken separately or together, charge Muslims with a very specific set of values—balance, toleration, love, moderation—and with serving as a bridge, connecting diverse peoples to one another, and to God:

> Muslims see all communities, Muslim and non-Muslim alike, to have been chosen by God. . . . The role Muslims have always envisaged for themselves in the arena of human history as the "middle community" does not mean that other human collectivities do not have their own God-ordained roles to play.

Rather, it means that each is brought into this world "to perform a function in accordance with the Divine Wisdom and Will." Consequently, Nasr says, "it would be a great mistake to underestimate the significance of the Quranic vision of community that most Muslims bear with their hearts and minds."

By Nasr's interpretation, someone trying to realize *umma* within the country in which he resides or is a citizen should not see faith and citizenship at odds but as complementary—to see his place of residence or citizenship as the place to demonstrate the practical compassion that *umma* calls for, the place to promote the middle way, a place to show how completely he lives by the doctrine of "one body."

Unveiled Truths

Prominent intellectual and literary critic George Steiner writes in *Lessons of the Masters* that "the pulse of teaching is persuasion," and that no one was better at this than Socrates, with his "charismatic spell" and the "witchcraft of his presence." Steiner mythologizes Socrates as someone who created a cult of personality, when most likely it was his unquenchable curiosity that fired his charisma. His "witchcraft" was nothing more than his insistence on using rational inquiry within a democratic community of inquiry and encounter as the most productive way to tap into one another's knowledge and to expand one's horizons. His "spell" was nothing less than the quest for a type of wisdom within a community imbued with *philia*.

Steiner considers Socrates a consummate teacher. But Socrates didn't teach. His pursuit, Socratic *seeking*, entailed a process in which there was a continual, mutual "transmission of knowledge, of technique and of values" among fellow seekers as they engaged in the process of inquiry itself.

Steiner goes on to say that Socratic teaching creates an intimate community of learners between "mature men and women on the one hand, adolescents and younger adults on the other." Indeed, the way of seeking that Socrates and his fellow inquisitors modeled creates even greater intimacy when employed in groups that transcend or bridge ages and cultures and walks of life—between toddlers and adults, between seniors and youth, between one culture and another, one society and another, one discipline and another, between rich and poor.

THIS COMMUNAL USE of compassionate questioning and reasoning was evident among the students with whom I gathered in Toronto.
In *Faces of Reason*, Canadian philosophers Leslie Amour and Elizabeth
Trott remark that Canada continues to embrace diversity today as it
did in the days of its founding, because it remains "young, open to the
influences of the outside world, and subject to the changing compo-
sition of its population." They note the pivotal role that the use of reason has played in Canada since its origins, and indeed must continue
to play if society is to perpetuate its founding ethos of openness and
inclusivity. Reason, they say, continues to be the principal deliberative
"device to explore alternatives, to suggest ways of combining apparently contradictory ideas, to discover new ways of passing from one
idea to another."

The authors say that Canada has been largely effective in avoiding
conflicts among a diverse population by creating common bonds of
understanding, in which reason is used not as "a device to defeat
one's opponent" but rather as a means "to find out why one's neigh-
bour thinks differently rather than to find out how to show him up as
an idiot." Such reasoning is necessarily imbued with *philia*, the sentiment that prompts one to be curious about and open to the thoughts
of one's neighbor in the first place.

Learning to Reason with Your Heart

Can reasoning for compassionate ends be taught? Can a professional
educator inculcate greater *philia* among her charges?

In *Cultivating Humanity*, Martha Nussbaum, in examining the state
of teaching in higher education in the United States, notes that universities increasingly are offering courses about non-Western cultures,

as well as on the ethnically and racially marginalized cultures in our own society. Such an approach might prove critical at a time when more people than ever from American society's lower socioeconomic strata, comprised disproportionately of ethnic minorities, are being excluded from higher education. No matter how stellar their high school achievements, fewer poorer students than ever are able to attend college because of federal cutbacks in grants and loans. Richard Kahlenberg, a senior fellow at The Century Foundation, notes that almost forty years after Congress passed the Higher Education Act, "low-income students are still much less likely to attend college than their wealthy or middle-class peers." Moreover, he goes on to say, "low-income students are virtually shut out of the nation's most selective colleges: Among the top 146 colleges, 74 percent of students come from the richest economic quartile and just 3 percent from the poorest." He says continued lack of adequate funding has led to the lamentable outcome that "smart, hardworking kids from low-income backgrounds" who "deserve a chance to go as far as their talents will take them" are being left behind. "These students represent a huge untapped resource for the country," Kahlenberg writes. "We can't afford not to give them genuine opportunity." Apparently, though, we can.

Perhaps, as a consequence of studying the singular obstacles of the nation's poor in advancing to institutes of higher learning, students of privilege who matriculate in our nation's best universities might be inspired to take the radical action of refusing to set foot in a classroom until and unless everyone deserving of admission was able to matriculate. Such studies might compel these students to believe that a vital part of the educational experience lies in engaging with people from a wide variety of socioeconomic and experiential backgrounds.

What if students of privilege had to study *themselves*, examine the impact of their own class and culture on others, and on how they view themselves in relation to those unlike them?

Although, as Nussbaum asserts, college campuses today are fulfilling more than ever "the original Socratic mission, really questioning *everyone*, recognizing *everyone's* humanity," genuine Socratic education would never be completely at home in universities; it must take place in large measure outside academic cloisters, in modern-day agoras, public places that are a magnet for bringing people together from different ethnic and socioeconomic backgrounds—people who would otherwise never have a chance to connect much less share their views and experiences, concerns, and achievements. This is among the best ways to ensure that today's students follow the inspiring example of Nussbaum herself, who for decades has been dedicated to improving the plight of marginalized women in the Third World.

What if each student, whether an engineer or biologist or student in literature or philosophy, had to apply her specialized knowledge in ways that enhance connections among and connectedness within her community and with those in other parts of the globe?

For Socrates, even this would not be radical enough. If he had his way, learning would never have been institutionalized; there would be no divides between disciplines, much less divides between one's formal learning environment and society at large. Moreover, all learning would spring from a question, or set of questions, that one was curious to answer—questions such as: What is my duty? How should I love? What kind of world do I want, should I want? What causes poverty? What does poverty cause?

To cultivate humanity as Socrates did, Nussbaum asserts that we must live the examined life that he exemplified, a life that "questions all beliefs and accepts only those that survive reason's demand for consistency and for justification," in which all humans "see themselves not simply as citizens of some local region or group, but . . . above all, as human beings bound to all other human beings by ties of recognition and concern." This, she says aptly, requires "narrative imagination," which she describes as "the ability to think what it might be like to be in the shoes of a person different from oneself."

Can one put oneself in another's shoes without walking another's walk for a while, without sharing directly another's trials and tribulations? Taking a course about the lives of others, reading books that expose one to a broad array of human experiences, can be a necessary step in developing greater compassion for those who are "different" from oneself, but these steps are rarely if ever sufficient.

Philia *Clash*

Greeks cultivating *philia* subscribed to the outlook that self and society aren't at opposite ends of a continuum but are interlaced. The more that this is so, the stronger the ties that bind self and society.

But when a single society or collective has within it groups that in large measure derive their respective identities from their opposition to one another, the strong sense of *philia* that the members within each of the groups share and that binds them together can be a type of "friendship love" that precipitates great civil strife within a community—the precise opposite ends to which the Greeks believed *philia* should lead in all cases.

Guess Who's Coming to Dinner

"We should come together as people of peace," I'm told by a man named Conor, the first to respond to our question "How should we come together?"

"This is the tenth year we're gathered here for Easter Sunday dinner," he tells me. "We see it as a small act of peace, Protestants and Catholics from one of the most divided communities in Belfast breaking bread at this critical moment in our history. How can we expect and demand our political and religious leaders to come together if we ordinary people don't break bread with one another?"

It is Easter Sunday, and Cecilia and I are in a restaurant in northern

Belfast, breaking bread with about twenty strangers. The working-class couples seated with us at a giant round table are about equally divided between Protestants and Catholics. Whereas in other places this would be no big deal, this is Northern Ireland, and the particular neighborhood where we are dining has been a frequent flash point over past decades for protests and clashes between the two sides. The restaurant straddles Protestant and Catholic neighborhoods and is along a common route for parade marches that commemorate uprisings or battle victories past and, depending on which side you're on, arouse either extreme ardor or ill will. Cecilia and I had just arrived in northern Belfast and were looking for a place to eat. As we stood outside a restaurant reviewing the posted menu, a sizable group of adults sitting inside, their children running around and playing underneath their dining table, saw us through the large picture window and waved us in. Even as we hesitated, they made room for us around their table. That was that.

We gather to hold a dialogue on the question "How should we come together?" as Northern Ireland's 1998 Good Friday Agreement between Protestants and Catholics is on the verge of unraveling. The historic power-sharing agreement, based on the principle of mutual consent, has been suspended indefinitely. Ordinary citizens fear a return of religiously based civil strife. The signing on April 10, 1998, of the Good Friday Agreement represented a historic breakthrough, bringing all sides to agree to share power and determine together the future of the Northern Ireland territory—whether it would remain part of the United Kingdom, as most Protestants would like, or whether it eventually would become an autonomous nation or part of the Republic of Ireland, as most Catholics would like. But pressing issues remain unresolved and have continued to fester to the extent that, as this dialogue takes place, the accord is in jeopardy.

"Is breaking bread sufficient in and of itself for people to 'come together'?" I ask.

"It can be a necessary ingredient, but never sufficient," says Aislin, forty-one, a housewife and mother of five. "And sometimes even breaking bread does nothing to bring people together. It can be just a show, as some of our politicians have demonstrated, with no real intent to reconcile differences. You have to break bread in the name of peace.

"If you want to come together, you have to 'go together,' like all of us here. We may live in different neighborhoods, have different ways of practicing Christianity, but we all believe, and we all are willing to make sacrifices to make that happen."

"Some of us here first got to know one another during a summer retreat for Catholics and Protestants," says Conor, who is Catholic and an unemployed bricklayer. "The retreat did more than I'd expected in breaking down the mistrust and animosity that's built up. We found common ground by talking about our experiences, realizing how similarly we've suffered. None of us in Northern Ireland has been unscathed by the Troubles. Shared suffering can be the glue that binds you. But if it's to lead to healing, then your common identity can't mostly be shared suffering, because that just creates a 'woe is me' victim mentality. From there, you have to agree together to do something positive, or you won't advance peace in the community at large."

"After we'd been venting for several nights," says his wife, Maire, a hairdresser, "I realized that my greatest animosity was towards me— over my endless griping and carping about the situation, and yet doing nothing personally to allay the hatred, nothing to stem any of the violence.

"It's easier to blame the political leaders, the radicals on both sides. But then I asked myself, 'What can I, a common person in northern Belfast, do to bring people together?' I realized that if I was to do my bit to be a person of peace, I had to make a piece of peace out of my little patch of the earth that I do have some control over—my house, my yard, but also my heart."

"What about when you're outside of your patch of the earth, and have less control?" I say.

"That's when my heart plays an even bigger role," she says. "I have to muster up courage, when I am out and about, to be warm to people outside my religion. My heart for peace gives me that courage.

Some of my neighbors don't take kindly to my showing anything more than the bare minimum of civility. But I've faced up to ostracism to be a person of peace. Sadly, I've lost some friends in the process, or, to put it more correctly, they've lost me. So be it.

"I do believe with all my heart it's how we treat each other in the everyday world—how we greet each other on the street, in the grocery store, at the gas station, the dentist's—that will be the biggest factor in the long run in whether we come together."

Soon after, Aislin says, "To come together with others, I first had to come together with myself. I'd felt just like that wall out there." She points down the road to the neighborhood's ironically named "peace wall," a drab and forbidding structure topped with barbed wire that separates the Protestant from the Catholic section of the neighborhood. "I had that wall inside me. If I'm torn apart within because of angers and fears I've harbored since I was a kid, I can't reach out to anyone. So I first had to work on unlearning all the prejudices and stereotypes I'd been brought up with before I could be or do any good to anyone else."

Aislin looks at her husband, Cioran, who manages a convenience store, and says, "We saw an interview on the local TV news with a man who lost his daughter in an IRA bombing. He talked about how his little girl's last words to him before she died were, 'I love you very much.' He said that because his child's last words were of love, in her honor and memory he could never bring himself to utter a single word of hatred for those who committed that barbarous act."

Says Cioran, "This man's message was, we adults have to be loving and forgiving like his beautiful child if we're to come together, and make sure no more innocents are killed in acts of hate. That father overcame all his natural impulses for hatred and revenge out of his love for his child."

"All we adults do is teach the love right out of the children," says Aislin. "After I saw that interview, I quit thinking I had to understand thoroughly all the reasons why I was divided inside before I tore down the walls inside me. I just tore them down. Ever since—in the name of all the innocents who've lost their lives and who would beg us to be peace people—I've done my best to reach out to people who historically have been on the opposing side and show kindness where before, at best, I'd shown indifference."

"I'm one of the people she reached out to," says Glendon, a machine tool operator, who is Catholic. "We work at the same plant. Aislin invited me and my family to join them for Easter dinner several years ago. We've been joining them ever since. Actually, those of us here today get together every month at least once to break bread. At Easter, we do it at a restaurant, but we're not Rockefellers. The rest of the time, we take turns having dinner at our homes. I'll tell you, I thought the braver thing was for us to meet at a public restaurant, but it takes even more courage to have these get-togethers at our homes. All of us have neighbors who've never had someone of 'the opposing side' in their homes. To them, we're traitors. They've put horrible graffiti on our homes, even left feces on our doorstep."

He sighs and then says, "Today, my father will gather with his mates to commemorate the 1916 Easter Uprising for Irish independence. He called me to complain that they were denied access to some of the traditional routes of their march. I tried to reason with him and say that the march glorifies violence and exacerbates division. He hung up on me. He's been more up in arms than ever since the Good Friday accord. He really fears that if the two sides come together, then Catholic pride will dissolve. If hatred of another is what it takes to have a strong identity, I'd rather not have a strong identity."

"The Good Friday accord is all about coming together: about building good out of bad, about healing," says Glendon's wife, Sandy, as she tries to keep a weather eye on her four rambunctious daughters. "With all its flaws, at least the major parties came together just enough so we could inch forward. Today of all days should be about resurrection, about new beginnings and renewed hope. Instead, the British military stationed here is on high alert, and people in many communities are afraid to go outside. It feels as if the 'Troubles' are starting up all over again."

The "Troubles" officially began on January 30, 1972, on a day known as "Bloody Sunday." That day, British troops opened fire, apparently unprovoked, on a Catholic pro-Republican march in nearby Derry. Thirteen unarmed marchers were killed. From that day until October 1997, more than twenty-five years later, when peace talks in Belfast commenced between the two sides, 3,600 died in this small territory of about 1.6 million.

"Even if the Peace Accords fall apart," says Kaitlin, thirty-five, a Protestant, "as long as we keep gathering like this, I'll have hope. You can't change what our ancestors did in the past—hell, you can't even change your parents or siblings—but you can change yourself. I'm the only person I have control over."

"But if others don't change as well, can you come together?" I ask.

"When others see how you've changed, they either distance themselves from you, or they're inspired to change too," she replies. "Even if it's just one person here and there, over time it adds up, and my theory is that eventually we'll be an unstoppable force for peace."

Conor tousles his son's hair and says to me, "I'm not sure I would have ever had the will to take risks in coming together if it weren't for the sake of our children. Kids today are so desensitized to violence. It's what they've grown up with. These children are the third generation since the Troubles began. For them, barbed wire and police fortresses are normal. They've seen so much hatred and violence among us adults. If they're allowed to grow up thinking that violence is normal, that division by religion is normal, they'll think coming together out of love and forgiveness is what's aberrant."

"I send my children to one of the interfaith schools in Belfast," says Conor's brother Liam, "so that being with people who are 'different' is no big deal. The biggest difference they see between one another isn't whether one of them is Protestant or Catholic, but whether one has blond or brown hair. Now, if they can ever teach us adults to see one another's differences that way, peace will be a done deal."

Thomas Hennessey writes in *A History of Northern Ireland* that "[p]erhaps the most dramatic development in education . . . has been the creation of integrated schools, which are attended in roughly equal numbers by Protestants and Catholics."

"A couple weeks ago," Cioran tells me, "we held a protest against sending our troops to Iraq. You wouldn't believe the motley group of people who came out—Protestant and Catholic hard-liners who'd never dreamed they'd show up on purpose at the same place, to protest in common cause against sending our boys and girls to a war they shouldn't be going to, a war they say is just fanning the flames of hate and extremism. Many of them are the same ones who fan the flame here! If they'd realize the hypocrisy of their contradictory stances, we'd quickly come together in real peace."

"There's a Gaelic word, *Corrymeela*, which means Hill of Harmony," says Aislin. "It's also the name of one of the most prominent peacemaking groups in Northern Ireland. Its aim is to make our community a shining Hill of Harmony, a model for other communities in conflict around the world. Right now, though, the hill is more like Mount Everest. There's still not yet a critical mass on both sides willing to make the climb. But those of us here won't wait for others. We're making the climb already. Once the rest see us up there enjoying the view, they'll come join us."

"If you asked the people on the fringes how we should come together, they'd answer, 'we shouldn't,'" Conor says to me. "There'll always be those who won't want to. They want a world of hate and fear. But we're fanatics too—for coming together out of love and forgiveness."

Cultivate Your Garden (or Park)

For the Greeks of fifth-century Athens, the outcome or product of *philia*, as they pushed and inspired one another to new frontiers of discovery and achievement, was a singular type of happiness called *eudaimonia*, which can be experienced only when all society's members have the opportunity and obligation to discover and develop the talents that best contribute to an evolving self and society. For this to come to pass, the Greeks believed that society had to be a laboratory that encouraged and created the conditions for continual experimentation, pushing outward the envelope for how the greatest human good might be achieved for everyone.

Philia brings about the ultimate coalition of the willing, a coalescing of people who genuinely want to be together out of desire rather than expediency. In Greece, over time the *agora*, or plaza of Athens, became renowned as the hemisphere's "*philia* mecca." It was the gathering place for Hellenic people of a welter of tribes, families, villages—a place where they not only sold and bartered goods but exchanged a bracing variety of ideas.

It Takes a Village Blackout

"The truth is, we're needy 24-7. But we only *show* we need each other in times of crisis," says Gwen. "That's fair-weather needing. There's neediness denial, a 'neediness blackout,' big-time in the Big Apple."

A cluster of us are sitting in a circle in Washington Square Park. Most are in the park tonight out of necessity, unable to make it to their homes in nearby high-rises, the outer boroughs of Manhattan, or the suburbs of New Jersey, New York, and Connecticut. Situated in the heart of Greenwich Village in New York City, the park for centuries has been an intellectual and social vortex near which such luminaries as Thomas Paine, Mark Twain, Edgar Allan Poe, Theodore Dreiser, Sherwood Anderson, and Eugene O'Neill once resided.

It is the night of the Big Blackout. The most expansive and expensive electricity stoppage in North American history has left millions in the dark from New York to Toronto to Detroit. The cascade of power station shutdowns struck Manhattan at 4:11 P.M. Sections of the city remained in the dark for more than twenty-four hours. Cecilia and I spend our summers in Manhattan; besides our outreach with marginalized groups throughout the tristate area, we hold weekly Socrates Café dialogues in the park, which has become for us a "*philia* magnet." Wouldn't you know that tonight was the night for our dialogue. The question we are examining—"When do we need each other?"—was proposed by none other than Gwen herself. The fifty-two-year-old, who has been a fixture at the park for decades, is a self-published, self-described avant-garde poet and novelist; she also is former owner of a small eclectic and dirt-cheap eatery that was long a community mainstay until her rent was more than doubled, effectively evicting her.

"After September 11, there was so much love," Gwen says as she leans against a large tree—her tree, she likes to make clear—near the center of the park, not far from the marble arch. "Strangers hugging strangers, people doing little and big things for one another without giving it a second thought. But after a while, that was that, and people became more distanced from one another, more rude to one another, than ever. It was like they couldn't stand how needy they'd been. After the crisis passed, they swung to the nth degree in the other direction."

Says Trent, one of the park's resident intellectuals, "Aristotle believed that in order for each individual to discover his *telos*, or purpose, he needed the help of all his community—and in turn he helped the community further discover its purpose. By his version of *telos*, you can't accomplish anything of worth without a lot of helping hands and hearts from friends and neighbors, and even the kindness of strangers who are part of your society."

"That's what we had for a while after 9-11," says Harold, an autodidact and Trent's friend and foil in intellectual repartee. "We were villagers again, acting out of a sense of connection, of *longing* for connection, like we know we need deep down but shun in the hurly-burly.

"Tonight, telos is everywhere. You know how you know? Look

around. Does anyone look worried and anxious, as you might expect? *Au contraire.* They are at peace, Why? Because this type of needy togetherness is their natural communal telos."

"Well, it's not *just* about *telos*," Trent chimes back in, determined that he and Harold never reach complete agreement on any subject. "*Telos* itself never can be all it can be without *philia*, Greek for 'communal love'. Without *philia*, you'd only need one another out of pure helplessness. But *telos* plus *philia* means you need one another as a matter of choice and desire, out of a shared longing to be part of a community where everyone can lead a more creative life than they could if left to their own devices. Sure, we can go it alone, but it's better to 'go it together.'"

"Can you ever really go it alone?" I ask. "Is need of others a basic and blanket element of the human condition, every second of our lives, no matter how much some might deny it?"

"I think so," says Monique, who lives in a nearby housing project and is in the park with her two young children to escape the oppressive heat in her apartment. "We need others for filling our basic needs and to fulfill our highest hopes. But we also need others to need us. Now, I don't know *telos* from *philia*, so I'll steer clear of that. I'll tell you this: when the blackout happened this afternoon, I was way up on 82nd and Madison. I'd just finished a job interview. I walked all the way down here as foot as I could to get my kids from the sitter. About every five blocks, there were people passing out water, just to be kind. I've never been treated so nice. They weren't doing it just for me, and they had no idea what my circumstances or troubles were. But it made me feel so good that they cared to give out that water to anybody who needed it.

"My interview didn't go well. I haven't had a job in over three years. That water was like an elixir. . . . It made me think, what if there were people like that passing out water every day, not because there's a crisis but just because they cared, because they knew that on a hot summer day, for all kinds of reasons, there'd be people passing by who'd need a drink of cold water, and that it'd make them feel better.

"There's also this: they needed me as much as I needed them. They needed people like me to need that water, so they could have that good feeling that comes from being needed. If nobody'd taken their water, they'd have been miserable."

"I hear you," says Harold. "I need these park people, even Trent. I need this park, and I like to think it needs us. We park people take care of it. We clean it up, keep it fairly spotless, to show it how grateful we are that it's here to give us a place that's conducive for gathering and reflecting. The police who kick us out late at night—except tonight, because they're on their best behavior, what with all these out-of-towners spending the night here—are the outsiders. This is our place if it's anyone's, our needful place. We're a wonderfully anarchic community, with our own tacit social contract. We look out for one another because we want to, and because we're not ashamed of being needy all the time.

"Our government, on the one hand, says we need it for essential services—like providing electricity—yet this preventable blackout is a sure sign that government no longer works at even the most basic level. We can't, and shouldn't, look to faceless institutions for succor—only to one another, face to face. Unlike society at large, we don't have to have laws to force one another to help out. We don't try to dupe each other that we're not needy, that we're some sort of rugged individualists. We know we're needy here, that our days would be dark without one another."

"We in the Girl Scouts brighten sad people's days, too, because we know how much we all need each other," says nine-year-old Tiffany. I'd been fretting, needlessly it turns out, that the highfalutin terms some participants were using would keep the kids on hand from participating.

"My mom could never find anyone else to help lead our Girl Scout troop," Tiffany goes on, "so she's doing it all herself. She was determined to do it, even though we may not be in the projects for long if my dad finds a job someplace else. Mom wanted to make it a tradition before we leave, so that all the kids who come through the projects after us—in need of fun and constructive activities and a group to be part of, where they can make great friends—can have it to look forward to."

Says Tiffany's mom, Trish, "I just believe that no matter how little time you live in a place, you still can make it better, more caring, so you can pay back others who were kind to you when you were in need."

"My mom tried to start a PTA group for our school," says Tiffany's friend Cherise, also nine. "No other parents cared to be part of it. She was a PTA of one. She works two jobs, and she still finds time to do it. She says all parents, *especially* poor parents, have to get together and get involved, to 'advocate' for poor kids, as she puts it, so their needs in education are met."

In what many consider to be a groundbreaking work, Robert D. Putnam, Dillion Professor of International Affairs at Harvard University, writes in *Bowling Alone: The Collapse and Revival of American Community*, that fewer Americans than ever are involved in any community and civic activities. Yet such associations are the lifeblood of a democracy, Putnam says. In them, citizens expend a great deal of what he calls "social capital"—"the collective value" of these "social networks." Drawing on a wealth of empirical evidence, Putnam asserts that we belong to few organizations, rarely take time to be neighborly much less to form friendships, much less take time to socialize with our own and other families, resulting in a "shared . . . civic malaise."

"My mom also started a community garden in a vacant dirt lot down the block," Cherise now says, enjoying that she has such an attentive group of listeners. "It used to be that people in our long-term shelter would just stay behind closed doors, and no one had anything to do with anyone else. Now everyone comes out to the garden, and we're all getting to know one another. We're having picnics and other get-togethers. I think that vacant lot needed us—and we need it. We made it pretty, and it gave us that good feeling Monique talked about. Before, everybody ignored it and one another. Now it's a gathering place."

Cherise looks at me and says, "No matter how long or short a time you're at a place, you should show how much you care about everyone else there—not because anyone expects it of you, but because you expect it of yourself."

"Is having high expectations for yourself a vital need?" I ask.

"Without them, why would I even get out of bed in the morning?" she says back.

Monique looks at the kids with unabashed admiration. "Out of the mouths of babes," she murmurs. And then: "I'm not in a position just yet to help with the Girl Scouts or the PTA, but you know what? If this blackout is still here tomorrow, *I'm* going to pass out cups of water— to rich, to poor, to whomever. It'll make me feel like I'm anyone's equal—not above anyone, just equal—equally needy. I'll do it because it'll give me that good feeling, and also because maybe somewhere down the road, I'll need that cup of water again, and I'll hope they'll do the same for me.

"We've got to start showing how much we need each other all the time," Monique then says. "There'll be other crises right around the corner. Every day is a crisis of some sort, usually of quiet desperation, because we don't feel connected. I'm not saying we have to go back to hug each other every second, but we should never be so cold and distant again, because rather than create the impression that all of us are self-sustaining, it just makes everyone feel they're needless."

Jack, an investment banker, seemed resigned to spending the night here, far from his home in Greenwich, Connecticut. Apparently content to listen and gaze at the stars until now, he takes a swig of warm beer and says, "I'm going to be depressed when the lights come back on. I'll return to life as usual, and it'll be like this never happened. I almost wish I never had to leave here. It feels like the most natural thing in the world to spend the evening here."

"I don't want to spend the night in a park," says Monique firmly. "I like having a roof over my family's head. Even though I live in public housing, we treat the place like it's our own. The staff goes out of its way to make us feel like *mi casa es su casa*. That makes me look up to them, realizing as they do that they may be helping us in time of need, but we're helping them too, giving them a chance to be a do-gooder.

"Besides, they know that the housing project is no more theirs than it is ours or anyone else's. Just like no one owns this park, or even a home that you buy and call your own. It's just yours for a short while. That's what all of us are anyway—stewards—taking care of other people and places as they take care of us."

Needful Things

Can we ever be so in tune with one another that we can come to know others' most heartfelt needs?

Martha Nussbaum stresses that to do so, we need to think of ourselves as part of a larger human community; only then will we become fully compassionate individuals, and develop compassionate institutions, ensuring that everyone's most fundamental "felt needs" are attended to. Nussbaum calls for a *philia*-type nurturing of our capacities via what she terms "affiliation," which is

> being able to live with and toward others, to recognize and show
> concern for other human beings, to engage in various forms of
> social interaction; to be able to imagine the situation of another
> and to have compassion for that situation; to have the capability
> for both justice and friendship. . . .

To Nussbaum, we cannot be inspired to develop and nurture this capability if we do not first recognize and live by the shared belief that all humans are born into a world that they "have not made and do not control," and that this renders us all in a state of "needy helplessness more or less unparalleled in any other animal species."

Today, though, because this is not the pervasive philosophy held by members of most developed societies, the many are rendered much more needy and helpless than others, while a select minority live as if they are above the fray, deluding themselves into believing that they are needful of no one and no thing.

As a result, today many newborns are brought into a world in which their needs are barely met. If an impoverished mother is starving or malnourished, or if a mother is drug dependent or infected with HIV or has another life-threatening illness, she is barely able to care for herself, much less attend to the needs of her newborn. Such a child may never have a chance to articulate or recognize this, because of the physical, neurological, and/or emotional damage she suffers as a consequence. Even poor and marginalized children who enjoy healthy births can quickly come to realize that they were brought into a world in which their most fundamental "felt needs" are being met only so they can meet and serve the needs of others. (Conversely, children of privilege can fast develop the view that the rest of the world exists for the sole purpose of satisfying their every felt need, real or imagined.) Our "felt needs" early on in our lives may originate from many sources, and in many instances may just as easily stem from our recognition that we can't (and perhaps, depending on circumstances, shouldn't) rely primarily on others, and that ultimately we must look foremost to ourselves to satisfy our needs if we are to survive.

But the most fundamental "felt need" is to *feel needed*, in ways that create healthy interdependencies that at the same time make us more autonomous. In her work with the United Nations, Nussbaum pioneered a "capabilities approach" to assess the needs of women in the Third World:

> The central question asked by the capabilities approach is not, "How satisfied is this woman?" or even "How much in the way of resources is she able to command?" It is, instead, "What is she actually able to do and to be?" . . . Users of this approach . . . ask not only about the person's satisfaction with what she does, but

about what she does, and what she is in a position to do (what her opportunities and liberties are). They ask not just about the resources that are present, but about how those do or do not go to work, enabling the woman to function.

To make this so requires far more than attending to each human's most basic physical needs. In addition, one must attend to other forms of "human needing" with a social, rational, and empathetic base, and in particular see to it that there is "appropriate education, . . . leisure for play and self-expression, . . . valuable associations with others." To gain satisfaction in the most self-fulfilling and socially redemptive way is not just tantamount to taking on works and deeds in which you feel genuinely useful; rather, you must also strive to ensure that those to whom you are reaching out feel equally useful and worthy, rather than just objects of your pity or compassion.

Bowling Together

In *Bowling Alone*, Robert Putnam expresses his great confidence in "our power to reverse the decline of the last several decades" and again become a society with thriving civic participation. He issues this call to civic duty: "Let us find ways to ensure that by 2010 the level of civic engagement among Americans then coming of age" in our society will not only "match that of their grandparents when they were at the same age" but in fact "will be substantially greater than it was in their grandparents' era." Putnam fails to take note of the vital role that those who came of age in the 1960s, who are now the grandparents of these children, must play. How can young people be expected to cultivate a sense of civic duty if this ideal has been largely abandoned by the most idealistic generation of socially conscious activists in our history? What's more, before we can be more civic-minded, we need to become more civil-minded. As the nonprofit *Public Agenda* reports, "a lack of respect and courtesy" is a pervasively "serious problem for our society."

Another of Putnam's civic imperatives is that we "spend less time traveling and more time connecting with neighbors." Of course we should spend more time with our next-door neighbors; but if we look at the globe as another type of neighborhood, then those of us privileged enough to do so should continue traveling, but in ways that enable us to get to know intimately and appreciate new cultures and different ways of world-viewing and world-making. Perhaps, with this objective in mind, if those of us in a position to do so traveled more, we might come to see how many societies live creatively with very little, nonetheless sharing everything they have; and see how many more live in abject conditions in which even basic subsistence is not a possibility.

The title of Putnam's book *Bowling Alone* stems from the fact that although more people than ever are bowling, the number of those bowling in leagues is down a whopping 40 percent from the sport's heyday of decades ago. Although the tradition of bowling is alive and well, Americans today tend to prefer bowling alone.

I was an inveterate bowler as an adolescent, taking part for years in a Saturday bowling league. League organizers purposely arranged it so our teammates were chosen at random at the beginning of each season. Not knowing whom my bowling teammates would be was a bit anxiety producing, and exciting; I knew that at the very least they'd share my passion for the sport. Invariably, I'd end up becoming fast friends with people I'd otherwise never have had a chance to get to know. During our many months together, I'd learn their philosophies and styles of bowling, their approaches to sportsmanship, to winning and losing, to life.

If we gather only with those most predictably like us, there is little room for the surprise of the novel and unfamiliar, for discovering new intellectual, social, existential terrain. We need to rediscover the tradition of communing with people whom we don't know very well. For even if, adhering strictly to Putnam's bowling analogy, we increase vastly the number of bowling leagues, but we always choose and vet our teammates, ours won't necessarily be a more participatory society in ways that promote *philia*.

Let's bowl together again. At least sometimes, let's have our bowling partners picked for us randomly rather than "knowing the score" in advance.

Love of Country

To the Greeks, *philia* was at the core of patriotism. Without friendship love, they did not believe there could be genuine love of country. The *philia* cultivated among friends was meant to extend outward in widening circles—to neighbors, members of the community at large, until everyone in the country shared it, creating a sense of solidarity, loyalty, cooperation, and common cause.

Patriot without a Country

"Love of country, in a democracy like ours, is speaking out and standing up for the weak and helpless," says Harriett, age ten. "It's taking their problems onto your own shoulders, righting the wrongs done to them."

I am with a group of elementary-age inner city children who are taking part with me in a dialogue on the steps of the nation's Capitol.

It is Independence Day, and, as always, I have extended invitations to our nation's congressmen, as well as to many hundreds of others I've met around the country who take part in philosophical discourse. On this July 4th, these children are the only ones who have taken me up on my invite, thanks to Mrs. Williams, their teacher of the previous school year, whose class I'd visited and who went to considerable lengths to arrange for them to join me today.

"Love of country is making sure all citizens have good books to read, clothes to wear, toys to play with," says Harriett's classmate Rachel. "It's seeing to it that all fellow Americans have a good, quiet, safe place to live and sleep—*and* making sure they all have good doctors and surgeons and nurses to keep them healthy."

"If people all around you are always coughing and sneezing because they're sick, and they don't have money to go to a doctor or buy medicine, that would mean their countrymen don't care about them," says nine-year-old Tina rather breathlessly. "Yet people in that condition can make everyone else around them sick. They go to work or school because they can't stay home to get well, because there's no one at home to take care of them, or because they don't have a home, *or* because even if they had a roof over their heads and someone to stay with, they still don't have any medicine or money to go to a doctor—*or*, if it's a parent and he called in sick, he'd lose his job."

"To love your country is to love your countrymen and -women like you would your own brother or sister or best pal," Harriett then says. "If *they* were sick, you *know* you'd do something about it to help them. And you *should* do the same thing for all your countrymen. Because if you don't make it possible for them to stay home from work, then everyone will get the contagious virus too. So more and more people will miss work and school and church, and the entire country will be worse off."

Then Jayson chimes in, "Love of country is the same thing as love of yourself. If you help out others in your country when in need, you're helping out yourself. You'll be making sure that when it's your turn to be needy—and we're *all* needy, sooner or later—someone will be there for you."

"All of us Americans should want *and* have to show this kind of love of country," says Rachel. "But some never will unless they have no choice. So it should be the law of the land."

"But then it's forced love, and that can't be love of country at all," says Jayson. "It has to come naturally, from your heart."

"None of you has mentioned the word *patriotism*," I say. "Are the examples you've given of how one should show love of country the same thing as examples of being a patriot?"

"Well, you can be a patriot without even having a country," says Harriett. "Our founding fathers were patriots way before the U.S. ever actually became the U.S. They loved so much the *idea* of a country where people had rights to life, liberty, and the pursuit of happiness that they were willing to sacrifice their lives to make it come true."

Tina tells me, "My friend's dad is fighting in the war in Iraq, even though he's not an American citizen." She looks at the White House in the distance. "I'm glad the president in the White House over there has hurried up the process to make people like him citizens—people who are fighting our wars against terrorism even though they aren't U.S. citizens. They love this country and what it stands for so much, in ways some of its own citizens don't. It boggles my mind."

"You know who's a great patriot?" says Jayson. "Our teacher here, Mrs. Williams. She says you can't really know *why* you should love our country if you don't get to know firsthand what makes this country so lovable. So she lets us practice freedom of speech. Like, once we held a freewheeling debate to decide whether we should be able to wear hats inside the classroom."

"And she's made us learn by heart all the Constitution and the Declaration, and we're trying to learn all the amendments," Tina tells me. "Mrs. Williams says people who immigrate here and become citizens know these things better than those of us born here. How can you love a country if you don't know all there is to love about it?"

Compassionate Patriotism

Martha Nussbaum believes there are inherent dangers in the type of
patriotism that is pervasive in America today.

> [o]ur sense that the "us" is all that matters can easily flip over
> into a demonizing of an imagined "them," a group of outsiders
> who are imagined as enemies of the invulnerability and the
> pride of the all-important "us." Just as parents' compassion for
> their own children can all too easily slide into an attitude that
> promotes the defeat of other people's children, so too with
> patriotism: compassion for our fellow Americans can all too
> easily slide over into an attitude that wants America to come out
> on top, defeating or subordinating other peoples or nations.

One might go even further and assert that if our citizens do not
believe that all humans are deserving of a world in which their basic
needs and higher hopes can be realized, then this could not conform
to what patriotism should be in a democracy such as ours, with a
Constitution declaring that all humans, not just Americans, are equal
with an equal right to life, liberty, and the pursuit of happiness. Such
patriotism might begin at our own doorstep but can never end there
no more than it can end at our own borders. Likewise, compassion
toward one's children that seeks to "defeat other people's children"
cannot be real compassion at all.

The "compassionate patriotism" that Nussbaum calls for would
require Americans to have the same high hopes and aspirations for all
people that they presumably have for other Americans. It would
require a type of nationalistic pride derived in large measure from the
cultivation of shared bonds of compassion that necessarily come to
extend further and further outward, far past one's own bounds. Jingoism and xenophobia have no place in this conception.

The practice of "compassionate patriotism" was a vital component of the democratic nature of ancient Athens. It led to the formation of broad confederacies that allowed more and more people in far-off places to enjoy the same freedoms enjoyed by Athenians. Athens' subsequent decline was marked by a proportionate decline in this practice, to the point that eventually Athens' leaders thought nothing about invading another land and slaughtering innocent people to get at the area's resources. Nussbaum writes that

> [c]ompassion and terror are in the fabric of our lives. . . . [W]e, like the Greek army, are not only victims but also causes of devastation in foreign lands. In the lives of Americans since 9/11, we do see evidence of the good work of compassion, as Americans make real to themselves the sufferings of so many different people whom they never would otherwise have thought about.

PART V

AGAPE

A Higher Love

In Hellenic Greece, *agape* was considered the highest form of love, self-sacrificial and unconditional love that springs from an overflowing within. Acting out of *agape* in all instances demonstrates one's love of humanity, that one's every gesture is an indication of seeing all humans as equal and equally deserving. Consequently, *agape* is the ultimate welcoming into the fold—but in a way in which the fold itself expands.

With *agape*, there is no expectation of reciprocal demonstrations from those on whom it is showered; rather, one imbued with *agape* gives freely, loves with no strings attached, with no thought of reward—and in doing so, even though this is not the expectation, one often receives even more in return.

Prison Diaries

"Who shows unconditional love?"

The question is posed even before I have a chance to take the chair set aside for me among the group of twenty-five. The man who asks the question, a longtime philosophy buff, is middle aged, an inmate at a maximum security prison that I have visited several times. Just like that, the dialogue has begun.

"My nine-year-old girl. When she bounds to me in the visiting room, she is unconditional love personified. I hope when she's older, and understands why I'm here, she'll still come straight into my arms. Even if she holds back, I'll know that that unconditional love is still there deep inside of her."

"My wife. She loves me 'for better or for worse.' She doesn't love me that way because she made that vow; she made it because that's how she loves me."

"My mom shows it. She tells me she'd love me just as much whether I'm in prison for life or I'm a scientist, though I know she'd rather I'd become a scientist. Her love makes me want to better myself. Who knows, someday I may be that scientist. I am this close to earning my associate's degree in mathematics. It was hard, but I'm making it, with her encouragement. I was going to say her love for me is with no strings attached, but she loves me with lots of strings attached—love strings."

"My dog shows me that kind of love. I may never see him again, may never again feel that wet tongue lick my cheek, never see that smiling 'I love you no matter what' face. A couple of times, I've kicked him, I'll admit it. That was the lowest. I can still see the hurt in his big watery eyes, but only for a millisecond. Then he's back to loving me every bit as joyful as ever."

"Do you show yourselves unconditional love?"

"No, that's not possible. Unconditional love is something others have for you, or you for others, but not for yourself. It would just be too weird to say, 'I love myself unconditionally.'"

"I don't see it that way. To say I love myself unconditionally just means I'm not going to give up on myself. No matter how many others say I'll always be a poster child for badness, unconditional love for myself is what inspires me to be pure goodness from here on out."

"Unconditional love is only for fairy tales. That's the only place it exists."

"That's the kind of world I want for my daughter, a fairy tale world where everybody shows everybody unconditional love, where they shower so much attention and affection and forgiveness and understanding on one another that the world couldn't be more peaceful and loving if it wanted to. Maybe someday, if everyone believes in this love as much as my nine year old, and shows it as much as she does, it'll become a reality. Wouldn't that be something?"

The Last Crusade

"We should live love," says Jeff, a developer from Albuquerque, New Mexico. He is the first to respond to my question "How should we live?" Socrates said this was the most important question a human being could ask and answer at a time when Athens' golden era was no more, when institutionalized religion soon would become the norm, and when *agape* was being reconceived by Greeks as a kind of love that could be engendered only by divine intervention.

"We should share our love, spread the love in everything we do," Jeff goes on to say. His voice, so soft you have to strain to hear him, contrasts with his imposing figure and stern demeanor. He and his family are among about fifteen with whom I am scrunched together under a fellowship tent in a large field in Flushing Meadows-Corona Park, New York. I had not expected an interfaith group, all of whom have come out to hear Billy Graham's message. They are not just members of Christian denominations but also include Sikhs and Jews. Indeed, such diverse gatherings are not altogether a rarity here among the nearly 80,000 who have come from around the globe on a sultry summer afternoon to experience the last day of a three-day evangelical revival that has drawn more than a quarter million. In a career spanning more than a half century, Graham, now eighty-six, the elder statesman of the Protestant evangelical movement, has spread his version of the gospel to well over 200 million people in 185 countries, and has been a spiritual advisor to every president since Dwight D. Eisenhower. By holding his final crusade here, Graham has come full circle: In New York City in 1957, at the cusp of a tumultuous era that would launch the civil rights and radical political movements of the 1960s, Graham held his longest-ever revival. Though it had been scheduled to last no more than a couple of weeks, it went on for a full four months. Graham's message of unconditional love and universal fellowship touched a chord far and wide.

"How do you live love, share the love?" I ask.

"By doing what we're doing now," Jeff replies. "Look at how diverse this gathering is, both inside and outside this tent. It's a love-in. That's what evangelism is supposed to be about: creating a tent that can include everyone. The tent has to be of a special type of spiritual material, one made of God's love, so it's capable of infinite expansion. Reverend Graham has always preached that whether or not you believe in God exactly as he does, whether you are a lost soul or found, he loves you just the same, and hopes you love him just the same—because God loves all, saint and sinner, believer and nonbeliever, equally. He says in one essay that 'some people seem to have such a passion for righteousness that they have no room left for compassion,' though an evangelical's mission is to show 'great kindness and mercy' to one and all, 'in compassion and love.'"

"Is there a string attached?" I ask. "Do you act lovingly towards others with the hope of converting them to your way of Christian living?"

"My love is without conditions, though my hope is that, yes, they will come to a life of Christ, as I have," says Jeff's wife, Carly. "But if I treat them differently if they didn't, that would make me the ultimate hypocrite. Jesus is my guide. He practiced *agape*, the word for love that often appears in the original Greek-language versions of the Bible. It means 'unconditional love.' It's a love where you totally surrender yourself to the task of making this world more loving.

"This is what my husband and I try to do, though imperfectly, in the name of Christ's love," she continues. "We give generously of our time and money to charitable causes. For instance, we volunteer to build homes for the homeless or for those who live in decrepit housing. This is a Christian project, so of course we do have a Bible reading when a family moves into a new home, and we do give them a Bible and say a prayer to the Lord, because our actions were inspired by Christ's love. But the home is theirs, with no strings attached. Whether they accept Christ into their lives and hearts or not, the home is a gift of unconditional love."

"So unconditional giving is a key part of living a life of unconditional love?" I say.

"It should be," says Eric, an Evangelical who came from Birmingham, Alabama, to be part of the revival. "Yet if we millions of Evangelicals ever gave till it hurt, out of love to make this Earth heavenly for everyone, there wouldn't be over 45 million Americans without health care. There wouldn't be record levels of poverty and homelessness."

Eric then goes on to say, "Our governor, Bob Riley, tried to pass a tax reform referendum that would have vastly improved the quality of life of the poor in our state. He said it was 'immoral' that we weren't doing more for them. The governor proposed the reform because, he said, 'according to Christian ethics, we're supposed to love God, love each other, and help take care of the poor.' He risked his political career to practice his 'Christian duty.' The referendum was overwhelmingly defeated. Now our evangelical governor, who was preaching a message of unconditional love—of making Alabama a place where everyone could live with hope and dignity—is considered a pariah in a state with one of the highest percentages of Evangelicals anywhere."

"What, if anything, is the message conveyed from this in terms of 'how should we live?'" I ask.

"That you should live as an Evangelical who only talks about most deeply held religious values; but don't you dare attempt to put those values into practice, don't dare to live the type of radical love that Jesus would have you live."

"We have a word, *khalsa*, which means 'path of love,'" says Gurjeet, a biochemist and father of six. A Sikh who is now a resident of Birmingham, Gurjeet and family accompanied Eric and his family here. Gurjeet has attended Billy Graham–led evangelical revivals since Graham ventured to Gurjeet's homeland of India decades ago when Gurjeet was a boy.

"Our holy scripture begins with this insight by Guru Nanak, the founder of the Sikh faith: 'We are neither Hindu nor Muslim. We all are created by God as human beings.' That is also what Reverend Graham preaches. Far from saying you should abandon your chosen faith, what matters is that you never lose sight of God—that in living by a noble faith, you do not dwell on practicing elaborate rites and idol worship, but on cultivating your heart and mind to be 'as God.' You do that by dedicating yourself to what we Sikhs call *seva*—selfless, loving devotion and service to your fellow humans."

Says Gurjeet's wife, Naima, "Guru Nanak observed that the Hindu priests and Muslim imams of his day lived in great luxury, while their flock starved." In her spare hours, Naima delivers food to elderly shut-ins. "They preached unconditional love and caring, while they propped up and benefited from the artificial caste system that kept down the people they were supposed to be serving. Guru Nanak was from a Hindu family of a high caste, and could have chosen to enjoy a life of great privilege, but he rejected it. All that mattered was to do his part to live in ways that created a world of greater social and economic justice, of charity and love."

"Do you walk the path of *khalsa*?" I ask.

"I try to, but will never do so as he did," Naima replies. "Like Jesus, Guru Nanak has set the bar very high. He provided us with guideposts for living, and urged us in his scriptural writings to work an honest and ethical job, to practice *seva* in everything we do. He believed that all our dealings, large and small, impact people's lives, and we should act so that they'll be moved to live a life of unconditional love. In trying to live this way, I can say that I have seen firsthand the wisdom of

Guru Nanak's words; just the slightest gesture of kindness can transform someone."

"It's easy to 'live love' when there's no tensions," says Gurjeet. "It's
when there's a conflict or tragedy that your faith is put to the test. A
Sikh was the first person murdered in a hate crime in the U.S. after
the September 11th tragedy—killed because he wore a turban and
was mistaken for a Muslim. The man who shot Balbir Singh Sodhi
yelled out from his pickup truck as he pulled the trigger, 'I stand for
America all the way!' But that killer no more stood for America than
a Sikh would have if he had reacted in an 'eye for an eye' way and
then declared 'I stand for Sikhism.' It's when you're most set upon
that you must 'live your faith.' If you react to hate with love, then you
demonstrate that you live by the laws of *wird*, the laws of God's grace
and love."

"Like *agape*, *seva* seems like grace in action," says Jeff. "John 4:7–8
tells us to 'let us love one another, for love is of God, and all who love
are born of God and know God.' When you love another, you're showing God's grace, showing you are his conduit. Even if you don't claim
to believe in God, when you reach out to others in a loving way, you're
living as a child of God."

"When you don't show love to others, are you a child of God?" I ask.

"You are, but you're not living as if you are," Eric replies. "So many
people here have come because they feel unloved, because they're crying out to be loved, or because they don't know or understand love
and want to. They're looking for a certain kind of love—nonjudgmental, no strings attached—and this is the place to find it. Everyone
has a home under Billy Graham's tent."

Says Carly, "Stories are legion about how [Graham] has transformed the most hate-filled people into the most loving. Reverend
Graham has taken to heart Matthew 5:44, where God says 'Love your
enemies. Bless them that curse you, and do good to those who hate
you.' He's been responsible for miraculous transformations with former KKK members, with murderers, with haters of all kinds, who've

been inspired to spend the rest of their lives living with unconditional love, restoring and repairing all the hurt they've done."

Says Gloria, from Connecticut, "There's a Hebrew word, *tikkun alum*, that essentially means that you repair the world by saving one life." A close friend of Carly's since the days when they lived in the same university dormitory in Boston, Gloria practices reform Judaism. "You don't have to look at 'saving a life' in a grandiose way. It can just be saying 'hi' to someone who's terribly down and out, recognizing him or her as a fellow human being who matters."

Says her husband, Andrew, a high school teacher, "In Jeremiah 31:3, the Lord says 'I have loved you with *ahev*,' which is Hebrew for 'everlasting love,' and that he has 'drawn you with loving-kindness,' or *hesed*, a Hebrew word which is 'love in action.' These two words together are God's grace in action, and are very similar to *agape* and *seva*. They inspire people to live restorative, transformative lives of love."

"By loving others as yourself, you are loving God with all your might, as Deuteronomy commands."

We fall silent and listen to Reverend Graham speak. Though his baritone voice is noticeably weak, when he says 'God loves everyone here,' his message appears to be as powerful as ever, judging from its impact.

"At the end of today's revival," Carly says to me, 'Reverend Graham will do what he always does—invite people to come on stage and join him in the Lord's love."

"I will go," says Naima, to the surprise of many here. "Like Reverend Graham, we Sikhs invite people of all belief systems to join us at our *gurdwaras*, our places of worship, so we can connect, learn from one another how better to live as conduits of God's love. Many of the Christians here with us in this tent have come to our *gurdwaras*. It is how we have become friends and learned about one another's beliefs, and how, in many ways, we have much in common. I used to have a lot more prejudices about Evangelicals than I do now, though too many still would have you believe that to live a life of faith, you have to practice fire-and-brimstone, fear-and-damnation preaching.

All in all, though, I have to say that my once-rigid prejudices are much more 'elastic' now that I know the hearts of these people here.

"And now I want to embrace Reverend Graham, this man of god who walks *khalsa*. He knows that you combat extreme hate with extreme love, extreme ignorance with extreme illumination."

"I'll go with you," Jeff says to Naima. He stands up, but before he leaves, he tells us, "Once, after I became born again, I went to hear Jimmy Carter give a Bible class at Sunday School in his hometown of Plains, Georgia. He talked in gentle tones, like Reverend Graham here, about living a life of compassion, of giving everything you have to make the world more just. He's done that all his life, walking the walk. He never just dusted off 'compassion' and used it for electioneering.

"I used to consider myself 'holier than thou,'" Jeff continues. "When some of my friends didn't join me in becoming a born-again Christian, I distanced myself from them. I wore my faith on my sleeve in an arrogant way. I believed I'd seen and felt something they hadn't, and that that put me above them. Instead of sharing God's love, I closed myself off from the world. Lately, I've been calling up my old friends and begging forgiveness. One by one, they're letting me back under their tent. Their unconditional forgiveness has been a great lesson in humility. Like Reverend Graham, they live in tents made of God's love."

Conditional Unconditional Love

In *The Four Loves*, renowned Christian apologist C. S. Lewis (1898–1963), author of the children's classic *Chronicles of Narnia* series, professor of Medieval and Renaissance Literature at Cambridge University, and a Fellow in English at Oxford, sets apart *eros, storge,* and *philia* as human-derived types of love, whereas *agape,* he says, is "Divine Gift-Love, the love that is God Himself." If the three forms of human love are not blended with *agape*, he says they cannot be fully or properly exhibited and are doomed to be distorted. In Lewis' view, humans cannot experience *agape* if they do not first accept God into their hearts, because this is the only way they can be a conduit of God's love and practice the one type of love that is of a "wholly disinterested" sort. Someone acting out of Christian *agape*, he asserts, desires solely what is "simply best for the beloved."

But to know what is best for a beloved, or anyone else, you would have to be wholly *interested* and, in an abiding way, devote a great deal of effort to discovering her deepest hopes and needs and desires. If one can be interested heart and soul in another, and still has the wherewithal to do what is best for the beloved, come what may, with no thought or expectation of personal reward, then one has moved further toward pure unconditional love.

On the other hand, what is wrong with reward, and does it have to be at odds with unconditional love? If I derive great personal satisfaction from having helped someone, from a beloved friend to a relative stranger, should this sense of fulfillment I derive negate any sense that my act was with no strings attached? If I help others in such a way, and they in turn are inspired to help me and others advance in the same way, practicing quite deliberate acts of loving-kindness in their own right, though this was not my expectation, does this dilute or detract from the "unconditionality" of my action?

IS THERE SUCH a thing as unconditional love? Is unconditional love desirable? Isn't our way of loving, our philosophy of love (including unconditional love), always conditioned by our cultural, religious, and social mores? Is love without attachment not so much unconditional as it is without mooring, without direction or clear purpose?

What if there were such a thing as unconditional, purely self-sacrificial love that gibes with Lewis' notion of *agape*, and we aspired to love others in this way? If those who are the recipients of such love do not share our worldview, if they do not agree with us about what *agape* is or should be—or if they do not believe in it at all—can one ever be said to have shown them unconditional love? What if the recipient does have a notion of unconditional love, yet believes it can be best demonstrated in ways precisely the opposite of those of the person who aspires to show it? Would the true gesture of unconditional love be to abandon one's own notions of *agape* in favor of acting in ways that accord with the beliefs of the prospective recipient?

What if unconditional love is more contingent on the recipient than on the person dispensing the love? Such might be the case if the recipient's response to your gesture is one in which she receives your gesture, understanding its intent, even though by her belief system it is by no means an act of unconditional love.

What if your heartfelt gesture goes against the grain of someone's own beliefs—if, for instance, you insistently offer steak dinners, after spending every penny you have on them, to a famished family whose religion, unbeknown to you, prohibits the eating of animal flesh? Yet the family nonetheless accepts it because it can see how much it means to you, even though it entails no inconsiderable sacrifice on the family's part. It would seem that the family's love is more unconditional than that of the giver, that the family is in fact the one giving.

C. S. Lewis asserts further that it is only by Christian *agape* that one can "love what is not naturally lovable; lepers, criminals, enemies, morons, the sulky, the superior, the sneering." Only God's grace allows one to love such people, and so the best translation of *agape* today, in Lewis' estimation, would be "charity." Who determines who is lovable and not so? Who or what determines who is a criminal, an enemy, a moron, sulky, superior? Societal standards? The religious? A bit of both? The criteria themselves that anyone would use to label someone in such ways, so they could then be unconditionally loving to them, would actually seem to obviate the possibility of unconditional love.

Genuine *agape* would seem to require that you dispense with all such pejorative labels, that you see yourself as flawed and foibled as (if not more so than) anyone, that you never put yourself above anyone. What if unconditional love meant that you set no preconceived parameters on what loving can mean and be, that you are fully open to new possibilities of love, to new belief systems about love, new applications? What if love in its highest incarnations could be realized only if humans were its source, creator, catalyst, and conduit? Could such a love still be divine?

Love without Limits

Joseph Campbell (1904–1987), renowned for his studies of comparative mythology, notes in his classic *The Hero with a Thousand Faces* that Christian nations, whose banner is supposed to be one of unconditional love, "are better known to history for their colonial barbarity and internecine strife than for any practical display of unconditional love." This, he says, is in stark counterpoint to God's paramount injunction: "Love your enemies, do good to those who hate you . . . bless those who curse you . . . he who strikes you in the cheek, offer him the other. . . . do unto others as you would have them do unto you . . . ," to give freely to all who ask. Campbell says it's no great thing to love those who love you, "for sinners also love those who love them." What matters, according to Campbell, is to go the next step and love unconditionally those who don't love you and who in fact might hate you profoundly. This is the type of love that Socrates tried to model, and it is a type of love that many paradigmatic figures throughout human history have modeled, from the Buddha to many Christians with an abiding social conscience, such as Dr. Martin Luther King, Jr.

WHAT SHOULD *ALSO* matter, these people have showed, is to love not only those who don't love you, as Campbell says, but to let yourself be loved by those whom you are not predisposed to love—to leave yourself open and vulnerable to new possibilities of love. If you do not do both—loving those who don't love you, but also allowing yourself to be loved by those you do not love—then you are loving only when you have control over the "loving situation."

BERTRAND RUSSELL FINDS the morality of the Christian Bible untenable—but not, as one might expect, on the grounds that it is illogical, inconsistent, and indefensible. Rather, as he says in his famous work *Why I Am Not a Christian*, Russell much prefers the Buddha and Socrates to Jesus or anyone else who holds that there is a hell: "[N]o one really profoundly humane can believe in everlasting punishment." Further, Russell says he admires the disposition of Socrates toward those who differed with him, and even were repulsed by his approach to being in and of the world. Socrates never declaimed against those who did not agree with him or would not listen to him. He never exhorted his followers, after receiving his unjust death sentence, to exact revenge on his persecutors. Instead, he told them to reach out to others, in love, more than ever.

Such a disposition, Russell finds, "is far more worthy" than that advanced in the New Testament, which he says states that anyone who does not believe in Jesus and heed his injunctions will not be able to "escape the damnation of hell" and "shall not be forgiven . . . neither in this world nor in the world to come."

True Christian Love

Lev Tolstoy (1828–1910), the great Russian novelist, pacifist, and Christian anarchist, has a much different perspective than that of Bertrand Russell on Jesus and the type of love he epitomized. In *My Religion*, Tolstoy writes:

Almost from the first period of my childhood, when I began to read the New Testament, I was touched and stirred . . . by that portion of the doctrine of Christ which inculcates love, humility, self-denial, and the duty of returning good for evil. This, to me, has always been the substance of Christianity; it was what I loved in it with all my heart.

Tolstoy found disagreeable the dogma of institutionalized Christianity, which he believed strayed far from the teachings and practice of Christ. He says he was "driven from the Church by the strangeness of its dogmas, and the approval and support which it gave to persecutions, to the death penalty, to wars, and by the intolerance common to all sects." But he was never driven away from Christianity itself and what he saw as its ennobling tenets of unconditional love.

A *NEWSWEEK* ARTICLE on the Reverend Billy Graham notes that his version of evangelism is one "rooted in decades of reflection on the virtues of faith, hope and love—love for all God's creatures." It quotes Graham as saying that his life "has been a pilgrimage—constantly learning, changing, growing and maturing," with the result being that he has "come to see in deeper ways some of the implications of my faith and message, not the least of which is in the area of human rights and racial and ethnic understanding." This was the version of Christian love that Tolstoy also embraced, and that he and Graham believe was practiced by Jesus.

For God's Sake

The Old Testament offers one of the most unforgettable examples of unconditional love—not of God for man, but of a man for God. The

Book of Job relates that no matter how utterly God forsakes Job, his most faithful and righteous son, no matter the hurts that God heaps upon him as he takes away his health, his wealth, his loved ones, Job's love for God remains steadfast. That Job cried out in anguish and bewilderment—"Oh God, why have you forsaken me?"—in no way reflects that his love for God is wavering in the slightest, but rather that he is in anguish that he apparently has been forsaken by one he himself could never forsake.

The punishments leveled on Job were for no sin he committed. Thus he reluctantly concludes that his omnipotent God is not wholly beneficent, but capricious: "The Lord giveth, and the Lord taketh away." Job is suffering simply because God wants him to, testing whether he will still love Him when he is tormented relentlessly for no reason. God has His doubts about the fortitude and steadfastness of Job's heart, but Job passes the test. Job's revelations about God's nature do not drive him away from his love of or faith in Him, but amazingly serve to deepen his love and show just how unconditional it is.

Danish existentialist philosopher Soren Kierkegaard (1813–1855) notes that in the very worst of times, when "Job's house was a house of sorrow," Job nonetheless continued to love and extol God: "Blessed be the name of the Lord." Kierkegaard lauds Job as "a teacher of men who had no doctrine to pass on to others, but who merely left himself as a pattern to succeeding generations, his life as a principle of guidance . . . his own deeds as an encouragement to the striving."

THE CONCEPTION OF God depicted in the Book of Job is similar to the conception that the Greeks of antiquity had for their gods, who in their almightiness could be vain and thin-skinned and capricious, capable of doing as much harm as good as they strove to see whether the human heart would remain good and loving no matter what befell them. Whereas humans came to understand the nature of God or their gods, the converse is not true: humans were forever capable of surprising their gods by doing the unpredictable, and continuing to love them even when they did nothing to deserve it. Job, for one, showed his God that he was worthy of His erstwhile beneficence by loving him just as unconditionally when treated hatefully as when treated lovingly.

Job does question God's actions and motives; he does wonder why God would allow the guiltless, the pure, to suffer so. Job does have his own ideas of how the world should be, of how the righteous should be treated—but he accepts God's will unconditionally, loving him just as much, just the same. Job stays the course of love in love-less times.

SOCRATES SEEMED TO consider the question: How should one comport oneself in a world in which there is senseless suffering? His answer: one should be more loving than ever, especially when the one suffering senselessly is oneself. He did not lash out at man or immortal when unjustly sentenced to die. He did not cry out in embitterment or anguish. His approach to living and dying was such that no matter how just or unjust events were that befell him, he would remain true to exhibiting and cultivating the type of love that he believed made existence a blessing. Like French philosopher Simone Weil, he believed that it was in a world in which there was a dearth or absence of love that one should be more loving than ever, or love would wither on the vine.

SOCRATIC AGAPE HAS elements of what the Hindus would call *karuna*, a love based on the ideals of showing mercy and compassion, even to the merciless and those without compassion. Socrates was devoted to bringing out the divine love he believed was within us all—a type of love of which we ourselves, not the gods, were the source and conduit.

Prayer

Walter Kaufmann, the late social philosopher from Princeton noted for making Friedrich Nietzsche an official member of the academic philosophic canon, was raised in a Protestant family in Germany. He decided on his own to convert to Judaism—not knowing at the time that his parents had converted from Judaism to Protestantism. When Hitler came to power in Germany and Kaufmann, then a teenager, came to the United States, he planned to become an orthodox rabbi. But he eventually left his faith, though he never abandoned his love for religion and the timeless lessons be learned from it.

> The conception of gods provides a setting for an aspiration that reaches out beyond all physical objects. It makes possible a language in which superhuman love and gratitude, despair and grief, can be expressed. A heart fuller than seems warranted by any event in this world can relate itself to the divine and voice passions that seem to transcend human relations. In prayer . . . [p]assionate feelings, inhibited in speech with others, find an outlet in jubilations, thanksgiving, complaints, and accusations for which suddenly there is an ear. . . .

However, such sentiments as those Kaufmann says provoke prayer are not superhuman, but extremes of human emotion that demand an uncommon outlet in order to give full expression. One need not subscribe to any conception of or belief in gods to pray in the manner he describes and for the reasons he elaborates. One may cry out to the universe in uncontainable grief or joy, perplexity or despair, without seeking in any way to transcend human relations but rather to deepen them. Although Kaufmann says prayer is "an intensity of devotion [that] can be achieved which in a dialogue with other human beings would scarcely ever be possible," prayer itself can be a poetic and cathartic form of dialogue—putting one in touch not with a transcendent divine but bringing out and giving voice to the divine within.

When my mother was stricken with cancer, I prayed in my way, though I'd long ago left the religious traditions of my mother and father—Methodist and Greek Orthodox, respectively. I prayed because no other kind of response would do—not because my heart was fuller than seemed warranted but because such fullness of heart was surely warranted for one I loved immeasurably. My prayer was a response that gave voice to this fullness.

Eternal Love

In addition to all his work in the abstract and sometimes abstruse field of logic, the Nobel laureate Bertrand Russell also lived with great heart; he was an outspoken and passionate advocate and activist for world peace, human rights, and social justice. Yet he never deemed that a man's deeds could outlive his own mortal span. The logical premises that served as the parameters for Russell's worldview would not permit such a perspective. Russell wrote in the celebrated essay "A Free Man's Worship" that

> no fire, no heroism, no intensity of thought and feeling, can preserve an individual life beyond the grave. . . . [A]ll the labors of the ages, all the devotion, all the inspiration, all the noonday brightness of human genius, are destined to extinction. . . .

But this view belies the fact that Russell himself was deeply influenced by the likes of Socrates and the Buddha, whose "heroism," whose "intensity of thought and feeling," not only "preserve[d] an individual life beyond the grave" but perpetuated it, inspiring people of disparate cultures and traditions ever since to live in ways such that their acts of love, no matter how short or long their mortal life span, would continue ad infinitum. Although it is true that the intentions of most are such that their doings in the world begin and end with their own conscious moment—because once they are gone, they will not be able to continue to reap personal gain—there have always been those exemplary humans—including Russell himself, though he tried to argue against this—who have operated from a different set of ideals and motives, who have a logic of a different color; their love is as close to eternal love as human love can get.

There is a vignette recounted by editor Al Seckel in a collection of Russell's essays on ethics that recounts something Russell told his wife: "the universe is unjust" and "the secret of happiness is to face the fact that the world is horrible, horrible, horrible," and that only once you accept this brute fact can you "start being happy again."

Socrates, on the other hand, believed that the universe, even in its most unjust and horrible moments, was essentially good, and that it was a wonderful thing to be alive; the secret of happiness was to grasp that every moment—particularly, perhaps, the moment one died, and the way one went about it—was an opportunity to bring about the change one wanted to see in the world.

Karl Jaspers notes that Socrates, just before his death, sets an unforgettably great example:

> where consuming sorrow seems in place, there springs [from Socrates] the great, loving peace which opens the soul. Death has lost its meaning. It is not veiled over, but the authentic life is not a life toward death; it is a life toward the good.

Or a life toward love—so much so, as Jaspers points out, that even "in his last moments. . . . [Socrates] is lovingly aware of every living human reality." If he had not gone about dying as he had gone about living, he would not have set an abiding example for his co-inquirers. His death was the catalyst for a "recasting of their own hearts," so that from there on out they "would leave the Athenians no peace." They would not join the herd and become false prophets who cry "peace, peace" when there is no peace. Much less would he have become for posterity "the Socrates who has stirred men ever since," who thought and lived in such a way that "does not permit a man to close himself" but instead "opens men's minds and invites the risks of openness." But Jaspers should also have noted that to become genuinely open to a variety of human experiences, one must have an open heart, as did Socrates. As Jaspers wrote:

> Where the influence of Socrates is felt, men convince themselves in freedom; they do not subscribe to articles of faith. Here we find friendship in the movement of truth, not sectarianism in dogma. In the clarity of human possibility, Socrates meets the Other as an equal. He wants no disciples.

Yet Socrates does "point to pathways that we too can travel" if we take his quest for cultivating a passionate heart for our own.

The Rhythm of Love

Hazrat Inayat Khan, the first Sufi master of the West, was brought up in a family of musicians. Khan himself became a premier player of classical Indian music, for which he gained renown even in his local environs, which teemed with accomplished musicians. At the behest and encouragement of his spiritual teacher, he traveled to the West "to harmonize the East and West with the harmony of [his] music." Over time, Khan came to realize that the thread that connects everything in every dimension of our world—existential, mystical, physical, moral—is rhythm. Everything has a rhythm of a sort, and what one must do, he theorized, was strive to discover how to bring these rhythms into harmony.

In his timeless work *The Music of Life*, Khan writes that "the whole universe is a single mechanism working by the law of rhythm." He does not mean that this reduces the universe to some sort of mechanical, clockwork entity that can be understood only by ever greater scientific reductionism. Rather, the epiphany that rhythm was nature's "hidden law" led to a transformation in Khan's approach to life, such that

> every soul became for me a musical note. . . . Now . . . I harmonize people instead of notes. If there is anything in my philosophy, it is the law of harmony: that one must put oneself in harmony with oneself and with others.
>
> What repulses us or attracts us in a person . . . is his rhythm. One person is rhythmic, and his influence is soothing; another is out of rhythm, and he upsets everybody.

Even a so-called right action can go awry if the person carrying out the action is out of rhythm with himself and his world. For instance, if someone with good intentions declares to a person who is treating others in an unnecessarily angry and combative way, "You have done wrong," unthinkingly believing that the direct approach is always the best, all he may succeed in doing is fanning that person's rage even more rather than calming him down, much less supplanting his hateful rhythm with a loving one. Such a person, to Khan, "has failed to put his empathetic rhythm in sync with the person with whom he is interacting." He is also out of tune with himself; not only is he blind to the underlying problems of the person in a rage, he is not in touch with his own reasons for acting as he does, and with his own underlying hopes and desires, fears and frustrations. As a consequence, according to Khan, he can have no real idea whether his act will do more harm than good. Indeed, he cannot even know if his act is well-intentioned, because there has been no proper self-examination, there has been no attempt to ask and answer questions such as, Why is that person angry? Might it be constructive anger, even anger motivated out of love? Why would I calm down such a person? How might

I best do so? What do I need to understand about this angry soul to change his disposition? What do I need to understand about my own soul, my own intentions and dispositions?

If we make no effort to gain genuine insight into the person we are confronting or encountering, in tandem with confronting ourselves, we are tone deaf to the rhythms at play. So, in Khan's view, we cannot be of service because we have not made it our life's work to be a "master of rhythm." Socrates, too, in a conversation with his youthful friend Glaucon, said he believed that we can never know how to help a person if we first don't take the time to discover what he first really needs, and lacks. Only then are we equipped to do what Greek observational philosopher Aristotle, following Socrates, characterizes as knowing when and how "to be angry with the right person, to the right degree, at the right time, for the right purpose, and in the right way." He might have added, when and how to show love.

Gift of Life

In the Greek classic *Alcestis*, by playwright Euripides, Socrates' contemporary, Admetos, king of Thessaly, will die of a terminal illness unless he can find someone else willing to die in his stead; then the gods will reverse his fate and allow him to go on living. No one in the city will exchange his life for that of the king except his young wife, Alcestis. The mother of their children, in the flower of her years, without a moment's hesitation accedes to his request—an act of unconditional love if ever there was one.

The chorus asks, "What other woman, anywhere on Earth, would do what she has done?" and remarks that although you often "hear men and women swear they love somebody more than themselves," those are "easy words," and "proof of the oath is hard."

The playwright emphasizes that none of his kingdom's elderly, not

even Admetos' own ancient mother and father, "two walking cadav-
ers" as they are described in Ted Hughes' translation, would give up
their lives for the king, even though they will meet their maker any
day themselves. Who is to say whose life is more valuable? Is someone's life less so just because she has lived more years? Or can that
make it more precious, depending on how she has lived it, and what
wisdom she might have to impart?

Way of the Warrior

"We are here . . . to be warriors!"

The sudden transformation in voice and bearing of the diminutive
and frail eighty-nine-year-old woman startles me—but no one else
gathered with us. I am encircled by a sizable group in Soweto township in South Africa, a country of 45 million that in 1961 gained its
independence from the United Kingdom, then became known as the
Republic of South Africa. Soweto, a short distance from the nation's
chief industrial and economic center of Johannesburg, was created by
the apartheid regime to keep the area's growing black population—
made up largely of workers and their families who had come here
from outlying provinces in hope of greater economic opportunities—
cordoned off from the opulent white neighborhoods nearby.

We are on Vilakazi Street, on the very block where the renowned
Soweto uprising was fomented to break the yoke of systematic
oppression of black South Africans. This is the only street in the world
where there resided two Nobel Peace Prize winners, the anti-apartheid leaders Nelson Mandela and Bishop Desmond Tutu. Bishop
Tutu still makes his home with his wife here in Soweto, a township
with a current population of about 3.5 million. Just down the block is
Nelson Mandela's tiny frame home—still riddled with bullet holes,
chilling reminders of numerous attempts by Afrikaner police to assas-

sinate him. The house is now a museum to which visitors flock from all parts of the globe.

On June 16, 1976, about 30,000 black students from Soweto schools and universities gathered on this block for a peaceful protest in opposition to a new government policy that would have made Afrikaans, the language of their oppressors, which their own teachers did not even speak, the only permissible language for school instruction. The Afrikaner police shot tear gas and bullets into the crowd, and shortly thereafter, thirteen-year-old protester Hector Pieterson was killed. The effect was the precise opposite of what the police anticipated; it hardened the protesters' resolve. As the day progressed and word of the killing spread, the students were joined by children and the rest of the members of their community, including the elderly, in facing down the police. By day's end, twenty-three demonstrators were killed by official government count, though it is estimated that the actual death toll approached or exceeded two hundred. The violent police action sparked nationwide protests, which did not end until the apartheid regime itself came to an end, nearly two decades and thousands of lost lives later.

AN ELDERLY WOMAN, Siboniso, is the first to respond to my question "Why are we here?" she has just attended an "after tears" gathering. "Since the uprising first began, this has been the day of the week we've buried our dead," she says to me on this Saturday, three days before the tenth anniversary of the National Freedom Day celebration, when South Africa rid itself of apartheid.

"The grandmother and Zulu warrior we buried today lived to witness nearly a decade of freedom for her homeland. She was with all us grandmothers on the front lines, fighting for freedom. We put our bodies in front of our young ones so we'd take the bullet in their place, hoping they would live to see a better day. Like all of us, her reason for being, her 'why,' was to risk everything for freedom—for the sake of her children and grandchildren, but also her ancestors. A true warrior never really dies, because she has given her life to her people, her heritage. There's no separation between the past, the present, and the hereafter for a warrior. Even if we'd all died, the universe would still pulse with our story."

"We stood tall," says her ninety-one-year-old cousin. "My name, Zindzhi, *means* 'warrior.' You strike a woman, you strike a rock. The Afrikaners thought we would break. But we were the movement's secret weapon. We feared nothing. We have been raised since our infancy in the warrior tradition."

She then says to me, "It is good you asked 'Why are we here?' rather than 'Why am I here?' because, to a warrior, there is no 'I' apart from 'we.' To a warrior, like Siboniso said, physical death is nothing to fear, because your spirit, your deeds, your love and courage live on forever."

"A warrior's ultimate why, then, is to risk her life selflessly in the name of her heritage?" I ask.

Says ninety-eight-year-old Paki as he strokes his snow-white beard, "Selflessly but not needlessly. A warrior does give his or her life to the tribe, not just in combat but in everyday life, teaching the younger members our language, our culture, our values and ways. One of our core values is to act wisely, never to sacrifice our lives, never to take anyone else's life needlessly, not even that of your brutal oppressor."

He smiles a bit sheepishly. "I haven't always acted as wisely as I ought," he admits. He pulls up his shirt and shows me a scar from a bullet wound. "At the *doye doye*, the protests, a white policeman came up to me and said that I should be glad that he didn't shoot me, because I was just a cockroach. I slapped him. This is what I got in return. I slapped him quicker than thought, on behalf of all my people.

"Today, I regret I slapped him," he says. "Our principal tribal belief is that physical force should be a last resort, that moral and intellectual force must be our primary weapons over brute force."

Ayize, in his late thirties, says with exasperation, "Where is this moral and intellectual force now? Why isn't it being deployed on behalf of all those still left out of the new South Africa? Our leaders might as well tell us young people, based on how they neglect us, 'You have no why any longer. You have served your purpose, now go away.' We have no education, no skills, no jobs. We still live in shanties, without sewage, water, or electricity.

"Because of the way we've been treated, we don't ask, 'Why are we here?' but instead, 'Are we here?' We're invisible. I was a warrior, as were my friends here, like all the grandmothers and grandfathers here. Yet our leaders who called on us to abandon our educations and take to the streets, who now control the government purse strings, have not fulfilled their promises to us."

An article in *Africa Today* says that "[t]en years into liberation . . . the slums and shanty towns of urban South Africa proliferate and the racial and class divides are even more sharply accentuated," with the "misery index" for black South Africans "as grim as ever and decent employment as well as educational empowerment . . . the illusory pipe dream they were under apartheid." *Time* magazine reports that "too much still remains the same" since the end of apartheid. Although all the nation's citizens are free "to move where they want, say what they want, vote for the party they want," the reality is that "huge divisions remain between white and black, rich and poor, urban and rural."

Says Ayize's friend Mosala, also in his thirties, "Sometimes it seems these days there's almost as many divisions between blacks and blacks as between blacks and whites. I know you can't remedy generations of inequality in just ten years. Some black South Africans who now live the good life, who work for the new government or receive grants from it, have turned their backs on the rest of us. They've forgotten the warrior tradition, that ours is a collective 'why.' There's still a battle to be waged and won—a battle for opportunity and equality for us all—so we all have a 'why,' a reason for being." Mosala looks at Ayize, then at me and says, "Everyone here knows that my friends and I steal cars to survive. We go into Johannesburg and steal from the whites. We feel now that our primary 'why' is our own self-preservation. Bishop Tutu said ours is now 'the Rainbow nation'. But black still isn't a color in the rainbow, and until it is I can't answer the question 'Why are we here?' "

Says Ayize, "So many of the whites who remained here after apartheid still live with the same wealth, with their mansions and barbed wire fences." He points to the palatial residences on a hill in the distance. "Decades ago, they built water and sewage systems, strung up telephone wires and electricity cables, that went to their homes but circumvented Soweto. They're still permitted to live outside society, so they are being denied the opportunity to feel part of the 'collective why' that's supposed to be what the new South Africa is all about—all for one and one for all."

Comments Mosala, "With the end of apartheid, all of us, black and white, were supposed to feel like we're in this together, that ours is a shared why. But the disparities just grow. Crime is soaring. Poverty and disease are rampant. I'm one of millions of South Africans who is HIV positive yet has no access to drugs. Where are the leaders whose why is to take care of the weak and vulnerable, so we can have lives of meaningful purpose?"

According to *Time* magazine, South Africa has "the dismal distinction of having more HIV-positive citizens than any country in the world: more than 5 million, or one of every nine people. Complaints of government foot-dragging come from all fronts."

Eventually, Siboniso tells me, "Everything he says is true, and it is so important that those left out continued to speak up and out. It is what Nelson Mandela himself would want them to do. We have a special name for Nelson Mandela—*Madiba*, which means 'father of the people' in the language of his Tembu tribe, of which his father was chief. Even though he's officially 'retired' now, he's still our conscience. He points out that none of us has taken the high road altogether—especially when it comes to how despicably and with what prejudice South Africans of all classes and colors have treated those who have AIDS.

"Madiba's own son, fifty-four-year-old Makgatho, died recently of AIDS. Madiba tells us that unless we cherish and treat as equals not only all our brothers and sisters with AIDS, but all who are still left out of the 'rainbow,' then we'll never be all we can be as a people, and so we'll diminish our shared 'why.' He insists that we face openly all our prejudices and shortcomings, especially the stigma still attached to those who suffer the tragedy of AIDS."

Says a man named Sehloho after a while, "I am filled with admiration for these warriors from Soweto." His particular comment, at this juncture of the dialogue, coupled with his boisterous good nature, clearly seem incongruous to the other participants.

He then says, "I myself am a warrior from KwaZulu-Natal province. I came here months ago to find good work and make a better life for myself and my family, now that we blacks are free to live and travel wherever we choose to. Conditions are miserable back home—and, yes, they are challenging here too. But I was brought up to believe that if I enter the world under poor and wretched circumstances, I should blame no one, and I should feel no self-pity. My creator thought so highly of me, and thought I had such inner strength, that he was sure I could overcome the harshest obstacles—and in doing so inspire my brothers and sisters to do the same.

"It's my obligation to my creator to fulfill this 'why' of mine, to show him that he was justified in his high expectations of me. I will one day be boss of a big company, with a fine house and a big yard for my children—my creator's reward for my persistence in the face of all obstacles."

This final comment doesn't sit well with one participant, a precocious fifteen-year-old named Mandi. "Are we here just to see to it that we all can have what the whites here have enjoyed for so long?" she says, looking at us one after the other as she speaks. Few are able to hold her penetrating gaze for long. "Or are we here to create a new type of society? My friends say they're so happy now that they have the same right as whites to go to the shopping malls and eat at McDonald's. They don't care about our higher purpose to their heritage, or to those who come after. They just live for personal enjoyment, here and now.

"We need to continue to be warriors," Mandi says. "We need to continue to fight for opportunity for all our people, here and in the rest of Africa, but to build a new type of sharing and caring and loving society. If we don't, what would our ancestors say? What would my parents who died during the protests say? What will history say, if all we do is see as our 'why' to become like people everywhere else?"

Loving Tradition

Ghanaian philosopher Kwame Gyekye, who received his PhD in philosophy from Harvard, believes that a culture's ability to evolve a more humanitarian set of moral imperatives hinges on "its capacity . . . to adopt itself to new situations and demands . . . its capacity to constitute itself into a credible and viable framework for human fulfillment." Gyekye writes in *Beyond Cultures: Perceiving a Common Humanity*, that indigenous African cultures, with all their flaws, offer by far the best "framework that enables its participants to flourish," because traditional societies strive to create "an adequate social setting for human fulfillment." Gyekye believes that emerging democracies in African nations need look no further than their own indigenous traditions and adopt them to today's needs. Gyekye points to a traditional indigenous proverb that says, "A person cutting a path does not know that the part that he has cleared behind him is crooked," which means that it is up to the generations that follow to "take a critical look at their cultural heritage with a view to eliminating or amending the 'crooked' . . . aspects of that heritage."

Although the limitations of any particular epoch or society make it impossible for any culture to claim that it has come up with the best value system and cultural practices, not just here and now but forever, Gyekye asserts that what matters most is that a given culture continually strive to achieve the ends of promoting the well-being of all humans—not just those within its culture but everywhere, acting in ways that strive to ever widen the circle of inclusivity. In doing so, it will have displayed a "morality of a shared humanity."

Gyekye notes that all cultures that share this ethos will obviously have at least somewhat different takes on how best to grapple with the most pressing human problems they face, not just because they have different cultural dynamics but because they have varying resources and capacities with which to address these problems. Nonetheless, he points out, traditional cultures in places as far flung as Greece and Asia and Africa aimed in their singular ways to further the material and mental well-being of humans. Modern cultures across the globe, he says, must again strive, singly and together, to achieve the original aims of human culture.

Madiba

In his biography, Anthony Sampson attributes Nelson Mandela's ability to emerge from his twenty-seven-year imprisonment in Robbens Island without any telltale "signs of the familiar deformations of power" because of "the fortitude and resilience" of his fellow African National Congress (ΛNC) inmates, who, like him, believed only in achievements for the good of their community as a whole. But just as important a factor was the difficult and daunting journey of self-confrontation that Mandela embarked on while behind bars. It was a journey in which a happy outcome was by no means assured. Surely Mandela's strong familial-type ties to his fellow inmates were critical to his successful struggle, but also critical was his desire to live up to his own father's high ideals of the paradigmatic figure that a tribal leader must be—for his immediate tribe and, in adherence with the dictates of his worldview, the tribe of all humans—that enabled Mandela to face up to his demons and grow into the person

who left Robbens Island as one whom the entire citizenry could identify—to such an extent that his story became, as Sampson writes, "the
nation's story."

BISHOP DESMOND TUTU, Mandela's former neighbor in Soweto
and fellow winner of the Nobel Peace Prize, writes that Mandela's
"ghastly suffering" during his nearly three decades in prison was "not
a waste" by any stretch. The Nelson Mandela who entered prison was
unrecognizable from the one who exited. When he first was confined,
Mandela was a young man justifiably angry with the many unjust
wrongs perpetrated on his people, himself unjustly sentenced for daring to demand that the oppressed of his nation be given the same
rights that in most of the civilized world are considered inalienable. In
Mandela's prison years, Tutu says he "began to discover depths of
resilience and spiritual attributes" which in part sprang from his new-
found ability to accept and even appreciate the weaknesses and faults
of others. First, he had to see them in himself. It was this frank recognition that he had many of these traits himself that led his inspired
cultivation of compassion and gentleness. Consequently, his prison
years proved invaluable in his metamorphosis into the nation's moral
and political leader, inspiring the vast majority of South Africans of
all ethnicities and backgrounds to come to view one another "as
brothers and sisters." Tutu stresses that such a societal transformation
did not come about without considerable effort: "fights with our family are often the most vicious," because it is human nature that "we get
upset the most with those we love the most."

IN HIS AUTOBIOGRAPHY, Mandela writes that "out of the experience of an extraordinary human disaster . . . must be born a society of
which humanity will be proud." He said that "the doors of the world
have opened precisely because of our success in achieving things that
humanity as a whole holds dear." More accurate would have been for

him to say that South Africa is achieving things that the rest of humanity *should* hold dear, and often claims to but rarely has, judging from its concrete actions. To do this, Mandela himself achieved something that humans rarely do; he engaged in and emerged from a harrowing self-examination that makes or breaks a person. For Mandela, much more than his own personal growth was at stake; the evolution of his nation hinged on his ability to see his enemies every bit as much as his allies as his people if he was to play the pivotal post-apartheid role in South Africa that was expected of him.

Mandela was influenced considerably by Martinique-born black social philosopher Frantz Fanon (1925–1961)—who fought against the pro-Nazi Vichy government, and in the 1950s took part in the Algerian liberation movement, after which he served as that country's ambassador to Ghana. Fanon warned in his seminal book *The Wretched of the Earth* that there loomed the real possibility that long-subjugated indigenous Africans, once liberated, could end up undermining their own liberation if, upon gaining freedom, they did not dispense with the vestiges of the master-slave mentality. Fanon believed that the only way to avoid this pitfall was if all those engaged in liberation movements sought, from the outset, to forge a new collective identity for themselves—one comprising the most humanizing elements of their traditional indigenous moral-cultural heritage. This, he maintained, was the most promising route for sculpting a national consciousness that effaced all vestiges of colonialism. To create such an identity, Nelson Mandela believed that he first had to be a liberation movement of one, freeing himself from self-imposed subjugation.

To Mandela, the pivotal act of reconciliation was not principally the Truth and Reconciliation Commission he helped spearhead, but the dissipation of the vestiges of the practical attitudes of apartheid—among blacks and whites but within them as individuals as well, and this required self-reconciliation. He asserted that without self-understanding, reconciliation ultimately would prove "transient, the ode of false hope on the lips of fools." From the moment he walked out of prison, Mandela was determined to free from their shackles both oppressed and oppressor, because otherwise he himself would never be genuinely free. For to Mandela, being free "is not merely to cast off one's chains, but to live in a way that respects and enhances the freedom of others." According to Mandela, "A man who takes away another man's freedom is a prisoner of hatred; he is locked behind the bars of pure justice and narrow-mindedness." Mandela unlocked himself from such bars, showing how unfettered love for self and for others went hand in glove. By doing so, he set his nation free, allowing its citizens to come together by choice as a radically new type of tribe of which his ancestors would be proud, what with their cultivation of ancestral values based on mutual warmth and empathy.

Ikigai *Arrested*

"I'm not comfortable discussing this question," Keiko says adamantly. She seems to carry authority with the rest of those gathered with us; they stay silent, all looking downward.

I've just posed the question "What makes life worth living?" It looks as though the dialogue will end before it has begun. But then Sadao, a businessman on lunch break sitting on a bench adjacent to those we occupy—and who at first had looked annoyed that we'd encroached on his tranquility—says, "No, this is a question we Japanese need to discuss."

Looking askance at the woman who thinks otherwise, he says to me, "We have a term in Japanese called *ikigai*. It means literally 'that which makes life worth living.' *Ikigai* is the fundamental driving force of our society. What happened here happened because we had horribly misplaced and misguided *ikigai*."

We are gathered in Hiroshima Peace Park, seated near the epicenter where, on August 6, 1945, the American B29 bomber *Enola Gay* dropped an atomic bomb and detonated it 1,500 feet above the Earth.

After a second atomic bomb was dropped on Nagasaki, the Japanese surrendered, and World War II ended. By the end of 1945, more than a third of Hiroshima's inhabitants had died; tens of thousands more died in ensuing years from radiation sickness. The only structure that was not completely decimated here at ground zero is just behind us, its twisted steel dome left untouched.

Keiko, forty-two, who had voiced her opposition to this question, now sighs and says, "Well, deep down, I agree we need to discuss this question. Yet if I ask myself 'What is my *ikigai*?' then I have to question the way I'm living now, and that makes me very uncomfortable."

She shortly goes on to say, "My husband has a good secure job as a financial analyst. I'm a traditional housewife and mother. I always thought I'd be a real nonconformist. But I'm more conformist than my parents. So I try not to think anymore about *ikigai*, because that makes me think about my youth, when *all* I thought about was *ikigai*, and how I was going to make a great difference in the whole world as an artist and activist.

"I was so passionate, so in love with life," she says, her voice breaking with emotion. "In our culture, there are two types of love. One is *koy*, which is 'the beginning of love,' like your first romance with another person or with life in general. Then there's *jyo-netsu-tek-na-ay*, a higher form of love, which means 'loving passion.' You're so in love with the world, and all those in the world with you, that you have this passionate conviction to do everything within your capacity to make the world itself a place that reflects your love."

She looks around at us and says, "For most Japanese today, this second stage no longer comes to pass. Its development is arrested, because we've settled for so much less than we should. We live lives of passion, but our only commitment is to our self-gratification. This base passion is a type of love, *geki-jyo*, but it is purely reckless and selfish. It is heedless about how it affects others. This is the type of love I know that I am as guilty of pursuing as most Japanese.

"So when you asked this question, I almost wanted to run from here. But now I want to think about this question some more. Because

I want to figure out how I can recapture the *jyo-netsu-tek-na-ay* I once had, so my 'loving passion' will rub off on my children, and they will make a difference in the world."

"*Ikigai* can also be translated as 'worth of life,' " says Takako, also a housewife and mother, after a considerable pause. "But it's a *kind* of life worth that implies reaching out to others. We have a word for love of family, *kazokuay*, and a separate word for love of country, *aykokushin*. The literal translation of these would be 'heart for family' and 'heart for country.' I'm wondering now if you can really love your family or country as much as possible if you don't also have great 'heart for the world.' During World War II, we had 'heart for country' and 'heart for family,' but a fanatical type in which we saw ourselves as superior to the rest of the world, and destined to lord over everybody else. We'd duped ourselves into thinking it was a noble *ikigai* when it was just the opposite.

"Today, the pendulum has swung in just the opposite direction, and none of us would give our lives for our country. We only live for ourselves, our immediate family and small group of friends, and close our hearts off to everyone and everything else, as if nothing outside our narrow bounds has worth. This seems a form of fanaticism, in its way, and I'm thinking now about whether it has 'negative worth.' Because if we had the right kind of 'loving passion,' which is the source of all true *ikigai*, we would also be thinking constantly about how to act in the world in ways that make everyone better off—maybe starting off with family and country, but always trying to widen the circle so it includes more and more of the world."

"Many aren't even committed to family anymore," says Takako's friend Kazu. "Divorce rates are skyrocketing."

An Associated Press report that came out around the time of my visit says that Japan's divorce rate has risen "to a record high . . . reflecting an increasing number of middle-aged and older couples who are parting ways."

She goes on, "Extramarital affairs are rampant. We have thousands of detective agencies whose specialties are spying on families—either on spouses suspected of cheating, or children suspected of doing the most horrible things. Our society is like a soap opera, about sordid pleasure and intrigue. We claim that marriage and family are sacrosanct, but it's not true. The only sacrosanct thing is 'me me me.'"

There is a pensive and somewhat tense silence before Sadao shares with us: "As a 'company man,' I'm indoctrinated to believe that my work should be my *ikigai*. Everything changed when my daughter was born.

"I'm an executive at one of our major banks. Every night, after a twelve- to fourteen-hour workday, I go out with my colleagues to one of the clubs nearby for drinks and to watch the women dance. It's expected of us. But nowadays, I leave as soon as I can excuse myself. I just want to be at home with my precious child."

He closes his briefcase and puts it aside, then says to us, "*Ikigai* has so much meaning packed into it. It also means 'the source of power to live.' My daughter is that source for me. She makes me want to be a knight in shining armor, to do pure good for the world, so the world she'll grow up in will be one of people filled with loving passion and commitment for one another. So my 'heart' for my child gives me greater 'heart' for the world at large.

"Now I'm committed to making Hiroshima a better place. I want to serve her, be of service to her—but in the opposite way of our typical tradition of *amae*, Japanese for the indulgent love of [parents for their child] so the child will then be dependent and subservient to us. No, I want to create a world that gives my child the conditions to soar, with no reciprocity. This is the love of *ai*, the type espoused by Japanese Buddhists, which is selfless and yet comes out of passionate love, in my case out of passionate caring for my child and a passionate desire to make the world a better place for her."

He goes on. "All of the geisha district in Hiroshima that was decimated by the bomb has not just been replaced, but expanded. It reflects the lower, reckless types of passions people have today. I'm spearheading a movement in my neighborhood to protest plans to build a gambling house there. This is one small thing I'm trying to 'do good' now, even though I must say that I'm doing so at risk of advancement in my career, since my company frowns on what I'm doing. But I do it even so, for my daughter."

"Can love of work ever be your most passionate and loving way of demonstrating how much you value all people, and that you're doing your utmost to make everyone's life more worth living?" I ask.

"It can be, yes," says Haruhide, who had joined us soon after we began, after seeing that we had expropriated the area to which he normally retreats during lunchtime. "A few old-timers who run our corporations still believe theirs to be a noble *ikigai*. I'm auditing a firm that is in terrible financial straits. I told the owner point-blank that he had to let go hundreds of employees. He refused. He said he would rather go into bankruptcy, even fold the entire company, than lay off a single employee, because of the commitment he'd made to give them work for life. At a time when most companies will do whatever is necessary to stay afloat, he still operates from the belief that if a company can't take care of its own, then it doesn't deserve to exist. His *ikigai* is to take care of those he has made a commitment to, because in his view they're his extended family."

"For me, if I'm to fulfill my noble *ikigai*, I must advance in my professional career," says Akashi, thirty-eight. "I have to work and battle ten times as hard as my colleagues. But I do so not just to achieve a high professional status for selfish reasons, but so in the long run I'll be in a position of greater influence to improve the plight of those of my fellow Burakumin, who face the worst kinds of discrimination here just because of their ethnicity."

The Buraku, a minority ethnic group in Japan, have been victims of harrassment and discrimination since the seventeenth century, when they were considered "untouchable" and were forced to live as virtual slaves. Today, there are about 3 million Japanese of Buraku ethnicity. Despite the country's antidiscrimination laws, which were enacted in the 1960s, they still face inordinate hurdles in assimilating into mainstream society.

Makio, a schoolteacher, has joined us after seeing our careworn sign that has, "Welcome to Socrates Café" in numerous languages, including Japanese. Cecilia and I tote it with us around the world when we hold spontaneous dialogues in public settings. Makio is waiting for his sixth grade charges visiting the nearby Peace Museum. He says, "I· also derive most of my sense of worth, my noble *ikigai*, from my work. The most loving thing I can do for my country is make sure the children under my wing receive the kind of education that sees to it they never fall sway to prejudice, racism, and fanaticism.

"That's becoming more difficult to accomplish," he tells us. "The new directives from our Ministry of Education have eliminated moral education as a mandate. Their priority is to educate children to compete in the business world. Our only task as teachers is to enable them to pass with flying colors the highly competitive standardized tests, so they can matriculate into the best technical and business universities."

"Even so," Makio continues, "I still try to incorporate some class time for thinking and reflecting, in the context of our *dowa*, or 'peace,' education program here in Hiroshoma, which is aimed at preventing discrimination, particularly against the Burakumin, and at building bridges of peace."

Until now, Kaoru, eighty-one, has been silent. Now she says with considerable passion, "I applaud what our education ministry is doing. They're only trying to reinstill discipline among our young people. Children can't have *ikigai* if they don't have boundaries. At home, there's no discipline; parents are so permissive. My grandchildren are spoiled little monsters. Training children to become productive members of society, as our ministry wants, is the best—and last—hope that they will become moral beings."

Just before my visit to Japan, Prime Minister Junichiro Koizumi convened his full cabinet to discuss the growing problem of youth crime. A *New York Times* article quoted one high-ranking government official lamenting that "[a]mong the youths the basic notion of not being a nuisance to others has declined, and adults are responsible for that. There are many parents who won't admit their kids' wrongdoings. They say, 'Why pick on my child?' Parents used to apologize: 'I failed to raise and discipline my child properly.'

Kaoru's best friend, Urui, also eighty-one, is dressed in a traditional kimono. She nods and says to me, mystified and outraged, "A teenager stole my bike. You might not realize what a serious transgression this is. Until recently, no one would ever think of stealing someone's bike. It just isn't done. But the old values are disappearing. The only love among the young is love of self-gratification, of cheap thrills, even stealing what isn't yours, if it gives you a rush. Our ministry is just trying to teach children discipline and respect, which are the values that make life most worth living. The values children have today—that society owes them everything and they owe society nothing—are counterproductive to *ikigai*."

As if they had been waiting offstage to join our dialogue on cue, a group of elementary-grade Japanese schoolchildren suddenly approach after seeing our sign.

When I tell them about the question we are discussing, one boy, Mamoru, who has come here from the historic city of Kyoto, says to me, "To know your *ikigai*, you have to come to this park and go to the Peace Museum, which tells about the horrible bomb that was dropped here. After today, my *ikigai* is to make sure that this can never happen again, that only the best can happen, so life is more worth living to people everywhere."

The elderly women who had just railed against kids are clearly startled by his remark.

Chiemi, a sixth-grade girl, then says, "Once I leave here, after a few days have passed and our classroom activities about this are completed, I'll probably be so involved in my regular life that I won't think anymore about my visit to Hiroshima."

She shakes her head and then says, "No, I refuse to forget. I'll just have to think of Sadako first thing every morning when I wake up."

Sadako Sasaki was two when the atomic bomb was dropped on Hiroshima. When she was diagnosed with leukemia a number of years later, a friend told her that Japanese legend had it that if you folded a thousand paper cranes, you'd be granted any wish. A talented runner, Sadako's wish was to race one last time for her school track team. She immediately set about folding paper cranes. She died of leukemia at age twelve, in 1955, of what the Japanese had come to call the "atomic bomb disease." Sadako died before she could fulfill her wish, but not before she'd made more than six hundred paper cranes. Her friends and classmates completed her project. Then they led an effort to have a monument built to honor Sadako and all children who died as a result of the atomic bomb. The nationwide fund-raising effort they galvanized culminated in 1958 with the erection of a monument at the Peace Park that features Sadako holding a golden crane. At the bottom of the monument is an inscription: "This is our cry, our prayer: Peace in the World."

Wakusa, her teacher, says to me, "These kids are the same age as the 9,000 middle-school students who were sent out on the morning of August 6, 1945, to build firebreaks to protect Hiroshima residents from air raids. Many of those who survived that horrific day made it their life's work to promote peace, out of love for humanity. To them, it was the only genuine *ikigai*, the only thing that gave any sense of worth to their remaining life on this Earth. The *hibakusha*, the survivors, became rescue and relief workers, teachers and pacifists and pro-democracy activists. They fanned out all over the world to work for global peace."

Says Chiharu, another fifth-grader, "Most people only come here to the Peace Park during the annual commemoration day. My grandfather, a *hibakusha*, comes here early every morning, every day, *except* on commemoration day. He says the problem is that most people only think about what happened here one day a year, when we must think about it every day. His two brothers and four sisters, his parents and grandparents, all died.

"He tells me it's up to me to carry on his *ikigai* for him when he dies, not just out of love for him but out of love for making this a beautiful, peaceful world. He reminds me that the Japanese aren't the only ones who suffered, that hundreds of thousands died at our hands all over the world.

"Grandfather sometimes quotes a Japanese philosopher: 'We must stop the chain reaction of atoms through the chain reaction of human beings.' Doing what we can to make what he calls a 'chain reaction of love' must be the *ikigai* of every person in this world."

A Chain Reaction of Human Beings

The philosopher whom the fifth-grader quoted was Ichiro Moritaki (1902–1994). The atomic bomb detonated while he was sitting in his schoolroom in Hiroshima, writing in his diary. The blast left him severely disfigured and partially blind. The *hibakusha* became a peace activist, founding a group that sought the permanent ban of all nuclear testing. Every time a nuclear bomb was tested in his lifetime— 475 times in all—Moritaki protested in Hirsohima Peace Park.

Moritaki says he was "ashamed of the first half of my life," that before the atomic bomb was dropped, he "worked hard so our country would not lose the war." Afterward, he made "an about-face" and began "thinking about how our civilization should be." Moritaki said that atomic bomb survivors' *ikigai* must be to "teach the next generation about the horror of nuclear weapons" so that never again are "so many people's lives . . . mercilessly taken," and so that ultimately all people come to "experience the sanctity of life."

How does one come to keenly recognize that life is as achingly precious as it is fragile? What if one holds the view that life is *not* sacred? One might argue that human history has been dominated by acts of inhumanity, showing that most cultures of most eras do not believe that life is sacred at all.

Do you first have to experience personal tragedy, some degree of loss or deprivation, to understand or appreciate the sanctity of life? Or can such an experience diminish its sanctity? Moritaki, for one, believed that in order to experience the sanctity of life, one must practice, in all one's interactions, "benevolence and the politics of love."

A Life Not Worth Living

In *What Makes Life Worth Living?* anthropologist Gordon Mathews examines the modern-day significance of the Japanese term *ikigai*. He came to find that ostensibly "to many Japanese their *ikigai* was clear: their total commitment to their families and companies." But more often than not, further interrogation revealed that this was what they *thought* their *ikigai* should be, not what it genuinely was. It turned out that "for many this commitment seemed unsatisfactory," from "the employee laboring for a company he hated but couldn't quit" to "the mother pushing her children to excel in an examination system she detested" to a young person "dreaming dreams certain to be crushed." Consequently, Matthews notes how challenging it can be to discover anyone's true *ikigai*, which he equates with "one's deepest sense of social commitment." It might "portend a dark future" for society if individuals do not have to develop *ikigai* that is true to themselves and responsible to others, because a society's worth is determined by the extent to which it creates the conditions necessary to "enable self to feel a sense of connection to larger meaning."

Ideally, autonomy and social conscience are not on opposite ends of a continuum but part and parcel of each other. One's *ikigai* must be permeated by *jyo-netsu-tek-na-ay*, a loving passion for all the world's peoples; it must reject *geki-jyo*, extremely reckless, hedonistic, and self-gratifying love in which one is unconcerned about the effects of one's acts on others.

Voice of Conscience

Prominent Japanese philosopher and ethicist Watsuji Tetsuro (1889–1960) asserts in *Ethics in Japan*, one of the first works by a Japanese philosopher to gain renown in the West, that the Japanese term for individual, *ningen*, denotes someone who gains self-fulfillment by seeing herself as part of the "totality" of humans, someone who is working toward realizing the "happiness of society" and ultimately "the welfare of humankind." According to the dialogue participants at Hiroshima, this conception virtually no longer exists. Yet to Tetsuro, an individual cannot exist without subscribing to it. Such an individual is one whose consciousness inspires her to be a "voice of conscience . . . heard from the standpoint of the individual's independence and not from that of the animal crowd."

The quintessential noble individual, in Tetsuro's estimation, was Socrates, who heard, and heeded, this voice of conscience like few others. It was this voice of conscience that compelled Socrates, at great personal risk, to stand up to "the animal crowd." Socrates believed that his life had value only within a totality that cultivated "the most important kinds of human fellowship." Thus in this climate, Tetsuro writes, Socrates stood alone in continuing to embody, with *jyo-netsu-tek-na-ay*, loving passion, "the virtue of the citizen of the polis."

Value Creation

One of Tetsuro's near-contemporaries, the eminent philosopher Tsunesaburo Makiguchi, was abandoned by his parents and had to fend for himself starting at a tender age; he had scant hope of ever going to school. When he was a young worker, one of his colleagues recognized the devoted autodidact's potential as a scholar, and sponsored his studies in college. He invested wisely; Makiguchi became a stellar student, and upon graduation trained to become a professional educator. After receiving certification as a teacher and administrator, Makiguchi rejected the current educational paradigm, which stressed rigid discipline in order to produce obedient students. When he had his own classroom of students, he became a pariah with his peers by implementing a revolutionary model in which, as Makiguchi scholar Robert V. Bullough puts it, "the individual learner, not the school, is the center of the learning process," and the educational process itself "must extend far outside the confines of the classroom, into one's family, one's community and nation."

Makiguchi's efforts to implement his philosophy of education put him at ever greater odds with his superiors, yet he forged ahead out of deep concern over the rising tide of fanaticism in the days preceding World War II. Makiguchi vehemently opposed the government educational policy of *shokokumin*, the making of "little national citizens," who would unquestioningly do their government's bidding. He wrote that the objective of education "is not the piecemeal merchandising of information" but "the provision of keys that will allow people to unlock the vault of knowledge on their own." A staunch opponent of Japan's militaristic government, the devout pacifist frequently spoke out against the government's efforts to impose the Shinto religion on Japanese citizens. To Makiguchi, the pervasive lack of freedom of religion and expression were inimical to a tolerant and benevolent society.

Determined to deprive Makiguchi of a soapbox, the government had him arrested in 1943, branding him a "thought criminal." Despite repeated attempts to force him to recant and repent, he never yielded. On November 18, 1994, at age seventy-three, Makiguchi died in prison, but not before he wrote groundbreaking works on moral, social, and educational philosophy, all of which today continue to carry great influence among progressive thinkers and activists in Japan and abroad.

MAKIGUCHI WRITES IN *Education for Creative Living* that he shares Socrates' faith that there is "a certain inherent element of moral good in all persons." Like his hero Socrates, he believes it is the task of educators to tap into and nurture—and, most importantly, model—this inherent reservoir of goodness he believes we all possess, so everyone will be inspired to make a "full commitment to the life of society" and work toward the attainment of "true happiness" that can be realized only if all one's endeavors are undertaken "for the benefit of society, without the slightest thought of personal gain."

Makiguchi considered Socrates the "Teacher of Humankind." Makiguchi profoundly admired him for thrusting himself "right in the middle of the chaos of his times." Socrates' *ikigai*, he said, was nothing less than to "instill an ethos of world-citizenship in the younger generation." Facing remarkably similar circumstances in his own epoch and culture, Makiguchi made it his own calling to attempt to instill such an ethos in Japan.

I Am in You, You Are in Me

Feminist philosopher Haruko Okano writes in *Moral Responsibility in the Japanese Context* that "the doctrine of human relationships" has historically been the binding ethical principle for the Japanese people. Although theoretically it should serve as the "ideal base for the social-ethical life," in Japan today, she says, its practice has come to be deeply flawed, to the extent that there is virtually no "consciousness of responsibility," much less love and benevolence, for those who are outside of one's immediate group. To Okano, it is vital that Japanese citizens abandon selfishness and become pervasively steeped in what she refers to as feminist virtues of "autonomy, equality, mutuality and recognition of the other's otherness"—what Watsuji Tetsuro much more eloquently describes as "I am in you; you are in me"—so they can become a genuinely contributing and participatory member of international society.

Okano blames the resurgence of "the simple folk religion of

Shinto," which she describes as a "combination of primitive spiritual beliefs and ancestor worship" and nationalism, for helping to revive the once-widely held belief that only those of "pure" Japanese ancestry are "guaranteed happiness and peace." In such a belief system, there is "no differentiation between the world and self, others and self"; and all those outside one's homogeneous world have no meaningful existence (the classic narcissist view of things). To Okano, only when all members of society embrace diverse ways of world-viewing and world-making, only when they cultivate a "global perspective which incorporates diverse models" and see those who are unlike them as equals, can they become better people.

Never Again

Just before our tour group in the Czech Republic disbands, our guide asks if we have any last questions. Many are already drifting off when I blurt out, "What should we have learned?"

Some are frozen in place by my question. Others make an even more hasty exit. Those remaining don't say a word, as if waiting politely to make sure that no one replies to my question before they depart.

Finally, Jiri, an electrical engineer from Prague, says, "Almost all the young people who'd been part of our group were cracking up the entire time our guide was talking. They took pictures of themselves pretending to be hung or executed. They thought the whole thing was a joke.

"Those kids go to one of the best private schools money can buy, yet they were incapable of learning from here," he says. "Since some of their adult chaperones were cracking up with them, it's safe to say that they are not the appropriate role models to enable the young people to learn the primary lesson of this place: never again. When you see that type of behavior in a place like this, what *I* learn is, 'Never say never again,' because you see how such unfeeling and callous attitudes are still possible, and make places like this."

Says Damek, twenty-five, who is here today as a volunteer, "This is my first time back here in a while. I'd once worked here for several years. I have to say that when I first started, it was 'just a job,' and the visitors for whom I was guide could sense that. If they were moved by the message of this place, it was in spite of, rather than because of, me. Even though it was a time of high unemployment, and jobs were few and far between, I knew I couldn't, and shouldn't, keep working here if I couldn't do a better job. I began reading every book about places like this that I could get my hands on.

"From then on, I no longer gave a rote spiel. Instead, I shared facts *and* feelings. I could see the difference it made in how this place impacted most visitors in my group. What *I* learned is that before visitors could learn as much as possible from me, how a place like this could come to be, I had to dig deep into its history, and dig deep into myself, and be moved by its history, so I could feel its inhabitants in my soul and convey this feeling to the visitors. Even then, the best I can do is optimize the chances that some will learn 'never again' from their visit here. There are instances, like today, when that doesn't happen. Even if I know it's not my fault that I couldn't get through to those kids, I feel we've all missed out on, even wasted, an opportunity to help the young become better human beings."

"Is it wasted if you learn something from their behavior?" I ask.

Damek thinks about this. "Well, I must say I do learn from experiences like today: it re-instills in me how easily something like this can happen, as Jiri said. If a group of well-to-do, 'cultured' kids, with all the privileges and advantages, can pass through here and remain unfeeling and disconnected, then what happened here can repeat itself. Those who presided over and guarded this place must have been taught to feel so superior to the inhabitants, so above them, that there was no way they could feel their pain."

There is a stretch of silence before a woman named Marjeta, who is standing beside Jiri, looks at him and says, "If you want to teach someone about being an exceptional mechanic, you don't hand him a bunch of books to read. He has to spend time with mechanics, learn the tools of the trade by observing his work, how he interacts with others, and then by practicing himself. The same can be said about learning the tools of the trade for becoming a more sensitive human being. You do the teaching and conveying by example, by treating others in such a way that if tomorrow never comes, their last memory of you will be one of a caring, giving human being who's trying to make ours a more lovable world. And you hope that some of that rubs off on those you are mentoring.

"Here, miraculously, the Nazis didn't obliterate all traces of the inhabitants, as they did elsewhere," she continues. "They neglected to destroy hundreds of pictures drawn by the children who'd lived here. So we can imagine their faces, their sufferings and hopes. It's up to all of us who have visited here to remember those who drew the pictures, to speak about them, to our grandkids, our friends and neighbors, to anyone who will listen, to make 'never again' more a possibility."

"Should you still try to convey 'never again' to young people, even when it appears they aren't listening?" I ask. "Because in my experience as an educator, sometimes even the worst behaved really are listening, and they just don't know how to react. Or, in some cases, it can take months or even years for the message to sink in."

"Yes, we should always keep all windows of communication open," Angela, forty-two, says adamantly. "My community has witnessed firsthand what happens when there's a complete breakdown of communication and connection between adults and young people. I'm from Littleton, Colorado."

On April 20, 1999, Eric Harris, eighteen, and Dylan Klebold, seventeen, stormed Columbine High School, and in sixteen minutes of terror, killed twelve students and a teacher before killing themselves. It was the deadliest school shooting in U.S. history.

"I've heard many explanations about what Harris and Klebold did," Angela says. "Depending on whom you believe or talk to, they were part of a 'trenchcoat mafia' cult. They were pagans, devil-worshippers, they hated Christians, they hated blacks, they hated jocks, they were misanthropes, misogynists. What I haven't heard is, if they were really all of these things, how in the world could we have missed the warning signs? The truth is that everyone now wants to paint them as these stereotypical monsters, because it's easier than exploring a question like, 'Could my child, or my neighbors' or colleagues' child, do something like this too?'

"Eric Harris and Dylan Klebold seemed in many ways little different than a lot of adolescents," Angela continues. "After it happened, I began to wonder: What are we adults doing wrong? What aren't we teaching our kids—and what aren't they teaching us? Those two obviously didn't convey to those closest to them what was going on within them. Without psychologizing too much, the Columbine tragedy means there was a complete breakdown between those kids and the rest of their world. Either they didn't look at those they shot as human beings, or they didn't see themselves as human beings. Otherwise, they could never have done what they did. Coming here today, and listening to Damek's moving accounts, has taught me more about how you can become like that. But it's also taught me that I must do all in my power to make sure such tragedies never again come to pass."

"Before Columbine, I never considered questions like, what should our children be learning?" says Hank, a physician from Wichita who came here with his wife and daughter. He had been hovering on the periphery of our group as if deciding whether he wanted to be part of the dialogue. "We parents put onto teachers' shoulders too much of the responsibility for making our children considerate human beings. We need to be asking: What are we parents doing to make our kids become moral beings?"

"I don't see anyone intolerant or hateful like I do adults," says Hank's daughter Leslie, the one and only young person who has stayed on to take part in the dialogue. "Look at all the adults in the U.S. who've massacred people in the last years at their workplace; look at our war policies; look abroad around the world, from Darfur to

Somalia to Rwanda, where adults massacre other groups of adults and children. And these adults never ask themselves what message they're conveying to young people. And that's the scariest message of all.

"My social studies teacher inspires me to do what I can to make ours a world of 'never again,'" Leslie then tells us. "He motivates us to learn and think about new possibilities for ourselves—not just for when we become adults but right now. He makes us feel like we matter, and like everyone in the world matters."

Everyone still on hand seems reluctant to leave. After a long while, Marjeta says, "I'm glad they kept this building intact. But that's not enough.

"What if, just for one day, kids like those with our group who'd behaved so badly had to go through some degrading experiences. What if, for just one day, they had to go without food, were kept in a cold and drafty cell with a bed with no mattress or pillow and a filthy bathroom. I don't know of any other way to teach such kids 'never again.' As the philosopher George Santayana wrote, 'Those who cannot remember the past are condemned to repeat it.'"

"If you remember the past, is that enough to make sure it doesn't repeat itself?" I ask.

Marjeta mulls this over for a moment. "No. You have to then be inspired to act in ways that minimize the chances that the worst parts of our past will recur, that the worst parts of our nature will again be 'cultivated' as they were during the Nazi era. To do that, you have to learn to love not only your neighbor, but strangers on the other side of the globe, to see them as a sort of neighbor too. Because this is what human beings just like you and me are capable of, if for one moment we quit treating one another with the dignity each deserves. This is what happens."

Damek says now, "The Viennese psychiatrist Victor Frankl, who survived Auschwitz, said that 'everything can be taken from man but one thing: the last of human freedoms—to choose one's attitude in any given set of circumstances, to choose one's way.' That attitude, that way, has to be one of love."

As the sun sets on International Holocaust Remembrance Day, we disband and make our way out of Thereisenstadt concentration camp, about an hour from Prague in the Czech Republic. As we exit the camp, we pass under a sign that reads, *Arbeit macht frei*. "Work Will Set You Free."

Thereisenstadt

Thereisenstadt—or Terezin, as it is called by the Czechs—was founded in the late eighteenth century in then-Bohemia. It first served as a garrison to ward off invading troops during the Prussian-Austrian War. At the beginning of Nazi occupation, about 32,000 people, mainly Czechs who resisted the Nazis, were sent here. It subsequently was converted into a ghetto–concentration camp, primarily for Jews.

Nazi propagandists successfully passed off Thereisenstadt as a "model camp." They depicted it as an idyllic community, a "self-governed Jewish settlement area" and veritable "paradise ghetto" whenever Red Cross officials made a perfunctory visit (always with plenty of advance notice). During these visits, the camp's inhabitants had to play soccer, pretend they were tending gardens, put on performances of plays. And always, Red Cross officials would be feted to orchestral music performed by the camp's many stellar musicians. Once the Red Cross visit was over, the musicians were typically then sent on to another concentration camp.

Of the more than 140,000 who were sent to Thereisenstadt between 1941 and 1945, only about 16,000 survived. Only 4,000 survived of those who were sent from Thereisenstadt to other camps. Most were sent to Auschwitz, the largest Nazi concentration camp, where more than 1.5 million Jews and a half million others, mainly gypsies, Poles, and Soviet POWS, were killed in its four gas chamber centers, and another 300,000 prisoners died of starvation or disease.

Of the 15,000 children who inhabited Terezin, only 100 survived. On May 8, 1945, Soviet troops liberated the camp.

Teaching "Never Again"

In the book *Can It Ever Happen Again?*—a collection of essays and statements about the Holocaust—one person is quoted as saying, "Maybe it wouldn't be the Jews again. . . . but . . . why couldn't it happen in any civilized country at any time if people are really blinded by their own problems and hate?"

What about those of us who are not blinded by hate, yet put on blinders?

Anne Frank wrote in her diaries that she was amazed she hadn't "dropped all my ideals" because "they seem so absurd and impossible to carry out" under present circumstances. Even so, she held tightly onto them "because in spite of everything I still believe that people are really good at heart." Even though she could "feel the sufferings of millions," she wrote that whenever she looked up "into the heavens," she concluded "that it will all come out right, that this cruelty too will end, and that peace and tranquility will return again."

Surely part of the reason she held out such strong hope lay in the fact that although most German gentiles were utterly indifferent to the plight of the Jews, there nonetheless were a number who were supremely "good at heart" and risked their lives by hiding Jewish families in their homes.

GERMAN SOCIAL PHILOSOPHER Theodor Adorno (1903–1969), in his famous essay "Education After Auschwitz," asserts that the "premier demand upon all education is that Auschwitz not happen again." To Adorno, all debates about education's ideals are "trivial and inconsequential compared to this single ideal: never again Auschwitz." But it is precisely the debate about education's overriding ideals that can help ensure there is never again an Auschwitz. To help ensure this, one must work to eradicate the conditions not just of war but of intolerance and hatred and racism—to educate for empathy by example.

In trying to come to grips with how the Holocaust happened, Adorno says that many well-intentioned people attempted to explain it away by saying that during the Nazi era "people no longer had any bonds." He calls this explanation illusory, as if "an appeal to bonds . . . would help in any way" to avoid a Holocaust. But it would help.

Philosopher Kristen Renwick Monroe, of the University of California-Irvine met and interviewed at length some of those Anne Frank would consider "people really good at heart"—European gentiles who risked their lives during World War II to rescue Jews. Monroe writes in *The Hand of Compassion: Portraits of Moral Choice during the Holocaust* that "human connection was the key. Their sense of being connected to the Jews through bonds of common humanity was what drove the rescuers to do the impossible."

Holocaust survivor and noted novelist and philosopher Elie Wiesel says in "The Courage to Care" that, for such people, "it was a natural thing to save people, to remain human." Kristen Monroe notes that the choices these rescuers made was not the way of "the scholarly world dominated by rational choice theory," which assumes that people will act in the most rational way, and so would never heedlessly risk their lives. But it may be that supremely irrational times demand supremely irrational choices. Or it may be that the most rational choice of anyone with a social conscience is to do precisely what the rescuers did, striving to realize Anne Frank's hopeful vision in the face of hopelessness, even if it led—as it did in many cases—to their own deaths.

Monroe says that the rescuers' "[r]esistance to genocide" wasn't simply "an affirmation of universalism in which every human being is entitled to right and equal treatment by virtue of being born." Rather, it represented "a cherishing, a celebration of all the types of difference—individual and group—that allow for human flourishing." Yet, she says, it was their very ordinariness—one of them, a Polish student, hid eighteen Jews in the house of the German major that she was caretaking; another, a Danish policeman, helped orchestrate the rescue of 85 percent of the Jews living in his country—that "encourages us to look deep within our souls and ask if we, too, do not possess this possibility."

IF YOU AREN'T able to identify with people who aren't just like you, are you really "civilized"? If you know that other humans are suffering in the most unspeakable ways, yet you can't bring yourself to identify with them in any respect, are you really "innocent"?

THE MOTHER OF Bono, the rock singer and social activist, died of a brain aneurysm when he was fourteen, prompting him to question deeply how life could be so unfair. Instead of retreating from the world with understandable bitterness, he has tried to wrap his arms around tragic hurt and suffering everywhere; his mom's loss served to make him cognizant of how precious each moment is, or should be, for all humans. A devout Christian who was raised as an Anglican, Bono has been acutely sensitive to the preventable deaths of those who are not considered so precious, particularly the marginalized of the Third World, its children in particular. In an interview in *Paris Match*, he excoriates people of the developed world for allowing millions of children and adults to die of AIDS in Africa "because we aren't sharing those drugs" that can prevent or waylay the outbreak of HIV into full-blown AIDS. He believes that "history will judge us harshly. . . . We're present for a new Holocaust and we don't even budge." He said he is taking two of his young children to Africa so they can see firsthand the tragedy that is unfolding there. "I want to shape them, gently, to be aware of the world."

Victor Frankl (1905–1997), whose experiences as a prisoner in a Nazi death camp were the basis for his seminal writings on human survival and man's innate search for meaning, places human beings in two broad categories: "the 'race' of the decent man and the 'race' of the indecent man." He says that "[b]oth are . . . everywhere," and "penetrate into all groups of society." Frankl believes that "no group consists entirely of decent or indecent people." But the fact is that some groups are primarily decent, based on their shared code and ways of acting in the world, and strive to be ever more so, whereas others predominantly are not, because their shared code doesn't seek or allow for such ends.

The indigenous people of Chiapas, Mexico, where I live part of the year, make the distinction between a "human being" and a *basil winik*, a "*true* human being." To them, a human being does not merely have the ability to reason, much less be endowed with certain physical traits, placing them neatly within the Aristotelian classification system. These indigenous people believe that to determine whether someone is a true human being, one has to examine all her deeds, and only then can determine whether she is "really good at heart."

Anne Frank believed that it was primarily up to young people to show the rest of us the way to making this a better world, because "older people have formed their opinions about everything." However, for the young, she says, "it's twice as hard . . . to hold our ground," particularly in "a time when all ideals are being shattered and destroyed, when people are showing their worst side."

Her writings have inspired many to devote their lives to making a reality the type of world she envisioned. Many have likely found, as she did, that "the difficulty in these times" is that "ideals, dreams, and cherished hopes rise within us, only to meet the horrible truth and be shattered"—but these people have also found the wherewithal to continue with their hopeful quest, with more determination than ever, with the notion that if people assume the worst outcome, it can easily become a self-fulfilling prophecy.

ADORNO ASKS "WHETHER there can be life after Auschwitz." More fruitful to ask, in the spirit of Anne Frank: What kind of life can there be, should there be, after Auschwitz? What are we willing to do to make this life a reality? What rather indelible message must we convey to others, and to ourselves? How can we become worthy messengers?

Empathy

Can you "teach" empathy?

Theodor Adorno does not believe that the better we treat children, the better they'll treat others, because such children, in his estimation, will have "no idea of cruelty and harshness in life" and so have no idea how to identify with those who do. Does that mean that you "spare the rod and spoil the child" and that harsh punishments are best? Do you have to first suffer cruelty and harshness yourself to identify with others who have suffered so, much less be compelled to do something about it?

To have empathy, must you first have to have experienced harrowing and vulnerable moments in life—to have experienced tragedy, or at least some moments fraught with loss and sorrow, moments of humiliation, of marginalization—ever to be able to "feel the pain" of others who have had such experiences similar or worse? To understand, much less curb, the violent impulses of others, do you have to be aware that you possibly harbor them yourself, and even may have acted on them in some way?

Daniel Goleman, a pioneer in the emerging field of "emotional literacy," contends in *Emotional Intelligence* that "the emotional lessons we learn as children at home and at school shape the emotional circuits, making us more adept—or inept—at the basics of emotional intelligence." This makes childhood and adolescence pivotal opportunities for developing "the essential emotional habits that will govern our lives." To this end, he calls for the broad implementation of "empathy training" as an integral part of a young person's formal classroom education. But surely, in tandem with such training, there must be "emotional modeling." Adults must strive to be paradigms of empathy themselves if children are to be expected to develop and practice such skills. Paradigmatic figures throughout human history have shown that at least some adult humans are capable of dramatic self-transformation, even at advanced ages as they try to model the change they hope to see in the world at large.

Although we will always be "prisoners" of our emotions, we can be "wardens" too, cultivating and constructing those emotional responses that best enable us to become more humane. To Goleman, the stakes in realizing this end can't be higher:

> [T]he sobering reality of the shootings at Columbine High School and the string of related tragedies in our schools highlights the need for us to offer this education of the emotions to our nation's children.

In *Upheavals of Thought: The Intelligence of Emotions*, philosopher Martha Nussbaum asserts that all intelligence has its emotional component, just as all emotions have their intellectual-rational component. Although to Nussbaum—the one Western philosopher today devoted to a comprehensive examination and understanding of emotions from interconnected conceptual, functional, and empirical standpoints—emotions that "shape the landscape of our mental and social lives" are not wholly cognitive appraisals; yet we are capable of offering an ever *more* rational and accurate assessment of why we experience a certain set of emotions in a given context. Even those emotions that seem purely instinctive or intuitive can and must be understood intellectually, in terms of why they arise and how they are put to use, and in terms of their rational makeup. Nussbaum maintains that as we cast more rational light on them, they no longer remain relegated to an ineffable realm; and as we further plumb and attempt to articulate them, we are no longer such prisoners to them, because such insight helps us constructively channel our emotional responses.

She further asserts that once emotions "are suffused with intelligence and discernment," and so "contain in themselves an awareness of value or importance," then they "cannot . . . easily be sidelined in accounts of ethical judgment, as so often they have been in the history of philosophy." This in turn, she believes, should compel us to do the hard work of grappling "with the messy material of grief and love, anger and fear, and the role these tumultuous experiences play in thought about the good and the just." By this view, emotions can serve as our constructive ally in public life, enabling and inspiring us to cultivate a type of functional and compassionate love that can aid us in everything from developing and implementing transformative social and economic policy to moral and civic education. Nussbaum believes that cultivating emotions in this way is a win-win

> two-way street: compassionate individuals construct institutions that embody what they imagine; and institutions in turn, "influence the development of compassion in individuals."

Its implications for an enlightened "political community to extend to its citizens the social basis of imaginative and emotional health" cannot, in her view, be overestimated.

Destroying Destructive Emotions

Near the outset of the new millennium, a group of prominent scholars—with specialties in fields such as Eastern religion, philosophy of mind, psychology, and cognitive neuroscience—converged from across the globe to gather in Dharamsala, India, with the Dalai Lama to hold a series of intensive dialogues. Their primary objective, Daniel Goleman recounts in *Destructive Emotions: How Can We Overcome Them?* was to examine how and why "destructive emotions eat away at the human mind and heart," and to explore ways to "counter this dangerous streak in our collective nature."

Some participants from the Western world at first attempted to draw sharp distinctions between the ways different cultures view what emotions are and where they come from, maintaining that these variations stem from culturally opposing notions of the self. They distinguished between the Western view, which features an independent self separate from others, and in which, consequently, emotions are experienced individually and apart from others from the Eastern notion of an interdependent or even effaced self that cannot exist apart from a greater social matrix. Such emotions are intertwined with this matrix; they are never experienced in isolated, individualistic ways. So it is, they maintained, that a destructive emotion for someone from Asia would be one that keeps a person from contributing optimally to society at large, whereas for someone in the United States, it would be one that inhibits individual accomplishment and self-actualization.

But the Dalai Lama resisted attempts to make neat and tidy distinctions between notions of self and their role in destructive emotions based on perceived cultural differences between the East and West. He noted that there still are very strong family and community structures in many Western nations and cultural groups, belying the notion that individualism reigns universally in the West. He also pointed out that there are still a number of insular societies with decidedly individualistic bents in many parts of the East, belying in turn the notion that cultures from the East uniformly subscribe to a notion of an interdependent self.

The Dalai Lama aspired to discover areas of commonality; dwelling on putative differences, he believed, could be more a way of justifying current ways of behavior than of offering fruitful ways to overcome humankind's darker side. The Dalai Lama noted that Buddhists don't think in terms of positive and negative emotions, but instead emphasize the notion of "mental afflictions," or *klesha*, which breaks down into two principal types. One of these is cognitive in origin and features a distortion that "stems mainly from a skew in thoughts and ideas"; the other is more inherently an emotional bias that creates "attachment, anger, and jealousy."

Inspired by the Dalai Lama's approach to the subject, the scholars meeting with him eventually concluded that people everywhere can cultivate greater empathy within their particular cultures by first and foremost "viewing others as if each sentient being is your own mother," because this will naturally engender "a sense of fondness, cherishing, gentleness, affection and gratitude."

But many do *not* hold endearing views of their mothers. For them, simply learning to view one another as "sentient beings" would be a step forward.

Lost without Her Love

My wife, Cecilia, had been away from our home in the insular mountain outpost of San Cristobal de las Casas, in Chiapas, Mexico, for an extended visit to an indigenous community in the state's tropical lowlands. A longtime activist in the movement for indigenous people's rights in Chiapas, Cecilia periodically teaches in a "classroom without walls" and holds philosophical dialogues with indigenous children in the outlying areas who have no opportunity to go to formal school. The community that she was visiting in this poorest of Mexico's states has been a sporadic flash point for conflict since the armed Zapatista rebel uprising was first launched in 1994.

Of late, tensions again had been mounting. When Cecilia did not return home at the promised hour, and did not answer my many calls

to her cell phone, I became worried enough to take a bus to the community. I then walked the streets, showing Cecilia's picture to anyone
who'd look. Several indicated to me in their indigenous tongue, then
in halting Spanish, that they had seen her, but not since hours earlier.
I kept looking, to no avail. Long after nightfall, I returned home.

I became convinced that the worst had befallen Cecilia. I notified
the police, and was getting ready to muster enough composure to call
her family. I hesitated for a long while, hoping that somehow, some
way, Cecilia would find a way to get in touch and let me know she was
okay. At last, though, I picked up the phone. Just as I began dialing,
Cecilia walked through the door. I collapsed on the floor and cried.

A GOOD WHILE later, when I was in more control of myself, I considered the thoughts and feelings I'd experienced. I'd entertained
notions of lashing out at the world, of wreaking revenge on those who
had taken the life of this person who was compassion personified,
who like no other I had ever known loved with all her heart and mind.
It was seductive, in a way, to channel my emotions this way. Yet I know
she would have wanted me to go on living a life of love, more so than
ever, and to forgive the unforgivable—even to make something positive out of tragedy. In doing so, I would have been following the
example of my Greek relatives on my grandmother's side who had
lost a family member in the terrorist attack on the World Trade Cen
ters. They established a charitable foundation in his name, honoring
his memory with an act of enduring compassionate love in response
to an act of hate.

Because my Cecilia—who treats the poorest human souls like the
most precious beings they are, and who is dedicated to making their
world more just—is alive and well, I can't begin to know the pain of
anyone who suffers the loss of a loved one through an act of hate. Since
that harrowing experience, though, I do try to seize each day with a
redoubled commitment to do what I can to make ours not just a less
indifferent and more tolerant world, but one where more and more

people come together out of love to bridge the divides between them. I try to do my bit by fomenting forms of dialogue that thrive on the consideration of an array of perspectives. In these discussions, our out-pourings of concern aren't confined to post-catastrophic responses, natural and man-made, but are aimed toward creating conditions that prevent such tragedies in the first place.

HARRY FRANKFURT, A moral philosopher from Princeton, says that love "creates reasons" to live. But as Socrates showed, reason itself can create, and deepen, love for those things that make us more human, that make our world more loving and caring. I believe that all of us have to nurture our reasoning powers in ways that contribute to making this a more love-filled world.

The right kinds of love can inspire you to live in ways that have lit-tle, if anything, to do with mere expediency. They can enable you to better seek the good within yourself and others, no matter how hate-ful they (or you) seem, so they can see and seek it too, then perhaps go the next step and transform themselves.

SOCRATES HAD FAITH that once we knew "the good"—and he believed we all were capable of knowing it and, deep down, wanted to know it—we'd spend our lives realizing it. By this view, the reason there is so much preventable pain and suffering in the world is that people don't know "the good," but once someone shows them the way, they will devote their lives to the task. He had what one today might call "Socratic faith." Many think that his faith in people was naïve, that many then and now *do* know the good and simply choose not to follow the path of the good themselves.

Yet Socrates himself steadfastly believed the best in people, even in the worst of times, even when he was unjustly sentenced to death. If you believe the worst in people, he felt, then they'll be all too happy to comply and show you their worst. On the other hand, if you believe the best in them, perhaps—even if just once in a blue moon—they will be inspired to bring out the goodness within and act accordingly.

AMERICAN PHILOSOPHER, SCIENTIST, and mathematician Charles Sander Peirce (1839–1914) asserts, like Socrates, that hatred isn't at the opposite continuum of love at all. In *Chance, Love and Logic*, Peirce says hatred is an imperfect attempt at love, a "perversion by those who don't understand what love is," so it is incumbent upon those of us who do know to serve as abiding models of what he calls "cherishing-love." Never undertaken in the name of the abstract, this love is directed "to persons . . . to our dear ones, our family and neighbors . . . whom we live near"; but it is also directed to strangers in ways that show them we consider them *like* neighbor and family and dear ones.

When Love Is Absent

A Christian who was never at home with institutionalized Christianity, French philosopher and social activist Simone Weil (1909–1943) wrote this in *The Need for Roots*: "Initiative and responsibility, to feel one is useful and even indispensable, are vital needs of the human soul." To Weil, any society that fails to meet these vital needs of all its members is "diseased." Further, she asserted that it is the duty of those in a position to bring about redemptive social change to devote themselves to seeing that the world is "restored to health," and they should be held morally accountable if they failed to do so. Weil was in the French resistance, and refused any medical or material succor when she contracted tuberculosis (she would not accept any more assistance than she believed those fighting the Germans at the western front would receive). She sacrificed her already-fragile health working at factories and farms to bring greater attention to the plight of the marginalized. Raised in Paris as an agnostic in a wealthy family of intellectuals of Jewish descent, Weil believed that the issue is not how much of your-self and your resources you should give to creating a more humanitar-ian, egalitarian world. Rather, to her, the only issue is, in what area of service to humanity should you spend yourself completely?

Weil so identified with the poor that she made their plight her own—not out of pity but out of her belief that every human mattered equally. She held too, just as importantly, that one can discover God's love only in situations in which His love is absent—that it is in times of greatest "affliction," when God's love is nowhere to be seen or felt, that one must personally see to it to fill the void with compassionate love. In doing so, one is not just acting as a conduit for God's love, one is its embodiment: "wherever the afflicted are loved for themselves alone, it is God who is present." By making whole what was empty, one is filling in the gaps of love that God purposely left so that humans would fulfill their highest purpose. In her view, it is not in intellectual pursuits, certainly not in theological speculation, that one comes to know and feel and express God's love, but in addressing the greatest sufferings of the poor, in trying to alleviate the preventable hurts of the world. For Weil, who died at age thirty-four, this is how one came to discover "love, true and pure." She believed that although "[t]hrough joy, the beauty of the world penetrates our soul," it is only through suffering that "it penetrates our body. We could no more become friends of God through joy alone than one becomes a ship's captain by studying books on navigation."

AS I WRITE this, I have just learned that Marla Ruzicka, twenty-eight, founder of the Campaign for Innocent Victims in Conflict—a humanitarian group devoted to helping families of innocent victims killed in the conflicts in Iraq and Afghanistan—was killed along with her driver in a suicide bombing in Baghdad. She died a victim of hate while carrying out an act of love; she was on her way to document that yet another Iraqi family's loved ones had been killed during an offensive by U.S. troops, so that she could then make her case to U.S. officials that this family was one of the thousands that should receive reparations.

Ruzicka, from northern California, with a comfortable middle-class upbringing, worked tirelessly to see that the military give recompense to all the families who had lost loved ones; she had raised more than $20 million on their behalf. She was alienated from much of the relief community because of her willingness to work with the military. As one article about her death said, she would be the first to point out that the tragic fate with which she met "happens to Iraqis every day and no one notices or even cares. There are no newspaper articles or investigations into what happens to them." To Ruzicka, demonstrating that one cherished the culture of life meant acting in ways that showed how much every human being's story mattered and counted, that "each number" of yet another person killed has "a story of someone who left a family behind."

The only reparation Ruzicka would want from all of those touched by her beautiful life and tragic death is the same as Simone Weil requested—that others be themselves inspired to convert acts of evil into works of beauty, to fill the absence of love with great compassion, to ensure that the story of each innocent killed in conflict is remembered and perpetuated in a way that transforms ourselves and our world, so that such tragedies become less likely.

But Ruzicka would also want us to discover the story of the bomber who killed her and her driver—how he could be driven to commit an act of unbridled hatred, how he might even have been duped into thinking it was an act of love for his god—and what might have been done to steer him along a different path, one of genuinely unconditional love, that would have made the prospect of committing such an act of unconditional hate unthinkable to him.

UNCONDITIONAL LOVE IS something that many from disparate cultures and belief systems believe is a vital objective. Is unconditional hate, or hate of any degree, ever a worthy goal?

Before deciding that hate is okay, it might be worthwhile to ask: in what way am I hateful? In what way might others consider me detestable? If I turn a blind eye to the hurts of the world, am I contributing directly or tangentially to the types of inequities that prevent others from having adequate housing, health care, education? If so, would those living in society's margins have a right to hate me? If I am in any way culpable, should I hate myself?

PART VI

SOCRATIC
LOVE

Platonic Love

The term "Platonic love" has long been associated with chaste love, a friendship love devoid of any hint of *eros*. Yet a compelling case can be made that Plato's dialogues on love, *especially* those touching on friendship love, have erotic overtones and components. Plato's dialogues and triangulating historic sources reveal that to Plato and Socrates, erotic love is intermingled with all other forms of love.

Platonic love *is* Socratic love. That doesn't mean Plato and Socrates came to the same conclusions about love, that they practiced love in precisely the same way, or that they always inquired into love, and experimented on matters of love, with precisely the same method. But they did at many junctures have similar ethos and ends in mind.

John Herman Randall, Jr., a philosophy professor at Columbia University for more than a half century noted for his work in Greek humanism, points out that "the human love from which the Platonic love of the *Symposium* sets out is . . . more disreputable than the notion usually associated with Platonic love," because it begins with the love of a younger man for an older one. When Randall calls this love "disreputable," he means that it is not at all "Platonic" as now conceived, charged with the erotic—a love that, as Socrates conveys, "transforms a passion of the body into a vision of the soul." It never divorces itself from the body but instead, Randall notes, is a combination of "imaginative experience with love as an animal fact." It is a love that ultimately inspires Socrates and Diotima, in one of the most eloquent pieces of philosophizing Plato composed, to

> unfold the science of love, what love is, and what it is good for. It is a vision, and an experience, an inspiration to perfecting, a human experience bearing fruits in achievement. . . . And it is reached, not by forsaking the human, earthly love, but by perfecting it in imagination.

Love Story

Randall believes we are so captivated by the dialogues on love because "[it] is an eternal theme, the most fascinating . . . nine-tenths of our literature is about it. And we always get slightly drunk on the talk about love." José Ortega y Gasset says that love, in the end, is itself more like a "literary genre," and that every love affair is a story crying out to be told, so that the rest of us can consider it, possibly learn and grow from it. He believes this was never better demonstrated and accomplished than in Plato's Socratic dialogues on love.

Martha Nussbaum says that Plato's "important strategy" in setting forth his philosophical views on love—namely, his novelistic approach to the detailed "imaginings of lives lived both outside and inside of the science of measurement"—made his accounts of love a more multidimensional and many-splendored thing:

> When, in the *Symposium*, he follows Diotima's speech with the speech of Alcibiades; . . . when, in the *Phaedrus*, he vividly describes the lives and feelings of rather different people . . . in

all these cases Plato seems to me to be doing the sort of tough work of imagination that is required for anyone who is going to make an informed choice in this matter.

Can we choose whom or how to love? Perhaps not completely, but our choices can be more, rather than less, informed. We can't decide how best to love or whom to love if we aren't privy to varied perspectives and values of love and approaches to love, of personas real and imagined, from the mythic Diotima to the historic figure Alcibiades. This is where love as literary genre, Nussbaum asserts in *Love's Knowledge*, plays a pivotal role in developing one's philosophical views on the matter:

> We need not just philosophical examples (which contain only a few features that the philosopher has decided are of greatest relevance to his argument); . . . [w]e need . . . works about people who live and value differently, to address us not just in and through the intellect, but by evoking nonintellectual responses that have their own kind of selectivity and veracity.

Plato incorporated literary license even with his most historically factual works in order to better convey the life of the mind and heart. He presented a variety of views on love via the interactions of compelling and complex personalities who engaged one another in ways in which, in the course of the dialogues, they came to grow and change and evolve their views, just as the reader does. Nussbaum believes that most philosophical theories of love fall short because

> they are too simple. They want to find just one thing that love is in the soul, just one thing that its knowledge is, instead of looking to. . . . show a complexity, a many-sidedness.

But Plato, taking his cue from Socrates, is one of the great and glaring exceptions to this among philosophers. Nussbaum says Plato, like the best novelists who "take our common humanity for their theme," shows us through his characters—no one more so than Socrates—"passionate love in . . . humanly recognized form." Thus the reader is able to relate to the loves of these characters and judge whether they are the best of which we are capable.

ORTEGA Y GASSET believes that love itself "reveals the character of the individual in which sentiment has found 'reason' to sprout and blossom."

> [N]o one loves without reason; whoever is in love has . . . a conviction that his love is justified. To love is, furthermore, "to believe" that that which is loved is, in fact, lovable for itself. . . . Love is not, therefore, illogical or anti-rational.

Perhaps it would be better to say that love should be part of reason, and vice versa. Love can be exhibited in illogical or irrational ways (and even these may be productive), but if we cannot step back and let reason enter at some point, we cannot know whether our intent or aims are genuinely loving in ways that uplift and liberate.

When love is not part and parcel of reason, it is bereft of its "reason for being" every bit as much as reason without love. Unreasoning love does not take the time to understand why one has chosen to love as one has, or what one's ends are, and whether what one takes to be acts and gestures of love are truly loving. Loveless reason has led some to walk a path that too often ends in brutality. Of all those who believe they are on the side of love, few take the time to reason why they love as they do, whether their love does more harm than good, whether it is narcissistic rather than imbued with vision and conscience, whether it might be admixed with hatred or resentment.

To experience love's full enchantment, Ortega y Gasset maintains that we must cultivate our capacity to see each human fully. To do this requires that one be "vitally curious about humanity, and more concretely, about the individual as a living totality, an individual modus of existence." This was Socrates' way in all his interactions, as recorded by Plato and Xenophon, among others. His polis, his family, his fellow inquirers, human civilization itself, were among Socrates' well-thought-out reasons for living, loving, and dying as he did. His cultivation of a passionate heart did not give him "rose-colored lenses" through which to see the world, but enabled him to see everyone and everything more clearly—with a warts-and-all realism tinged with imaginative and empathetic vision. Because he took the time to consider the movement and spirit, the process and ends and substances of love, from a plurality of human perspectives, Socrates showed us how to reason better, in ways that help to wed the sensual with the passionate, the imaginative with the reasonable.

A lover in the mold of Socrates believes: I think I'm right in loving this and not that, in loving in this way and not that, but I could be wrong; I do not believe that my philosophy of love and loving is necessarily best. Rather, it can be supported or refuted only by methodical inquiry with others, who also have carefully considered and cultivated passions that may be quite different from my own. It is critical that I weigh mine against theirs, seeking to discover what speaks for and against each. Moreover, I operate from the premise that there is always more to know about love and what I already know likely is always wrong to some degree, or at least is never altogether correct. I will not emerge unchanged from my inquiries on matters of love, no more than will those who inquire with me, and that is to the good. It is how we grow together as individuals and as a community; it is how we push outward the boundaries of knowledge about love and about loving in ways that, at their best, can help us sculpt a more participatory world.

Basic (Greek) Instincts

Nikos Kazantzakis' classic novel *Zorba the Greek* is also a classic example of love as literary and philosophical genre. Alexis Zorba, the protagonist of the novel, is a consummate free spirit who lives with seemingly unbridled passion. He is the antithesis of his boss, the story's anonymous narrator, who has rented in a Crete village a rundown mine that he plans to turn into a thriving operation, with Zorba as his improbable foreman.

Zorba throws himself into his work with as much zest as he does any other undertaking, but with little thought to method or outcomes. He tries one harebrained scheme after another to make the mine operation more efficient; the results are the opposite of those hoped for. Eventually the operation goes bust, and with it the aspirations of Zorba's boss to be a thriving capitalist.

But all is far from a loss. Zorba's boss, a quintessential rationalist, learns from his failed foreman a great deal about how to live a life of the heart. Such a life, the narrator comes to find, is far from mindless; in fact, it is quite mindful in its own way. Before he and his boss part company, Zorba shatters his boss's stereotyped notions of him as someone who lives with all heart and no mind, showing that he has given considerable and eloquent thought to what makes life worth living: "How simple and frugal a thing is happiness: a glass of wine, a roast chestnut, a wretched little brazier, the sound of the sea." Socrates also gave frequent encomiums to cherishing the simple pleasures of life, and at a time when his fellow Athenians scoffed at such a view. Zorba's boss, in the end, came to marvel at this "living heart" who, unlike most men, had not yet been "severed from mother earth." Herman Melville, in *Moby-Dick*, referred to "the calm self-collectedness of simplicity" of such salt-of-the-earth types as having "Socratic wisdom."

NIKOS KAZANTZAKIS (1883–1957) made of his own life a passionate pursuit. The prolific Greek novelist and playwright, born in Crete, studied philosophy under Henri Bergson (1859–1941), the French philosopher who won the Nobel Prize for literature in 1927 and whose philosophical works on human consciousness asserted that intuition was of more significance in man's development than intellect. Kazantzakis eventually earned a Doctor of Laws degree. His life was devoted to public service in one fashion or another. As director of the Greek Ministry of Public Welfare, he orchestrated the rescue of more than 150,000 people of Greek ethnicity from the Caucasus region of the Soviet Union. Whatever he did, he did like Zorba, who said, "Throwing yourself headlong into your work, into wine, and love, and never being afraid of either God or the devil." But one did such "throwing" not in a thoughtless way but considering deeply one's actions as carefully as one could every step of the way.

Kazantzakis believed not only that reason devoid of passion made life reasonless, but we must use reasoning in ways that make living a more passionate and participatory pursuit for all. As one of his biographers notes, Kazantzakis "gives value and dignity to the human condition by asserting that man himself, with passionate affirmation, may create the structure of his life and work."

Kazantzakis, like Zorba and Socrates, was an autonomous soul whose values went against the grain of the rather narcissistic ones that his society as a whole held dear. He believed that if one's way of living and loving did not have "regenerating significance," if in addition to cultivating our "inner life," it did not also hold promise of elevating the lives of others, it was a heartless pursuit.

KAZANTZAKIS WROTE THAT the one book he never tired of was Plato's *Symposium*, for it epitomizes "the great, the holy revelation of the Hellenic world," an era in which "(t)he religion of the Beautiful reigned." Kazantzakis was forever moved by the *Symposium* because its myth about love also mirrored the real way that the Greeks aspired to live back then. The fact that the Greek way of life and pervasive philosophy of love disappeared makes the existing myth even more poignant, particularly as it is told from "the lips of Socrates," the West's greatest lover, to whom love was "the most divine flight that the human mind has ever known."

James F. Lee writes this about ancient Greece in the context of his biography on Kazantzakis:

> Following the Peloponnesian War, Greece began to disintegrate. . . . Belief in the fatherland was no more. . . . The [new] protagonist on the stage was . . . the wealthy citizen, with all his lascivious passions and pleasures—a skeptic, materialist, and libertine.

The "reign of the Beautiful" was supplanted by the reign of ugly "every man for himself" narcissism. Kazantzakis explored in his writing whether such purely egocentric pursuits as had won the day would ever exhaust themselves, whether there might come a time when an individual and communal love life, once modeled in ancient Greece—a type of life with "Socrates as its symbol"—might again be revived. If this were ever to come to pass, he asserted that one "must heed . . . the lessons and wishes of the heart." One must be careful what one wishes for, and give thought to the types of loves that make for a meaningful existence.

KAZANTZAKIS' ZORBA IS typically explained away as one who is a slave to his passions, though he is no more a slave to them than he is to cold reason. Zorba tells his boss, an idolator of reason at the expense of all other forms of feeling and believing and doing: "You have money, health, you're a good fellow, you lack nothing . . . except one thing— folly." His boss takes himself so seriously, is so self-absorbed, that he has alienated himself from the joy and passion of being alive.

After Zorba's insightful and mordantly honest critique, his boss "nearly wept." He knew that what Zorba said was true, and he goes on to rationalize: "As a child, I had been full of mad impulses, superhuman desires. I was not content with the world. Gradually, as time went by, I grew calmer. I set limits, separated the possible from the impossible, the human from the divine, I held my kite tightly . . . ." What he still fails to grasp is that such impulses and desires were no more "mad" than "superhuman." Only as an adult did he come to reason them away, to concoct this mesmerizing explanation rather than change his life, because it was easier than recognizing that he had simply never dared to live.

Heartfelt Beliefs

English philosopher and mathematician William Kingdon Clifford (1845–1879), deeply influenced by Socrates, could just as well be speaking for the Greek philosopher when he writes:

> It is not only the leader of men, statesman, philosopher, or poet, that owes this bounden duty to mankind. Every rustic who delivers in the village alehouse . . . may help to kill or keep alive the fatal superstitions which clog his race. Every hard-worked wife . . . may transmit to her children beliefs which shall knit society together, or rend it in pieces. No simplicity of mind, no obscurity of station, can escape the universal duty of questioning all that we believe.

It is a duty born of love for humanity, out of love for discovering the wisdom that can best ennoble humans.

Only by having a set of heartfelt beliefs, and continually questioning and scrutinizing them, Socrates maintained, can one further sculpt a set of beliefs genuinely worth having and living by. Socrates saw this as his paramount responsibility. Clifford puts it this way:

> Our words, our phrases, our forms and processes and modes of thought, are common property, fashioned and perfected from age to age; an heirloom which every succeeding generation

inherits as a precious deposit and a sacred trust to be handed on to the next one, not unchanged but enlarged and purified, with some clear marks of its proper handiwork. . . . An awful privilege, and an awful responsibility, that we should help to create the world in which posterity will live.

Socrates believed that if we were going to do justice to our universe, we had to quit thinking in Manichaean, black-and-white terms and think instead in colors, entertaining objections and alternatives, passionately examining what speaks for and against each, then coming to warrantable truths that could be tested further. Taking a stand in the name of Socratic pluralism, Walter Kaufmann sought to provoke progressives of his day into realizing that anyone who is sure he has right totally on his side, and feels that everyone who differs with him is wrong, likely has much more in common with those fundamentalists whose views he considers abhorrent than he cares to acknowledge. Kaufmann believed that such a disposition was prevalent among thinkers of all political and philosophical stripes, swinging the pendulum of human sentiment further and further away from love.

It is because men think in terms of good and bad that they construct such pairs as love and hate. . . . What is the opposite of love? Is it hate? Or rather lack of love, which could mean ignorance of a person's very existence? Or indifference to a person whom we might be expected to love or whom we did love at one time? Or near-indifference coupled with a little irritation? Or a definite aversion, either faint or strong? Or envy? Or resentment?

Many people would say: Hate, of course. Others: No, hate is really much closer to love than is indifference; and as long as there is hate, love may be kindled. However that may be, hate and love are certainly not opposites; they are not even mutually exclusive, they often coexist and interpenetrate. Love and hate are neither two solid substances nor two liquids that can be mixed. "Love" is a highly abstract term that can be applied to very abstract configurations of feelings, thoughts and actions, and many of these configurations bear very little resemblance to one another.

Kaufmann, who lost loved ones in the Holocaust, nonetheless believed we should not altogether hate or detest even the most hateful or detestable person. He believed that a person should not be loved or hated solely because of his acts, and the beliefs on which they are based, because to him they are not the sum total of who he is or might be, no matter how despicable he may appear: "You should always remain mindful of the other man's humanity, and of the ways in which he is 'as yourself.'" This implies that one cannot hate—or love—blindly. Rather, in judging others, we should be sure to judge ourselves first, scrutinizing our own darker impulses, shortcomings, and blind spots. In fact, part and parcel of judging others should be even more rigorous judgment of ourselves.

To Socrates, "not hating" is not sufficient. Rather, we should love even the most hateful. He practiced what he preached, loving even those who had demonized him and orchestrated his death. If he didn't, how could he expect others to do so? If he didn't, others would say that loving in such a way was impossible. But he knew that if there's even one example of a person who demonstrates such love, then clearly it is possible.

Loving Inquiry

Does love have a nature, a duel nature, dueling natures? What if we dispensed altogether with all human constructs of love? Would the world, our world, be any different, any better or worse? Does love have an essence? Or is it that love is a great appearing act, that it makes its presence known only when humans engage in certain types of interactions with one another, and that this is the form and essence and nature of love? Is there an immutable form of love, or is it forever changing, evolving, or devolving? Is ceaseless change itself love's most immutable property? Does love have a hierarchy or hierarchies that can be revealed only in dialectic? Can a type of dialectic itself be love's highest expression?

Socrates inquired with others to discover answers to such questions.

IT SEEMS A commonplace that Socrates had disdain for the sophists and others who claimed to know what they didn't. To be sure, the sophists and their like showed themselves up in the course of inquiring with Socrates; his method made it a virtually foregone conclusion that those with logical lapses and loopholes in their views would make these flaws readily apparent. But if Socrates had had disdain for them, he wouldn't have engaged them in his dialogues. Only in this way can you discover what others'—and your own—views really amount to. Only with such total immersion can one do justice to anyone's philosophical perspective. Socrates himself would not embrace the Socratic method if divorced from his ethos of sympathetic immersion, the quintessential act of love, *arête* in action.

Love of Whole Persons

The premier philosophical scholar of Western antiquity, Gregory Vlastos, chides the theory of love expounded by Socrates in the *Symposium*, saying it fails in his view to "provide for love of whole persons," that it neglects to account for anything other than "love of that abstract version of persons which consists of the complex of their best qualities." Vlastos says that the intent of such a view, at least on the part of the scribe Plato—whom he calls a sexual "invert" incapable of

understanding profound passion, and whom he says is intent on cir-
cumventing the kind of "mad obsessive intensity which is commonly
thought peculiar to sexual love"—is to transcend love's sexual
aspects, so it is not tainted with "human flesh and color and other
mortal nonsense." Vlastos goes on to say:

> Plato's speculation structures love in the same way as it does
> knowledge in epistemology, the world-order in cosmology, the
> inter-relations of particular and universal, time and eternity. . . .
> In each of these areas the factors of the analytic pattern are the
> same: the transcendent Form at one extreme, the temporal indi-
> vidual at the other.

Yet in reality, the "transcendent" and the "temporal" are entwined.
To fail to recognize this is to fail to understand—much less be able to
weigh and measure against our own notions—Plato's and Socrates'
approach to love. Plato, no more than Socrates, believed we should
seek to love only in the abstract, to tease out love's universal qualities,
so we can better search for and discover, create love and evolve in the
particular—in particular beings, actions, places, situations, where
we'd otherwise never know or seek to look for it, much less be able to
recognize or nurture it.

Among the love objects that Vlastos considers abstract are "social
reform, poetry, art, the sciences, and philosophy." In his view, Plato
saw "that the aesthetic quality of . . . purely intellectual objects is akin
to the power of physical beauty to excite and to enchant even when it
holds no prospect of possession." But as Plato's Socrates demonstrated in his dialogues, such love objects can in their own way be passionate and sensual and intimate. It's not just that "the most abstruse
inquiry," and even "the elegance of deduction," can be a sort of possession, achingly personal and even to a degree physical, but that they
impact how people interact with one another, how they feel about
one another.

Some of our most intimately personal outpourings of love might take the form of social reform or scientific and artistic undertakings or philosophical inquiry. Into such vessels we might well pour our imaginative sympathy and concern.

DIOTIMA SAYS IN the *Symposium* that "the aim of *eros*" is to unfold and reveal beauty to us. "We are all pregnant in body and in spirit," she says, "and when we reach maturity our nature longs to give birth." This is what the great artists, scientists, and social reformers do.

In each instance we must become masters of the abstract as it relates to our field, the abstract informing the concrete, and vice versa, with the end of gaining in the quest for "the everlasting possession" of a love that is the daimon, the spirit and movement, "the mediator who spans the chasm" between human ideals and human realities, and inspires us to make our realities bear more resemblance to our ideals.

Robert Musil's exquisite novel *The Man Without Qualities*, which in essence maps the rise and fall of Austrian civilization preceding World War I, wonders via the book's protagonist Ulrich whether beauty is bound to be in the eyes of the beholder and, if so, whether conditional and relational elements can make of beauty something ever more profound, intimate, and everlasting as one's inner eye becomes more developed:

> Good heavens, if a gigantic matron were to have been sitting here in the shade, with a huge belly terraced like a flight of steps, her back resting against the houses behind her, and above, in thousands of wrinkles, warts, and pimples, the sunset on her face, couldn't he have found *that* beautiful? Lord, yes, it was beautiful. He didn't want to weasel out of this by claiming he was put on earth with the obligation to admire this sort of thing; however, there was nothing to prevent him from finding these broad, serenely drooping forms and the filigree of wrinkles on a venerable matron beautiful—it is merely simpler to say that she is old. And this transition from finding the world

old to finding it beautiful is about the same as that from a young person's outlook to the higher moral viewpoint of the mature adult.

It takes sublime work and effort to see beauty in the ostensibly old or ugly; it takes heart and mind and soul, with new lenses. But contrary to what Musil's character indicates, sometimes a child can have this "higher moral viewpoint" more than a "mature adult." It takes love to see love. This isn't circular once it is recognized that love is not just an entity but a process, a journey and principle and destination and objective. This is what Socrates recognized better than almost anyone. He showed us how we can use loving and reasoned inquiry as a means for opening ourselves up to the bracing variety of human experiences. He showed us how to take others' crosses and aspirations for our own. He showed us how to make it a way of life to seek out interactions with others in ways that ensure we are exposed to new artful and scientific, theoretical, and practical means and methods and ends of love, by becoming more connected to and falling more in love with our world, warts and all.

Revolutionary Love

To Socrates, for love to be deserving of its moniker, it has to have a revolutionary component. He did not believe that any existing agreement on, or widely held conception of, what love is should be overturned or supplanted easily. But our conceptions had to be testable and subject to emendation or overhaul if it turned out they did not best serve the ends of *arête*. Socrates himself was a pariah in his latter years for practicing a revolutionary sort of love. Today, his way is considered iconic of love that seeks to strengthen and deepen human connectedness. Socratic love is always capable of surpassing itself, based as it is on the premise that we should continually seek for new ways of being human that lead to greater human being.

Chivalry Is Alive

Was Socrates tilting at windmills, a delusional man whose aspirations in matters of the heart were unrealistic? Was he the Athenian version of Don Quixote?

Don Quixote made up obstacles as he went along in his misadventures. Socrates, on the other hand, was well aware of the real and formidable obstacles he was up against, but he was undeterred just the same—and even managed to see great beauty at a time when many people's behavior was ugly.

Smitten by tales of chivalry he read in romance novels, Don Quixote lived in a reality of his own fabrication, far removed from the pathetic actual world that to him was not worth living in, because it was a world in which chivalry was not possible. His romantic notion of how the world should be became for all intents and purposes the real world. For Socrates, living in such a world could never suffice, because it did not change its condition for the better for others. Still, he did have a romantic vision of the world, and he strove to make the real world one that meshed with his vision.

Don Quixote in effect supplanted reality with unreality, and lived accordingly. In acting "as if" the world were so, for him it did become so—all for the sake of his professed love for Dulcinea. All the loopy, tragicomic, anti-heroic, folly-prone events that followed were based on the way Don Quixote viewed the world. Call him delusional, a fool, a romantic to end all romantics; his way of living has touched both the funny bones and the hearts of readers ever since.

As different as they were, Socrates surely shared some of Don Quixote's traits. Anyone who takes on the world alone and autonomously, against impossible odds, in the name of love, is tilting at wind-mills. Yet to Socrates, the only life worth living was one permeated with honor and chivalry, idealism and *arête*. He acted in and on behalf of the spirit of the world he envisioned and believed could be realized, if only he could capture the imaginations of enough fellow Athenians, speak to their better angels, and inspire them to join him in his quest and take it for their own.

Unlike those who crossed paths with Don Quixote and saw just a madman—some were humored by him, some humored him, some did him at least as much harm as he tried to do them—many of those who crossed paths with Socrates were inspired to be like him.

What if at least a little bit of Don Quixote's way of viewing the world was contagious, and we all became "infected" by it? What if we all, like him, saw a homely maiden as a damsel, a barnyard nag as a magnificent steed, even a windmill as a monster in need of slaying, a threat to those we love? Socrates believed we must have vivid imagi-native lenses, but he also filtered his vision through a healthy rational-ist sensibility.

To "be like Socrates," one must also possess a bit of Don Quixote. Maybe the best quests are rather hopeless ones, though undertaken with great optimism, enthusiasm, and love. However, in the Socratic quest, one is not deluded like Quixote: one realizes full well that to some degree one is tilting at windmills, but one also knows that as long as the odds might be, one just might achieve the impossible.

Genius of the Heart

Friedrich Nietzsche (1844–1900), the existential philosopher renowned for his investigations into the genesis of human values and morality, calls Socrates in *The Gay Science* "the genius of the heart," the one person who knows how to descend into the depths of every soul . . . who teaches one to listen, who smoothes rough souls and lets them taste a new yearning . . . who divines the hidden and forgotten treasure, the drop of goodness . . . from whose touch everyone goes away richer, not having found grace nor amazed, not as blessed and oppressed by the goods of another, but richer in himself . . . full of hopes that as yet have no name.

Socrates was indeed a genius of the heart, but he taught others how to descend into the depths of their souls, showing them how to divine and reveal the treasure within.

THOUGH MISTAKEN IN equating all Socratic love with *eros*, Laszlo Versenyi nonetheless puts it best when he notes that, for Socrates, love is a continual process of becoming, for to him, "life is action: a process, a movement, a drive" that leads to higher human achievement, advancing true *arête*. Socrates believed, until his latter years, that no one practiced this love "in greater number than the Athenians." Socrates himself was its greatest practitioner by the time he was sentenced to death. Giambattista Vico (1668–1744), Italian philosopher of cultural history and anthropology, said of Socrates that he "derived his moral philosophy from the heavens." Rather, Socrates' philosophy of matters of the heart showed us the way to the heavens.

Love Letter

"I miss our rendezvous in the park," Alexandros says in his latest letter. He's been writing me about once a week. My dear friend and mentor has moved back to Greece—lock, stock, and barrel. When he told me of his decision during one of our get-togethers at Athens Square

Park in Astoria, Queens, he couldn't hide his excitement any more than I could my sadness.

"Democracy is strong there again," he told me. "Perched between the West and the Middle East, Greece can be a bridge between the two worlds. Gandhi said, '[W]ho can say what sores might be healed, what hurts solved, were the doings of each half of the world's inhabitants understood and appreciated by the other half.' Greece is perfectly situated as the place to facilitate this understanding and appreciation. Our friend Socrates would be proud of our revived democratic ethos and our outreach.

"Who knows," Alexandros then said, "maybe I can help in my modest way to make a difference. I just know I want to be part of it. When I was back in Greece for the Summer Olympics, I didn't want to leave. I realized that sometimes you can go back home again. I think my parents, God rest their souls, would want me to be wherever I can do the most good in the world, and now that is Greece."

It didn't take this voracious heart long, after returning to Greece, to figure out how he could "do the most good."

"I'm a language teacher for new immigrants," he writes to me. "There's so many refugees from Albania, from the former Soviet bloc countries, from the Middle East, who have come to Greece to find a place where they can live in peace and build a decent life for themselves and their children. Once upon a time, you would have had to come to America to do that.

"You'll be happy to know that as part of my class, I hold dialogues with the students, so I can learn about their culture, their values. Their passion for finding a way, in their limited Greek, to share who they are helps them develop their language skills much better than rote teaching. They are so thoughtful and hopeful. To me, immigration is a beautiful thing. It makes our world more colorful and vibrant.

"Maybe I'll eventually open a little café. It'll give my students a home away from home. And it'll provide us with a more suitable place to hold our dialogues, and share and discover our passions, convictions, and dreams."

He goes on to write: "Keep steering your life by that great-souled man Socrates, who made life more worth living—and more worth dying for—by investigating matters of the heart in ways meant to build bridges of love."

Never one to hide his sentiments, Alexandros signs off his letter in this way: "Now, my friend, let me say to you in the language of my students: *Te dashuroj. Asektem. Te iubesc.* Albanian, Kurdish, and Romanian for the Greek, *S'agapo.* I love you."

ACKNOWLEDGMENTS

The birthing of this book was as challenging and—thanks to my marvelous longtime editor Alane Mason—as rewarding as it comes. None of my accomplishments is possible without my wife, Cecilia, who teaches me more about love every day. The encouragement and friendship of John Esterle, visionary director of the Whitman Institute, as well as the steadfast support of the pioneering Institute itself, have made all the difference in my endeavors to make ours a more thoughtful, connected, and participatory world. I'd also like to thank Mary Beth Reticker, Winfrida Mbewe, Alex Cuadros, and Lydia Winslow Fitzpatrick, of W. W. Norton; Alessandra Rastagli; Vanessa Levine-Smith; Andrew Stuart; Felicia Fth, Leigh Haber; Teresa Alto; Don Boese; the marvelous Barry Kibrick and Bettylou Kibrick; Yoko Nishiyama; Takako, Hisa, and Arisa Hara; Carlos Loddo; Michael Toms and Justin Willis Toms; Josh Glenn; Sheldon Kelly; Bill Schulz; Walter Anderson; K. J. Grow; the late James Phillips, my uncle; Mike Holtzclaw; Sam Crespi; Nancy Damon; Vivian McInerny; Margot Adler; Tyla Schaefer; Lelia Green; Teri Cross Davis; Brian Lehrer; Cathie Lewis; Betty Luse; Cecelia Goodnow; Ken Lafave; Sheldon Kelly; Omar Jamal; Steve Steinberg; Georgia Tasker; Eric Darton (read his novel *Free City*); Katie Kehrig; Gwen Kehrig-Darton; Donald Hsu; Kelsey Phillips; Joe and Jen Siciliano; Jerry Spivak and Karen Northrop; Lynne Conybeare and Jim Benson; longtime pals Jake Baer, Nick DeMatt, and Steve Hornsby; Masako Ueda; Priya George; Laura Norin; Henri Ducharme; Randy Tong; Rebecca Nassif; Susannah Fox; Bill Delaney; Cathy Lewis; Mizgon Zahir; Roya Aziz; Clea Kore; David Williams; Marlene Carter; Stephanie Welter; James Riddel; Bo Emerson; Mandy Mankazana; Mabrouk Abairid; Leonardo Chapa; Valentina Chapa Sosa; Armando Chapa Zambrano; Lucrecia Vargas de Chapa; Armando Chapa Vargas; Gloria Leal Chapa; Estefania, Armando, and Luis Eduardo Chapa Leal; Sylvia Blaustein; Emily Shapiro; Salvador Ruiz Olloqui Vargas; Bill Glose; Yolanda Sosa; Javier Espinosa Poo; Maughn Gregory; Sam Sadler; Carole Brzozowski; Pamela McLaughlin; Bob Coles; the late Berta Zambrano de Chapa; Clay Morgan, who has been an inspiration in so many ways; Tom McGee; Pat McGee; Sean McGee; Marlene Carter; Dave Williams; Mat Lipman; John U. Lee; Mike and Fran Schiavo; Shirley Strum Kenny; Roy Nirschel; the fabulous Tom Conway; Bill Smith; Elizabeth Carter Tipton III QOA; M. R. Ying; Evan Sinclair and Hallie Atkinson; Jennie Savage; John Thornell; Giancarlo Ibarguen; Jeanne Smith; Tom and Tracey Flach; Leigh Williamson; Paul Reichardt; Anne Umina; Kevin and Susy Kelly; Shep Shaw; Kary Lewis; Colette Bancroft; Mike Kiniry; Mane Paredes; Kerri Miller; Jay Tolson; Mimi Geerges; Nicole Geiger; Abigail Samoun; Chris Clark; Bill Pennington; great hearts Larry and Sue Parker; Carol Horn; Tom Morris; Fred Anderle; Renita Jablonski; Craig Wilson; Michael Krasny; Tina Ratsy; Ken Lafave; John Geluardi; Tom Reynolds; Mary Ann Kohli; Kelly McGannon; John Wilkens; Lisa Feintech; Bert Loan; Paola Carbajal; David Blacker; Edd Conboy; Jose Antonio Ramirez Narvaez; Humberto Escalante; the late Melissa Wescott; Evora Jordan; Josie Hays; Auntie Bubbles Beloff; Elaine Rioux; John Rice Irwin; the late Alex Haley; Tom Seligson; Lynnette Harris; Todd Carstenn; Dennis Dienst; Katie Sieving; Park Jin Whan; Carol Reeve; Carla Narrett; Lolis Eric Elie; April Cage;

Anita Hamilton; Bill Smith; Jillian Hershberger; Joe Smith; Kiki Kapani; Michael Schwarz; Julie Mancini; and Miriam Feuerle. I'd like to make special mention of Bill Hayes. I met Bill, a retired postal worker, at one of the first Socrates Cafés I started more than a decade ago. He'd never read a word of philosophy, but upon attending our gatherings he became smitten with the discipline, and from then on read voraciously, particularly the works of the pragmatist philosophers, and he also enrolled in college courses in philosophy. Bill and I regularly got together in ensuing years, our friendship deepening during our many impassioned exchanges. Bill passed away the day I finished this book. I miss him very much. Finally, I'd like to thank all those around the globe with whom I have had the privilege of engaging in philosophical discourse, immeasurably enriching my life.

RECOMMENDED
READING

Martha Nussbaum is undertaking some of the most fruitful investigations in social philosophy of any modern Western philosopher. You can hardly go wrong in reading just about any of this prolific philosopher's works, which often break down the artifical divides between disciplines at the same time that they resuscitate the ethos and spirit and method of Socratic philosophy. I recommend in particular her *Upheavals of Thought: The Intelligence of Emotions* (Cambridge University Press, 2003) and *Cultivating Humanity: A Classical Defense of Reform in Liberal Education* (Harvard University Press, 1998).

Required reading should also be Princeton social philosopher Walter Kaufmann's many original works, including *Religion, Existentialism and Death* (New American Library, 1976), and *The Future of the Humanities* (Reader's Digest Press, 1977), particularly for those concerned with the state of higher education.

Virtually everything written by John Dewey is worth reading, but in particular his less pedestrian works, such as *How We Think* (D. C. Heath & Co., 1910), and the lamentably out-of-print *Logic: The Theory of Inquiry* (Henry Holt & Co., 1939), which is a must-read for those seeking to hone their philosophic method for undertakng fruitful investigations on pressing existential questions and all other matters of the heart.

Tsunesaburo Makiguchi's *Education for Creative Living* (Iowa State Press,

1989, translated by Alfred Birnbaum), where moral philosophy, values theory, and educational practice converge, is a compelling philosophical work.

In the realm of moral philosophy, one should explore Haruko Okano's "Moral Responsibility in the Japanese Context" in *Women and Religion in Japan* (Harrassowitz Verlag, 1998); Simone Weil's *The Need for Roots: Prelude of a Declaration of Duties Towards Mankind* (Routledge, 1995); Peter Singer's *Practical Ethics* (Cambridge University Press, 1993) and *Rethinking Life and Death: The Collapse of Our Traditional Ethics* (St. Martin's Griffin, 1996).

Among insightful works in ethical and social philosophy are Watsuji Tetsuro's *Ethics in Japan* (State University of New York Press, 1996) and Michele Foucault's *Madness and Civilization: A History of Insanity in the Age of Reason* (Knopf, 1973).

Recommended readings in philosophy of culture, consciousness, and social conscience include Frantz Fanon's *Wretched of the Earth* (Grove/Atlantic, 1976), *Black Skin/White Masks* (Grove/Atlantic, 1976), and *Toward the African Revolution* (Grove/Atlantic, 1988); Aiko Ogoshi's *A Feminist Criticism of Japanese Culture* (Miraisha, 1996); and Kwame Gyekye's *Beyond Cultures: Perceiving a Common Humanity* (Ghana Academy of Arts and Sciences, 2000), *Tradition and Modernity: Philosophical Reflections in the African Experience* (Oxford University Press, 1997), and *An Essay on African Philosophical Thought: The Akan Conceptual Scheme* (Temple University Press, 1995).